Calculator Analysis for Business and Finance

Note: The calculator keystrokes and descriptions used in this book were based on **The MBA** advanced business calculator with the *Algebraic Operating System* (AOS) entry method. The facts and information included will be generally useful when working with other specially dedicated business calculators, but the keystroke sequences described will only apply directly to The MBA™ calculator.

This book was developed by:

The Staff of the Texas Instruments Learning Center:

Roger F. Farish   and   Elbert B. Greynolds, Jr., Ph.D., CPA,
Associate Professor of Accounting
Southern Methodist University
School of Business Administration

Jacquelyn F. Quiram
Charles L. McCollum
Dr. Ralph A. Oliva, Educational Software Director

With contributions by:

Fred Roberto, Assistant Professor Real Estate and Regional Science
Southern Methodist University
School of Business Administration

David J. Springate, D.B.A. Associate Professor of Finance
Southern Methodist University
School of Business Administration

Rocky Armstrong
Joseph L. Curry
Ralph T. Dosher, Jr.
Lane L. Douglas
Patrick W. Lam
C. B. Wilson

Artwork and layout were coordinated and executed by:

Schenck, Plunk & Deason

ISBN 0-89512-015-1

Library of Congress Catalogue Number: 77-18313

Table of Contents

4. FINANCE

Introduction

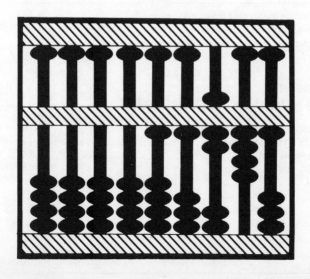

The Electronic Calculator: How and Why It Came About

I

Throughout the centuries, businessmen have looked for tools to help them handle the "numbers" part of their business more quickly and accurately. Your calculator represents one link in what has been and probably will continue to be an explosive evolution in technology. To a large extent, this evolution has been brought about by real and practical business needs.

As a human institution, business goes back quite a long way in history. As soon as Man began to trade the products of his labors for those of his neighbors, business was born. Very early, simple counting systems were developed for record-keeping purposes in these transactions, using tally sticks or some other small counters such as pebbles—with one counter representing one unit of the commodity. Historians usually consider the abacus, which originated in the Orient more than 5,000 years ago (and is still in use today), to be the first calculating device. For many centuries, there was little change in these simple devices, but by the 17th century, the evolution had begun to move again.

In 1642, the French scientist-philosopher, **Blaise Pascal,** invented the first actual "adding machine". It was a complex tangle of wheels, gears, and windows, but it enabled him to handle his father's business accounts more quickly. By the late 1600's, **Gottfried Leibnitz** had developed his more advanced machine, the *Stepped Reckoner,* which could add, multiply, divide, and extract square roots. Early attempts to manufacture calculators, however, produced highly unreliable results. It was not until 1820 that the first commercial machines handling addition, subtraction, multiplication, and division became available.

Another novel idea occurred during the early 1800's—the use of punched cards for data storage—and was quickly pressed into service in calculator data processing. In 1835, an Englishman, **Charles Babbage,** invented a machine that used punched cards to store numbers *and* the operations to be performed with them. His *Analytical Engine* was designed to handle a series of prewritten operations, use the results of one computation as input data for another, handle repetitive calculations (loops) and conditional transfers. It was the first "programmable" calculating device and a milestone in the evolution of today's calculators and computers.

The late 1800's and the early 1900's saw the introduction first of electricity and then a fast-growing electronics technology to data processing. By the 1940's, the Harvard Mark I computer had been developed, and the University of Pennsylvania ENIAC followed in 1946. Because of the speed made possible by all-electronic calculation, the ENIAC was more than 1,000 times faster than its electromechanical counterparts.

Computers by this time could handle highly complex mathematical computations and do them quickly and accurately, but their vast array of circuitry and vacuum tubes made them bulky and expensive—hardly feasible for the average business office. The development of the transistor, which replaced the vacuum tube, greatly reduced the size and cost of computers and increased their reliability. But computer technology was already searching for another breakthrough. The breakthrough came in 1958, when **Jack Kilby** invented the integrated circuit at Texas Instruments.

The integrated circuit (or IC) is a tiny "chip" of silicon, with complete electronic circuits, including transistors, diodes, capacitors, resistors, and their required interconnections, built into it, using a series of techniques which resemble photographic development processes. The equivalent of 10,000 operational transistors can be "grown" into a typical integrated circuit. Along with companion breakthroughs in display technology, these tiny devices have been a key factor in making hand-held portable calculators a practical reality, bringing the advantages of small size, reliability, and extreme cost saving to the computational machine. Today's highly complex and versatile "chips" make it possible for you to have an advanced professional and programmable calculator of your own.

Calculator Analysis

I

A new era is at hand, literally—the era of **Calculator Analysis.** Modern technology has placed the capability of instant problem-solving right in your hands in the form of the hand-held calculator. Bulky volumes of tables formerly needed to reference the necessary information can now be shelved. Resolution of the mandatory mathematics of money is now easier and far more accurate than dreamed possible just a few years ago unless, of course, you had a computer handy. Still, computers are a bit awkward to carry with you everywhere you go.

The power and portability offered by **The MBA**™ calculator can be the factors deciding the success or failure of a business opportunity. The most widely used financial and statistical formulas have been built directly into the calculator. With the added flexibility of accepting a program, the calculator can be adapted to your own business needs regardless of their complexity.

Timing is so critical in some cases that an "I'll call you later with these figures," just won't do. The small amount of time needed to master the vast potential of hand-held mathematics is an investment with continuous returns.

Calculator Analysis for Business and Finance

This book is designed to show you how to apply the power of **The MBA** calculator to your business and financial decision-making. Since the features and functions of the calculator have already been discussed in your Owner's Manual, we'll concentrate on actual situations occurring in the business world.

You'll find chapters covering interest and annuities, accounting, personal and business finance, bond analysis, real estate, marketing and forecasting, and statistics. In every case, we've tried to select real-life examples representative of the decision-making situations the business community works with every day. Generally, the problems in each chapter are arranged in order of their complexity, beginning with the simpler, less complicated examples of general interest in that field and progressing on to advanced, in-depth applications.

Many of the sample problems include brief programs. Often, these programs can be taken from one specific problem and applied to other similar situations. Consider them as "building blocks" or "modules" you can use to develop routines adapted to your own specific needs.

For quick reference, we have included an index at the end of this book. If you'd like to explore further on your own, a bibliography of our sources also appears with the index.

Notes About the Calculator

The comprehensive design of your **MBA** calculator provides easy resolution of the mathematical aspects of business and finance. The techniques applied in this manual make use of virtually the entire capability of the calculator. Here are some brief reminders to help you make efficient use of the calculator.

There are four clearing options available. Choice of the correct one for a given situation is important.

⌐CE⌐ clears number entries, assuming that a function key has not been pressed. It does not affect calculations with their pending operations, the fixed position of the decimal, or the contents of any memory. Programs are not affected.

⌐CLR⌐ clears the display and all calculations in progress. It does not affect the contents of any memory or a program.

⌐2nd⌐ **CM** clears only the contents of memories 0 through 7. It does not affect the display, a fixed decimal point, calculations in progress or a program.

⌐2nd⌐ **CA** is the same as turning the calculator off then on again. All memories, the display, a program, and any calculation in progress are all irrecoverably cleared. This clearing operation should be used sparingly, because it does clear everything.

An interesting feature of the calculator is that the memories used for storing financial information can be accessed directly through the financial keys themselves. Memory 3, for instance, contains the number of payments entered by pressing ⌐N⌐. This value can be recalled at any time by pressing ⌐RCL⌐ 3 or ⌐RCL⌐ ⌐N⌐. It is convenient to use the ⌐RCL⌐ ⌐N⌐ sequence because it is descriptive of exactly what you're recalling. The financial keys and their associated memories are listed below.

Financial Key	⌐N⌐	⌐%i⌐	⌐PMT⌐	⌐PV⌐	⌐FV⌐
Memory Number	3	4	5	6	7

Notice that they are in the same order that they appear on the keyboard. All you have to remember is the financial memories begin with memory 3 and go up from there. There is one key that should be used carefully. Entering a number with the ⌐%i⌐ key will cause the number to be divided automatically by 100. Check this with the following key sequence:

Action	Press	Display
1. Enter 5 to the %i memory.	5 ⌐%i⌐	**5.**
2. Recall the number from memory 4.	⌐RCL⌐ 4 (or ⌐RCL⌐ ⌐%i⌐)	**0.05**

Pressing ⌐STO⌐ ⌐%i⌐ , though, does not divide the value by 100. Try it.

This is a very useful feature in financial calculations because it allows you to enter interest rates directly as percentages, without converting them to decimal form first. The %i key converts entries for you.

You have the option of limiting the decimal point to display from 0 to 8 decimal places by the key sequence 2nd **FIX** **n,** where **n** is any number from 0 through 8. Turning the calculator off, then on, or pressing 2nd **CA** or 2nd **FIX** 9 removes any previously selected decimal setting and restores the floating decimal display.

Since most of the calculations in this book involve dollars and cents, we have used a two-decimal display in most places. Remember, however, that the calculator is really computing with its full capacity internally, even though the calculated result is rounded in the display. If you need to reenter a calculated result in another calculation, be sure that you obtain all the significant digits first by pressing 2nd **FIX** 9. Reentry of a rounded result can cause a slight variance in your answers.

A Note About This Book

This book has been written for a variety of readers with a variety of applications needs.

- *Chapter 1* contains a basic overview and discussion of compound interest and annuities situations.
- *Chapters 2-6* cover applications for an array of specific fields.
- *Chapters 7-9* provide applications of statistical methods to finance and business.

Regardless of your requirements in the world of financial mathematics, you should be able to find this book useful for both your personal as well as your occupational needs.

Money at Work

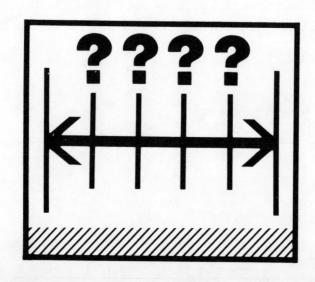

One of the most fascinating (and sometimes troublesome) aspects of using money is that it both *earns* and *costs*. That is, you can invest your money in a growth situation so that it earns additional money, or you can borrow from a lending agency, in which case you must pay for the use of someone else's money. Almost every day, you have to make decisions about money in your personal or professional life, and sound financial planning calls for a close look at the way money "works" and the alternatives that are available to you. Your calculator can be a powerful tool for you to use in making these decisions.

The Essence of Interest

Interest is the fee paid for the use of someone else's money. Interest can be money a bank or savings institution pays you for the use of your money. Or, when you borrow money, interest is the charge you pay for using the lending institution's money. The amount of interest paid depends on four factors:

1. The amount of money involved (called *principal*)
2. The interest rate (usually expressed as a percentage per time unit)
3. The length of time the money is borrowed or loaned
4. The type of interest (or the way the interest is computed)

There are two basic types of interest: *simple* and *compound.* There are also two basic ways of stating interest rates: *nominal* and *effective.* These are explored with methods shown for converting between the most common rates.

Simple Interest

The four interest factors for computing simple interest are related as shown below.

Simple Interest = Principal × Interest Rate × Time

Example: Suppose you deposit $1000 at 6% annual simple interest for three years. How much money would you have at the end of three years? The keystrokes for performing this type of calculation on your calculator are very simple.

Action	Press	Display
1. Clear calculator.	CLR 2nd CM	0.
2. Enter principal.	1000	1000
3. Calculate interest earned in one year.	X 6 % X	60.
4. Calculate interest earned in three years.	3 =	180.
5. Calculate total amount by adding the interest earned to the principal.	+ 1000 =	1180.

Notice that simple interest is earned on the original amount of principal only.

In simple interest problems, the amount of interest you earn depends not only on the interest rate, but on the way time is calculated for periods other than even numbers of years. For instance, a year may be assumed to contain 360 days or 365 days depending on the type of simple interest. You need to check with the agency or persons involved when making such calculations.

Compound Interest

1

Almost all borrowing, lending and savings situations involve compound interest. **Compound interest** means that when saving money you earn interest not only on the original amount of principal, but also on the *interest* that you have earned in each previous compounding period. In the borrowing situation, compound interest means that you pay interest only on the unpaid balance, not on the original principal borrowed. Consider the previous example, but with yearly compounding.

Example:

You deposit $1000 at 6% annual compound interest for three years. What amount of money will you have at the end of the third year?

Action	Press	Display
1. Clear calculator and select two-decimal display.	CLR 2nd CM 2nd FIX 2	0.00
2. Add 6% to your original principal of $1000. This is the amount you'll have at the end of one year.	1000 + 6 % =	1060.00
3. Add 6% to the $1060 you had at the end of the first year. This is the amount you'll have at the end of the second year.	+ 6 % =	1123.60
4. Add 6% to the $1123.60 you had at the end of the second year. **This is the amount accumulated at the end of third year.**	+ 6 % =	1191.02

The method used above is for manually calculating compound interest. Your calculator has special keys to make computation of compound interest easy.

- N key: Enters or computes the number of compounding periods.
- %i key: Enters or computes the interest rate per period.
- PV key: Enters or computes the present value of the investment.
- FV key: Enters or computes the future value.
- CPT key: Used in conjunction with the above keys to compute the unknown variable.

These keys use memory registers 3 through 7, so all calculations involving the financial keys should begin with 2nd CM or 2nd CA to clear these memories.

Now, work the previous example using these keys, instead of the manual method.

COMPOUND INTEREST

Action	Press	Display
1. Clear calculator and select two-decimal display.	CLR 2nd CM 2nd FIX 2	0.00
2. Enter the $1000 principal as the present value.	1000 PV	1000.00
3. Enter the 6% annual interest rate.	6 %i	6.00
4. Enter the number of compounding periods (3 years).	3 N	3.00
5. Calculate the future value you'll have in 3 years.	CPT FV	1191.02

The value of $1000 after three years at 6% simple interest grew to $1180, but with interest compounded yearly, it saw a greater increase in value (to $1191.02).

Nominal Rates: The Method Used in This Book
Interest rates are often specified as an annual rate with daily, monthly, quarterly, or semiannual compounding. For instance, 6% annual interest compounded monthly (when stated in the USA) usually means a 6% *nominal* annual interest compounded monthly.

A **nominal interest rate** tells you the compound interest rate for a convenient period of time, usually a year. A nominal interest rate of 6% annual interest compounded monthly means that the annual rate of 6% is divided by the number of months in a year (that is a rate of 6%/12 monthly interest, or 0.5% monthly interest). The nominal interest rate of 6% annual interest compounded quarterly, means that the quarterly interest rate is 6%/4 (or 1.25% each quarter).

Effective Rates
An **effective rate** is the rate at which you actually earn or pay for the period of time stated. In the USA effective interest rates can generally be used directly in calculations. Interest rates stated as 1% monthly interest, 2% quarterly interest. etc., are usually effective rates. In all cases involving interest, if there is any doubt in your mind about the terminology, check with the lending agency involved as there are dozens of ways interest can be calculated.

EQUIVALENT INTEREST RATES

What if you are given a monthly interest rate, and you need to know the semiannual rate, or the yearly rate?

Your calculator can easily make these sometimes difficult conversions.

Step 1: At the given interest rate find the value of $1 after 1 year.

Step 2: Find the interest rate for a given interval. Then enter the number of those intervals in one year and press `N`.

Step 3: Now press `CPT` `%i` to compute the equivalent effective interest rate.

Example: (Nominal to Effective Yearly Interest)

The interest rate on savings is 6% nominal annual interest compounded monthly. What is the equivalent annual rate (the *effective annual* rate)?

Action	Press	Display
1. Clear calculator and select two-decimal display.	`CLR` `2nd` `CM` `2nd` `FIX` 2	0.00
Enter monthly interest rate.	6 `÷` 12 `=` `%i`	0.50
Enter number of intervals in one year.	12 `N`	12.00
Enter $1 as present value.	1 `PV`	1.00
Calculate value of $1 at end of one year at given interest rate.	`CPT` `FV`	1.06
2. Enter number of time intervals in a year for interest you need.	1 `N`	1.00
3. **Compute the effective annual rate.**	`CPT` `%i`	6.17

Example: (Monthly to Semiannual Rate)

A certain interest rate is 11% annual interest compounded monthly. What is the equivalent semiannual interest rate?

Action	Press	Display
1. Clear calculator and select two-decimal display.	`CLR` `2nd` `CM` `2nd` `FIX` 2	0.00
Enter monthly interest.	11 `÷` 12 `=` `%i`	0.92
Enter number of months in a year.	12 `N`	12.00
Enter $1 as the present value.	1 `PV`	1.00
Find the value of $1 at end of one year at given interest rate.	`CPT` `FV`	1.12
2. Enter number of semiannual time intervals in a year.	2 `N`	2.00
3. **Calculate semiannual interest rate.**	`CPT` `%i`	5.63

COMPOUND INTEREST

Example:
(Daily to Monthly Rate)

Your bank pays 5¼% annual interest compounded daily. Since you make monthly payments you'd like to know the monthly rate.

Action	Press	Display
1. Clear calculator and select two-decimal display.	CLR 2nd CM 2nd FIX 2	0.00
Calculate daily interest.	5.25 ÷ 365 = %i	0.01
Enter number of days in a year.	365 N	365.00
Enter $1 as present value.	1 PV	1.00
Compute what $1 is worth at the end of one year.	CPT FV	1.05
2. Enter number of months.	12 N	12.00
3. Calculate monthly interest rate.	CPT %i	**0.44**

Note:

If you convert an interest rate to a shorter time interval, you may not receive all the interest you calculate! For example, when a quarterly interest rate is specified for a savings account, you may not earn any interest until the quarter is completed. An equivalent monthly rate would lead you to believe that you would earn interest after one month, but in reality the bank may only give you the interest at the end of the quarter.

Building and Using Time Lines

One of the most helpful tools in dealing with financial problems is a simple diagram of the situation called a **time line.** Time lines are usually horizontal lines, laid out and labeled to give you a picture of the value of your money as time passes. When drawing a time line, the first step is to lay out a horizontal line divided into equal intervals of time. The intervals should be chosen to represent the interest rate time interval. For instance, if you are dealing with monthly payments and interest, then you will want your time line divided to represent months.

Example:
(Solving for FV)

Below is a time line for a compound interest situation. If you deposit $958 (Present Value) at 0.6% monthly interest for three months, how much will you have at the end of the 3rd month (Future Value)? The time line for this situation looks like this.

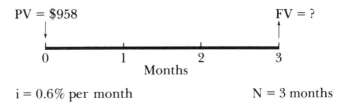

$$PV = \$958 \qquad\qquad\qquad\qquad FV = ?$$

$$0 \qquad 1 \qquad 2 \qquad 3$$

Months

$$i = 0.6\% \text{ per month} \qquad\qquad N = 3 \text{ months}$$

You can easily calculate the future value of your money using your calculator.

Action	Press	Display
1. Clear calculator and select two-decimal display.	CLR 2nd CM 2nd FIX 2	0.00
2. Enter present value.	958 PV	958.00
3. Enter monthly interest rate.	.6 %i	0.60
4. Enter number of months.	3 N	3.00
5. **Calculate future value of your money.**	CPT FV	975.35

Time line diagrams are used to help visualize financial calculations. It is often said that you have *moved* the money through time. In our previous example, you will have $975.35 at the end of the third month. You can see from the time line that you have moved the $958 forward in time by three months. At that time the $958 is worth $975.35. In a sense the $958 and $975.35 are the same amount of money, considered at different points in time. Here is the key concept involved in the use of a time line. *When you have several amounts of money to consider at different times, you can make a sound judgment only if all the amounts are moved to the same point in time for comparison.*

The interest rate used in moving money may be the interest rate you expect to earn, the current interest paid for savings accounts, etc., depending on your particular financial situation.

Often the tricky part of financial calculations is constructing the time line properly. It is often difficult to determine just what is meant by some financial terms, and in these cases it is always wise to ask questions of someone who is knowledgeable in such matters or consult a good reference book.

Now, using time lines and the compound interest routines built into the calculator, look at several examples. For simplicity, set the display to round to two decimal places in these financial examples. Remember, however, that the calculator is really working with its full capacity internally. If you want to check one of these answers for more than two decimal places, you can restore the display to a full 10 digits by simply pressing 2nd FIX **9.**

Example: (Solving for N)

Harry invested $10,000 in a get-rich-quick scheme. His initial investment is guaranteed, and he is earning 5½% interest compounded at the end of each year, but he cannot withdraw any of his principal or interest until the money doubles. How long will he have to wait?

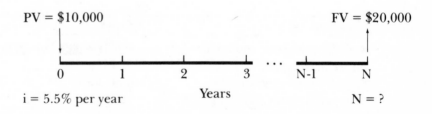

Action	Press	Display
1. Clear calculator and select two-decimal display.	CLR 2nd CM 2nd FIX 2	0.00
2. Enter Harry's initial investment.	10000 PV	10000.00
3. Enter amount he must have before he can withdraw.	20000 FV	20000.00
4. Enter annual interest rate.	5.5 %i	5.50
5. Evaluate how many years Harry must wait before he can withdraw any of his money.	CPT N	12.95

Example:
(Solving for PV)

A shipping line owes your company $20,000, payable at the end of five years. Your company can currently earn a 15% annual rate of interest on funds invested internally. Using this data, what is the present value of the debt? In other words, what amount could be invested today at 15% compounded annually that will grow to $20,000 or more at the end of five years?

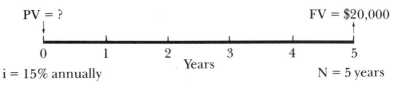

PV = ?   FV = $20,000

0   1   2   3   4   5
                          Years

i = 15% annually   N = 5 years

Action	Press	Display
1. Clear calculator and select two-decimal display.	CLR 2nd CM 2nd FIX 2	0.00
2. Enter number of periods.	5 N	5.00
3. Enter future value of debt.	20000 FV	20000.00
4. Enter annual interest rate.	15 %i	15.00
5. **Calculate amount invested by your company at 15% annually that would grow to $20,000 at the end of 5 years.**	CPT PV	9943.53

If a settlement could be worked out today with the shipping line for anything more than $9943.53, payable immediately, your company would benefit.

Example:
(Solving for FV)

You deposited an inheritance of $15,000 in a savings account on January 1 of this year. The account will earn 6% interest compounded monthly. What amount will be in the account at the end of 8 months?

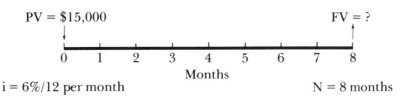

PV = $15,000   FV = ?

0   1   2   3   4   5   6   7   8
                    Months

i = 6%/12 per month   N = 8 months

Action	Press	Display
1. Clear calculator and select two-decimal display.	CLR 2nd CM 2nd FIX 2	0.00
2. Enter number of periods.	8 N	8.00
3. Enter deposit.	15000 PV	15000.00
4. Enter monthly interest rate.	6 ÷ 12 = %i	0.50
5. **Calculate amount after 8 months.**	CPT FV	15610.61

BUILDING AND USING TIME LINES

Example:
(Solving for i)

Don has the opportunity to purchase a piece of land. The initial cost of the land is $5,000, and it is projected to return $6,125 at the end of three years. Assuming yearly compounding, is the earning rate of the land greater than a 6% savings account? In other words, if $5,000 were invested and compounded to $6,125 in three years, what would be the annual growth rate?

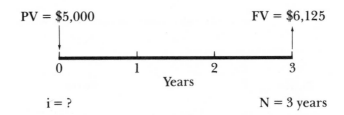

PV = $5,000   FV = $6,125

0   1   2   3

Years

i = ?   N = 3 years

Action	Press	Display
1. Clear calculator and select two-decimal display.	CLR 2nd CM 2nd FIX 2	0.00
2. Enter number of periods.	3 N	3.00
3. Enter cost of land.	5000 PV	5000.00
4. Enter projected return at the end of three years.	6125 FV	6125.00
5. **Calculate the projected rate of return.**	CPT %i	7.00

Yes, this investment would beat a 6% savings account.

Annuities

An annuity is a series of equal payments made at regular intervals of time. Annuities are normally classified into two types: **ordinary annuities and annuities due.**

Definitions

- *Ordinary annuities* involve payments made at the *end* of each payment period. Most loans fall into this category.
- *Annuities due* involve payments made at the *beginning* of each payment period in anticipation of receiving some service or as part of an investment program. Most leases are annuity due situations.

Your calculator is equipped to handle both ordinary annuities and annuities due easily. In addition to the keys already discussed in the compound interest examples, there are two more keys on your calculator that are used in calculations involving annuities with equal payments.

Key Definitions

- PMT key
  Enters the amount of the periodic payment into the calculation or is used in conjunction with the CPT or 2nd DUE key to compute the payment.
- 2nd DUE key sequence
  Takes the place of the CPT key when making annuity due calculations. 2nd DUE tells the calculator to compute the next pressed key value as an annuity due situation.

ORDINARY ANNUITY EXAMPLES

Example:

If you loan a friend $500 for three years at 6% annual interest compounded monthly, how much should the payments be?

Your friend will make 36 monthly payments beginning a month after you loan him the money. The situation, which is an ordinary annuity, looks like this on a time line.

$$PV = \$500$$

i = 6%/12 per month   N = 3 × 12 months

ANNUITIES

Now, find the payment amount with your calculator.

Action	Press	Display
1. Clear calculator and select two-decimal display.	CLR 2nd CM 2nd FIX 2	0.00
2. Enter interest per pay period.	6 ÷ 12 = %i	0.50
3. Enter present value.	500 PV	500.00
4. Enter number of payments.	36 N	36.00
5. Calculate payment amount.	CPT PMT	15.21

The payments you would receive each month are $15.21. Now, the future value of the payments is how much all 36 payments would be worth if you had deposited them in a savings account each month and earned 6% annual interest compounded monthly (the same as the loan rate).

6. Calculate future value.	CPT FV	**598.34**

Now fill in the time line.

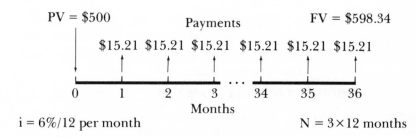

Here are the different representations of equivalent amounts of money. Having $500 now is financially equivalent to having $598.34 at the end of 36 months, or to having 36 monthly payments of $15.21, as shown, providing you deposit the payments at the same interest rate. The time line has been used to move a series of payments through time using the annuity formulas built right into your calculator.

If you do not deposit the payments you receive, you still receive 6% interest compounded monthly on your investment, along with part of your initial $500 back each month. The amount you receive in payments ceases to earn interest when you receive it! It must be reinvested to keep earning interest.

To further illustrate the equivalence of the present value and the future value of a series of equal payments (if they are deposited at the same interest rate), move the $598.34 backward in time 36 months.

1

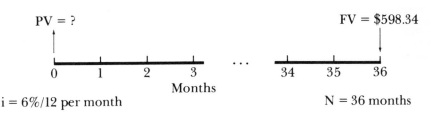

PV = ?   FV = $598.34

```
    0    1    2    3   ...   34   35   36
              Months
i = 6%/12 per month                    N = 36 months
```

Action	Press	Display
1. Clear calculator and select two-decimal display.	CLR 2nd CM 2nd FIX 2	0.00
2. Enter monthly interest.	6 ÷ 12 = %i	0.50
3. Enter future value.	598.34 FV	598.34
4. Enter number of payments.	36 N	36.00
5. Compute present value.	CPT PV	500.00

The present value is $500, as we expected.

Now to examine several annuity problems, showing you how to diagram each situation in a time line and solve it on your calculator. In these examples, tax effects are ignored for simplicity. Methods for handling taxes in business and financial calculations are discussed in later chapters.

ORDINARY ANNUITY EXAMPLES

Example: Solving for FV (Ordinary Annuity)

To establish a retirement annuity, you invest $500 at the end of each month in a savings account. The savings account pays an annual rate of 5¾% with interest compounded monthly. How much will you have in the account when you retire in five years?

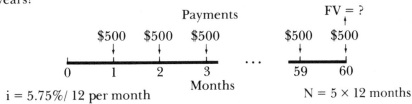

```
                    Payments                        FV = ?
        $500   $500   $500           $500   $500
    0     1     2      3     ...      59     60
                     Months
i = 5.75%/ 12 per month              N = 5 × 12 months
```

Action	Press	Display
1. Clear calculator and select two-decimal display.	CLR 2nd CM 2nd FIX 2	0.00
2. Enter number of periodic deposits.	5 × 12 = N	60.00
3. Enter periodic interest rate.	5.75 ÷ 12 = %i	0.48
4. Enter periodic deposit.	500 PMT	500.00
5. Calculate the accumulated amount immediately after the last deposit.	CPT FV	34661.80

**Example:
Solving
for PMT
(Ordinary
Annuity)**

Metropolis City wishes to establish a sinking fund to retire $100,000 of bonds at the end of 15 years. The fund pays 7.4% annually (compounded monthly), with the payments made into the fund at the end of each month. What should the amount of each payment be?

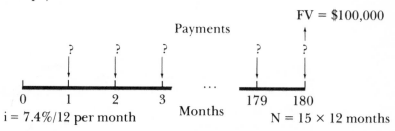

Action	Press	Display
1. Clear calculator and select two-decimal display.	CLR 2nd CM 2nd FIX 2	0.00
2. Enter number of payments.	15 ✕ 12 = N	180.00
3. Enter periodic interest rate.	7.4 ÷ 12 = %i	0.62
4. Enter required future value.	100000 FV	100000.00
5. Calculate periodic payment.	CPT PMT	304.67

Metropolis City must deposit $304.67 at the end of each month to reach its goal.

**Solving
for the
Amount of
a Final
Payment
(Ordinary
Annuity)**

When the loan payment amount is specified and the number of payments is calculated, the number often will have a fractional final period. This usually means that the final payment will be less than the previous payments. To find out how much the final payment will be, use the following procedure.

1. Clear calculator.
2. Key in all known quantities.
3. Determine the number of periods using the CPT N key sequence.
4. Enter the number of whole payments (omitting the fractional part) as N and calculate the present value at that point.
5. Subtract that amount from the original present value and reenter the result in the PV register.
6. Reenter the number of whole payments, *plus one,* into N.
7. Eliminate payment from annuity routine so that compounded value can be computed. If a value is stored in PMT, the calculator assumes an annuity situation exists and calculates accordingly.
8. Compute future value by pressing CPT FV. This amount is the final payment.

1

**Example:
Solving
for Final
Payment
Amount
(Ordinary
Annuity)**

Carolyn and Dan are borrowing $8000 to purchase a new van. The annual interest rate is 11.5% compounded monthly, and they want to pay $265 at the end of each month. How many payments will they have to make, and how much will the final payment be?

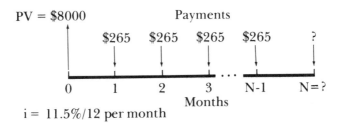

PV = $8000   Payments

$265 $265 $265 $265   ?

0   1   2   3   N-1   N=?
                        Months
i = 11.5%/12 per month

Action	Press	Display
1. Clear calculator and select two-decimal display.	CLR 2nd CM 2nd FIX 2	0.00
2. Enter data.	8000 PV	8000.00
	11.5 ÷ 12 = %i	0.96
	265 PMT	265.00
3. **Calculate number of payments.**	CPT N	35.81
4. Enter number of whole payments and compute present value.	35 N CPT PV	7848.16
5. Subtract this amount from original present value and reenter result as present value.	+/– + 8000 = PV	151.84
6. Add one to the number of whole payments.	1 SUM N	1.00
7. Eliminate payment from annuity routine.	0 PMT	0.00
8. **Compute future value.**	CPT FV	214.05

The result $214.05 is the amount of the last payment, to be made at the end of the 36th month.

Example: Solving for i (Ordinary Annuity)

You are evaluating a five-year project for your company which costs $13,100 initially and should generate $4,000 each year after taxes. Your company expects all projects to earn 14% annually. Will this project meet this earnings goal? What is its annual return rate?

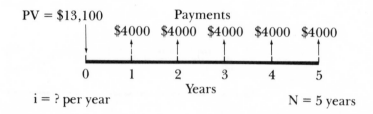

PV = $13,100   Payments
$4000 $4000 $4000 $4000 $4000

0   1   2   3   4   5
                      Years
i = ? per year   N = 5 years

Action	Press	Display
1. Clear calculator and select two-decimal display.	CLR 2nd CM 2nd FIX 2	0.00
2. Enter number of years.	5 N	5.00
3. Enter annual income.	4000 PMT	4000.00
4. Enter initial cost of project.	13100 PV	13100.00
5. **Calculate the annual rate of return on the project.**	CPT %i	15.99

The project will more than meet your company's required return rate with a return rate of 15.99%.

Note:

The calculation of %i takes a bit longer than other calculations because of the iterative sequence it employs.

ANNUITY DUE EXAMPLES

Example: Solving for FV (Annuity Due)

If your company deposits $6,000 at the beginning of each month in a savings account paying 6% annually, compounded monthly, what will the account balance be after six months?

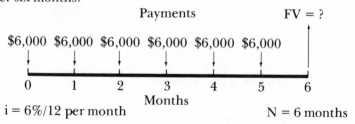

Payments   FV = ?

$6,000 $6,000 $6,000 $6,000 $6,000 $6,000

0   1   2   3   4   5   6
                    Months
i = 6%/12 per month   N = 6 months

Action	Press	Display
1. Clear calculator and select two-decimal display.	CLR 2nd CM 2nd FIX 2	0.00
2. Enter number of periods.	6 N	6.00
3. Enter periodic interest rate.	6 ÷ 12 = %i	0.50
4. Enter periodic deposit.	6000 PMT	6000.00
5. **Calculate the amount you will have after 6 months.**	2nd DUE FV	36635.28

(Leave your calculator on.)

To check to see how much difference it would make if you made the deposit at the *end* of each month (ordinary annuity) rather than at the *beginning* (annuity due), use the following key sequence

6. Store annuity due future value for later recall.	STO 0	36635.28
7. **Compute future value based on an ordinary annuity situation.**	CPT FV	36453.01
8. **Compare the two values.**	+/− + RCL 0 =	182.27

You will earn $182.27 more at the end of six months by making the deposit at the beginning of each month.

To demonstrate why this difference occurs, compare the time lines for both situations.

FV = $36,635.28

Annuity Due

	PMT_1	PMT_2	PMT_3	PMT_4	PMT_5	PMT_6
Cash Flow	$6000	$6000	$6000	$6000	$6000	$6000
Number of Months	0	1	2	3	4	5
Compounding Periods		1	2	3	4	5	6

FV = $36,453.01

Ordinary Annuity

	PMT_1	PMT_2	PMT_3	PMT_4	PMT_5	PMT_6
Cash Flow	$6000	$6000	$6000	$6000	$6000	$6000
Number of Months	0	1	2	3	4	5	6
Compounding Periods		1	2	3	4	5

For an ordinary annuity, interest will be compounded for one less month than in the annuity due.

ANNUITIES

Example: Solving for PV (Annuity Due)

On January 1, Howard and Dorothy's Bakery signed a five-year lease for a kneading machine. The annual payments are $2,500 payable at the beginning of each year. Using an annual interest rate of 7%, what is the present value of the lease?

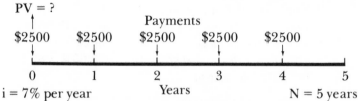

Action	Press	Display
1. Clear calculator and select two-decimal display.	CLR 2nd CM 2nd FIX 2	0.00
2. Enter number of years.	5 N	5.00
3. Enter periodic interest rate.	7 %i	7.00
4. Enter periodic payment.	2500 PMT	2500.00
5. Calculate the present value of the lease.	2nd DUE PV	10968.03

Example: Solving for PMT (Annuity Due)

Your company is leasing a warehouse to Smilin' Sam's Smuggling and Storage Company for twelve months, beginning January 1 of next year. The present value of the lease payments must be $75,000 to give you a minimum annual return of 11.5%. With payments due on the first of each month and ignoring tax effects, what will the monthly payments be?

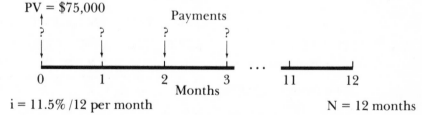

Action	Press	Display
1. Clear calculator and select two-decimal display.	CLR 2nd CM 2nd FIX 2	0.00
2. Enter number of periods.	12 N	12.00
3. Enter periodic interest rate.	11.5 ÷ 12 = %i	0.96
4. Enter present value.	75000 PV	75000.00
5. Compute periodic payment.	2nd DUE PMT	6583.04

Monthly payments of $6583.04 fulfill the 11.5% annual return requirement.

**Example:
Solving
for i
(Annuity
Due)**

Your company has a choice of either buying a machine outright for $49,000 cash or purchasing it on installments of 24 payments of $2,300 each, made at the beginning of each month. What interest rate is the seller charging for financing the installments?

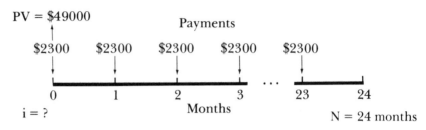

Action	Press	Display
1. Clear calculator and select two-decimal display.	CLR 2nd CM 2nd FIX 2	0.00
2. Enter number of periods.	24 N	24.00
3. Enter periodic payment.	2300 PMT	2300.00
4. Enter purchase price of the machine.	49000 PV	49000.00
5. Compute periodic interest rate.	2nd DUE %i	1.07
6. Calculate annual interest rate requested by seller.	✕ 12 =	12.78

Continuous Compounding

COMPOUND INTEREST

Some savings and loan associations and banks now charge or pay interest using continuous compounding. This method assumes that compounding takes place continuously over the time periods rather than at the end of each period. The formulas used are:

$$PV = FV (e^{-rn})$$
$$FV = PV (e^{rn})$$

where:
$$PV = \text{Present value}$$
$$FV = \text{Future value}$$
$$r = \text{Interest rate per time period as a decimal}$$
$$n = \text{Time period}$$
$$e = \text{Euler's constant (2.718281829)}$$

The calculator can be easily "taught" a calculation sequence. Up to 32 steps can be stored and used over and over. *Chapter 4* of the Owner's Manual contains all the details on how to construct and use these programs. Useful, prewritten programs are given where needed in this book and used as described in the example solutions.

With two simple programs, you can easily compute either present value or future value with continuous compounding. First, look at a program for calculating present value.

Program for Present Value with Continuous Compounding

Program Memory	Key Sequence	Program Memory	Key Sequence	Program Memory	Key Sequence
00 55	✕	11 42	R/S	22 00	
01 43	(	12 41	RST	23 00	
02 61	RCL	13 00		24 00	
03 22	%i	14 00		25 00	
04 55	✕	15 00		26 00	
05 61	RCL	16 00		27 00	
06 21	N	17 00		28 00	
07 84	+/−	18 00		29 00	
08 44	)	19 00		30 00	
09 18	2nd e^x	20 00		31 00	
10 85	=	21 00			

**Example:
Solving
for PV
(Continuous
Compounding)**

What is the present value of $10,500 received at the end of 6 years, using an annual rate of 8.5% compounded continuously?

PV = ?

FV = $10,500

0   1   2   3   4   5   6
Years

i = 8.5%, compounded continuously

N = 6 years

Action	Press	Display
1. Clear calculator and enter	2nd CA 2nd LRN	00 00
program.	Program 2nd LRN RST	0.
2. Select two-decimal display.	2nd FIX 2	0.00
3. Enter annual compounding rate (the %i key automatically converts it to a decimal as it stores the number).	8.5 %i	8.50
4. Enter number of time periods.	6 N	6.00
5. **Enter future value amount and calculate present value.**	10500 R/S	6305.20

The present value of $10,500 received in 6 years would be $6305.20.

**Program
for Future
Value with
Continuous
Compounding**

Program Memory	Key Sequence	Program Memory	Key Sequence	Program Memory	Key Sequence
00 55	×	11 41	RST	22 00	
01 43	(	12 00		23 00	
02 61	RCL	13 00		24 00	
03 22	%i	14 00		25 00	
04 55	×	15 00		26 00	
05 61	RCL	16 00		27 00	
06 21	N	17 00		28 00	
07 44	)	18 00		29 00	
08 18	2nd e*	19 00		30 00	
09 85	=	20 00		31 00	
10 42	R/S	21 00			

**Example:
Solving
for FV
(Continuous
Compounding)**

You have the choice of investing $5,000 in a savings account which pays 6% compounded quarterly or an account which pays the same rate, but compounds interest continuously. Which account will pay the most interest at the end of 3 years?

CONTINUOUS COMPOUNDING

Continuous Compounding Time Line

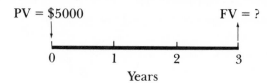

PV = $5000   FV = ?

N = 3 years

i = 6% annually, compounded continuously

Quarterly Compounding Time Line

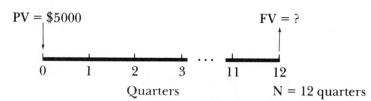

PV = $5000   FV = ?

N = 12 quarters

i = 6% annually, compounded quarterly

Action	Press	Display
1. Clear calculator and enter	2nd CA 2nd LRN	00 00
program.	Program 2nd LRN RST	0.
2. Select two-decimal display.	2nd FIX 2	0.00
3. Enter interest rate.	6 %i	6.00
4. Enter number of years.	3 N	3.00
5. **Enter amount of investment and calculate future value with continuous compounding.**	5000 R/S	5986.09
6. Store future value for comparison.	STO 0	5986.09
7. Calculate and enter quarterly interest rate.	6 ÷ 4 = %i	1.50
8. Calculate and enter number of periods.	3 × 4 = N	12.00
9. Enter present value.	5000 PV	5000.00
10. **Calculate future value.**	CPT FV	5978.09
11. **Determine difference in compounding types.**	+/− + RCL 0 =	8.00

You will earn $8 more in three years with continuous compounding.

Grawoig, Fielitz, Robinson, and Tabor, *Mathematics: A Foundation for Decisions*, pp. 286-294.

ANNUITIES WITH CONTINUOUS COMPOUNDING

Continuous compounding is also used when dealing with a series of payments (annuity). This is a useful technique in some capital budgeting situations. This method assumes that the cash flows are received uniformly or continuously during each period and computes the interest continuously during the period. The formulas used are:

$$PV = A \left(\frac{1 - e^{-rn}}{r} \right)$$

$$FV = A \left(\frac{e^{rn} - 1}{r} \right)$$

where:

PV	=	present value
FV	=	future value
A	=	amount of payment received uniformly during the period
r	=	interest rate as a decimal
n	=	number of time periods or payments
e	=	Euler's constant (2.718281829)

Again, two short programs can help you compute the present value and future value of a series of uniform payments with continuous compounding. First, look at a present value situation.

Program for Computing Present Value of a Series of Continuous Payments with Continuous Compounding

Program Memory	Key Sequence	Program Memory	Key Sequence	Program Memory	Key Sequence
00 55	$\times$	11 44	)	22 00	
01 43	(	12 18	2nd e*	23 00	
02 01	1	13 85	=	24 00	
03 65	−	14 45	÷	25 00	
04 43	(	15 61	RCL	26 00	
05 61	RCL	16 22	%i	27 00	
06 22	%i	17 85	=	28 00	
07 55	$\times$	18 42	R/S	29 00	
08 61	RCL	19 41	RST	30 00	
09 21	N	20 00		31 00	
10 84	+/−	21 00			

Example: A company has vending machines located in a busy airport. The machines are used constantly, 365 days a year, and each machine generates $6,000 revenue each year. Assuming a 12% discount rate with continuous discounting and cash flows, what is the present value, before taxes, of four years' operation of a machine? Contrast that result to the present value with discrete (periodic) compounding.

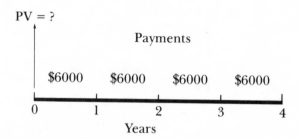

PV = ?

Payments

$6000 $6000 $6000 $6000

0   1   2   3   4

Years

i = 12% continuous compounding   N = 4 years

Calculating Present Value of a Series of Continuous Payments with Continuous Compounding

Action	Press	Display
1. Clear calculator and enter program.	2nd CA 2nd LRN Program 2nd LRN RST	0
2. Select two-decimal display.	2nd FIX 2	0.00
3. Enter discount rate.	12 %i	12.00
4. Enter number of periods.	4 N	4.00
5. **Enter annual revenue and calculate present value with continuous compounding.**	6000 R/S	19060.83
6. Store present value for later comparison.	STO 0	19060.83
7. Enter annual payment for calculation of present value with discrete discounting.	6000 PMT	6000.00
8. **Compute present value.**	CPT PV	18224.10
9. **Determine difference in compounding types.**	+/- + RCL 0 =	836.73

The difference in present values is $836.73.

Now, calculate the future value for an annuity invested uniformly over a number of periods and compounded continuously.

Program for Computing Future Value of a Series of Continuous Payments with Continuous Compounding

Program Memory	Key Sequence	Program Memory	Key Sequence	Program Memory	Key Sequence
00 55	☒	11 01	1	22 00	
01 43	(	12 44	)	23 00	
02 43	(	13 45	÷	24 00	
03 61	RCL	14 61	RCL	25 00	
04 22	%i	15 22	%i	26 00	
05 55	☒	16 85	=	27 00	
06 61	RCL	17 42	R/S	28 00	
07 21	N	18 41	RST	29 00	
08 44	)	19 00		30 00	
09 18	2nd e˟	20 00		31 00	
10 65	−	21 00			

Example: During the next five years, you will receive continuous payments amounting to $1,500 per year. If the payments are deposited in an account compounded continuously at 6.5%, what will be the value of the payments at the end of the five years?

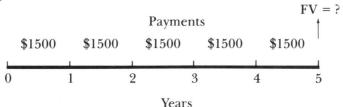

FV = ?

Payments

$1500 $1500 $1500 $1500 $1500

0   1   2   3   4   5

Years

i = 6.5% compounded continuously   N = 5

Calculating Future Value of a Series of Continuous Payments with Continuous Compounding

Action	Press	Display
1. Clear calculator and enter program.	2nd CA 2nd LRN	00 00
	Program 2nd LRN RST	0
2. Select two-decimal display.	2nd FIX 2	0.00
3. Enter interest rate.	6.5 %i	6.50
4. Enter number of periods.	5 N	5.00
5. Enter annual amount and calculate future value.	1500 R/S	8862.25

At the end of five years, the amount in the account will be $8862.25.

Reference: Grawoig, *et al*, *Mathematics: A Foundation for Decisions,* pp. 286-294.

General Annuities

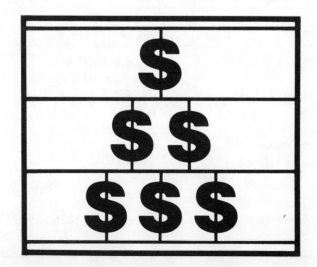

In *Chapter 1* we explored simple annuities, which were defined as a series of equal payments made at regular intervals of time. Each of our examples involved a situation in which the payment period and the interest compounding period were the same. The question now is, what happens if the payment period is different from the compounding period?

Definitions: *An annuity with a payment period different from its compounding period is defined as a* **General Annuity.** If payments are made at the *end* of the payment period, we are dealing with a **General Ordinary Annuity.** If the payments are made at the *start* of the payment period, the situation is a **General Annuity Due.** In this chapter general annuities of both types are discussed, solving for present value, future value, payment amount, number of payments, and interest rate.

The solution of most general annuity problems requires that certain conversions be made. Once these values have been found, the calculation can be solved as a regular annuity problem. The formulas for general annuities are:

General Ordinary Annuities   *General Annuities Due*

$$FV = \frac{CP}{s_{\overline{m/k}\,i}} \left(s_{\overline{n}\,i} \right) \qquad FV = \frac{CP}{a_{\overline{m/k}\,i}} \left(s_{\overline{n}\,i} \right)$$

and   and

$$PV = \frac{CP}{s_{\overline{m/k}\,i}} \left(a_{\overline{n}\,i} \right) \qquad PV = \frac{CP}{a_{\overline{m/k}\,i}} \left(a_{\overline{n}\,i} \right)$$

These formulas will be repeated and the terms defined where appropriate in the examples given in this chapter. As general background information, the terms

$$\frac{CP}{s_{\overline{m/k}\,i}} \quad \text{and} \quad \frac{CP}{a_{\overline{m/k}\,i}}$$

convert the general annuity payment to an equivalent simple annuity payment, for ordinary annuities and annuities due respectively, so that the equivalent payment period is equal to the compounding period.

In general annuity situations where you need to solve for the annual interest or return rate, you first find an estimated interest rate (r) corresponding to the payment period. You can then compute the annual interest rate for compounding periods with the formula:

$$\text{annual I} = m \left[(1 + r)^{k/m} - 1 \right] \times 100$$

Again, this formula is discussed in detail where appropriate.

For further information about general annuities, refer to *Mathematics of Finance,* third edition, by Paul M. Hummel and Charles L. Seebeck, Jr.

Present Value of a General Ordinary Annuity

If you know the payment amount and period, the interest rate and compounding period, and the life of a general ordinary annuity, you can determine the present value of the annuity with the formula:

$$PV = \frac{CP}{s_{\overline{m/k}|i}} \left(a_{\overline{n}|i} \right)$$

where:
PV	=	present value
CP	=	general annuity cash payment
m	=	number of compounding periods per year
k	=	number of payments per year
i	=	interest rate per compounding period (m)
n	=	number of compounding periods (m) per year × the total number of payments (g) ÷ the number of payments per year (k)
$s_{\overline{m/k}|i}$	=	future value of $1 payments, compounded m/k periods at i%
$a_{\overline{n}|i}$	=	present value of $1 payments, compounded n periods at i%

Example:

You will receive a general annuity of $2000 per year for six years that includes 8% interest, compounded semiannually. The payments occur at the end of each year. What is the present value of the annuity?

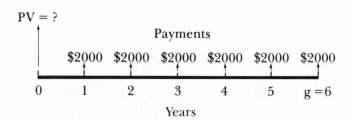

i = 8%/2 semiannually
m = 2 compounding periods per year
k = 1 payment per year

Action	Press	Display
1. Clear calculator and select two-decimal display.	CLR 2nd CM 2nd FIX 2	0.00
2. Enter $1 for payment.	1 PMT	1.00
3. Calculate and enter semiannual interest rate.	8 ÷ 2 = %i	4.00
4. Calculate and enter m/k.	2 ÷ 1 = N	2.00
5. Compute and store $s_{\overline{m/k}|i}$	CPT FV STO 0	2.04
6. Calculate and enter mg/k.	2 × 6 ÷ 1 = N	12.00
7. Compute $a_{\overline{n}|i}$ (Note: payment and interest rate already stored.)	CPT PV	9.39
8. **Calculate present value of general ordinary annuity.**	× 2000 ÷ RCL 0 =	9201.05

The present value of the annuity is $9201.05.

Future Value of a General Ordinary Annuity

Given the payment amount and period, the interest rate and compounding period, and the life of a general ordinary annuity, you can calculate its future value by the formula:

$$FV = \frac{CP}{s\,\overline{m/k}\,|\,i} \left(s\,\overline{n}\,|\,i \right)$$

where: FV   =   future value
CP   =   general annuity cash payment
m   =   number of compounding periods per year
k   =   number of payments per year
i   =   interest rate per compounding period (m)
n   =   number of compounding periods per year (m) × the total number of payments (g) ÷ the number of payments per year (k)

$s\,\overline{m/k}\,|\,i$ =   future value of $1 payments, compounded m/k periods at i%

$s\,\overline{n}\,|\,i$ =   future value of $1 payments, compounded n periods at i%

Example: Your company will receive payments of $3500 at the end of each month for the next 38 months, with interest at 7% compounded semiannually. What is the future value of the annuity?

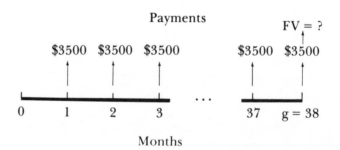

Payments

$3500 $3500 $3500 $3500 $3500   FV = ?

0   1   2   3   ...   37   g = 38

Months

i = 7%/2 semiannually
m = 2 compounding periods per year
k = 12 payments per year

Action	Press	Display
1. Clear calculator and select two-decimal display.	CLR 2nd CM 2nd FIX 2	0.00
2. Enter $1 for payment.	1 PMT	1.00
3. Calculate and enter interest rate.	7 ÷ 2 = %i	3.50
4. Calculate and enter m/k.	2 ÷ 12 = N	0.17
5. Compute and store $s_{\overline{m/k}\,\rfloor\,i}$	CPT FV STO 0	0.16
6. Calculate and enter mg/k.	2 × 38 ÷ 12 = N	6.33
7. Calculate future value ($s_{\overline{n}\,\rfloor\,i}$).	CPT FV	6.96
8. Compute future value of the general ordinary annuity.	× 3500 ÷	24343.25
	RCL 0 =	148175.29

The future value is $148,175.29.

Finding the Annual Interest Rate (General Ordinary Annuity)

If you know the payment amount and period, the compounding period, the life of the annuity, and either the present or future value of general ordinary annuity, you can calculate the equivalent annual interest rate with the formula:

$$\text{annual } I = m \left[(1 + r)^{k/m} - 1 \right] \times 100$$

where:

m	=	number of compounding periods per year
k	=	number of payments per year
r	=	estimated periodic interest rate per period g (g = the total number of payments made throughout the life of the annuity)

To solve for the annual interest rate, you first estimate the value of the periodic interest rate (r). Use the simple ordinary annuity key sequence for this step. Then you can use a short program to solve the equation for the equivalent annual interest rate.

Program for solving $m \left[(1 + r)^{k/m} - 1 \right] \times 100$

Program Memory	Key Sequence	Program Memory	Key Sequence	Program Memory	Key Sequence
00 61	RCL	11 12	CPT	22 00	0
01 00	0	12 25	FV	23 00	0
02 45	÷	13 65	−	24 85	=
03 61	RCL	14 01	1	25 42	R/S
04 01	1	15 85	=	26 41	RST
05 85	=	16 55	×	27 00	
06 21	N	17 61	RCL	28 00	
07 00	0	18 01	1	29 00	
08 23	PMT	19 85	=	30 00	
09 01	1	20 55	×	31 00	
10 24	PV	21 01	1		

FINDING THE ANNUAL INTEREST RATE
(GENERAL ORDINARY ANNUITY)

2

Example: Present Value Given

Your company is considering a four-year project which costs $40,000 initially, but is expected to generate quarterly after-tax cash returns of $4,000 at the end of each quarter. Assuming annual compounding, what is the expected annual return rate?

PV = $40,000

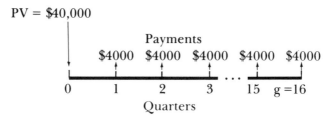

annual I = ?
m = 1 compounding period per year
k = 4 payments per year

Action	Press	Display
1. Clear calculator and	2nd CA 2nd LRN	00 00
enter program.	Program 2nd LRN RST	0.
2. Select two-decimal display.	2nd FIX 2	0.00
3. Enter quarterly cash return (CP).	4000 PMT	4000.00
4. Enter initial cost of the project.	40000 PV	40000.00
5. Enter total number of payments (g).	4 X 4 = N	16.00
6. Calculate estimated periodic interest rate (r). This calculation takes several seconds to complete.	CPT %i	6.15
7. Store number of payments per year (k) in memory 0.	4 STO 0	4.00
8. Store number of compounding periods per year (m) in memory 1.	1 STO 1	1.00
9. Calculate equivalent annual return rate.	R/S	26.98

The expected annual return rate is 26.98%.

(Keep calculator on for next example.)

FINDING THE ANNUAL INTEREST RATE
(GENERAL ORDINARY ANNUITY)

**Example:
Future
Value
Given**

A sinking fund is established to accumulate $38,000 at the end of five years. Your company deposits $475 in the account at the end of each month. Assuming quarterly compounding, what annual interest rate do you need to obtain on the account? (Use the program still in your calculator from the previous example.)

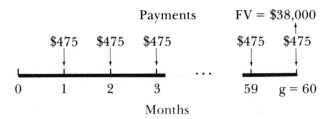

Payments   FV = $38,000

$475 $475 $475 $475 $475

0   1   2   3   59   g = 60

Months

annual I = ?
m = 4 compounding periods per year
k = 12 payments per year

Action	Press	Display
1. Clear calculator display and memories. *(Note:* this key sequence will not disturb your program.)	CLR 2nd **CM**	0.00
2. Enter payment.	475 PMT	475.00
3. Calculate and enter number of periods.	5 × 12 = N	60.00
4. Enter desired future value.	38000 FV	38000.00
5. Compute monthly interest rate (r).	CPT %i	0.94
3. Store number of deposits per year (k) in memory 0.	12 STO 0	12.00
4. Store number of compounding periods per year (m) in memory 1.	4 STO 1	4.00
5. Calculate annual interest rate.	R/S	11.33

The annual interest rate you need is 11.33%.

Solving for Cash Payment (General Ordinary Annuity)

If you know either the present value or future value of a general ordinary annuity and have the other pertinent information, you can calculate the amount of the periodic cash payment. The formulas are:

$$CP = \frac{PV}{a\overline{_{n}}|_{i}} \left(s\overline{_{m/k}}|_{i} \right)$$

$$CP = \frac{FV}{s\overline{_{n}}|_{i}} \left(s\overline{_{m/k}}|_{i} \right)$$

where:
CP	=	periodic cash payment
PV	=	present value
FV	=	future value
m	=	number of compounding periods per year
k	=	number of payments per year
i	=	interest rate per compounding period m
n	=	number of compounding periods (m) per year × the total number of payments (g) ÷ the number of payments per year (k)
$s\overline{_{m/k}}|_{i}$	=	future value of $1 payments compounded m/k periods at i%
$a\overline{_{n}}|_{i}$	=	present value of $1 payments compounded n periods at i%
$s\overline{_{n}}|_{i}$	=	future value of $1 payments compounded n periods at i%

Example: Present Value Given

A firm is considering a project that costs $10,000 initially and has a ten-year life. If the firm wants to achieve an 18% annual return rate, compounded monthly, how much of a cash return must be generated by the project at the end of each quarter?

PV = $10,000   Payments

0   1   2   3   39 g = 40

Quarters

i = 18%/12 per month
m = 12 compounding periods per year
k = 4 payments per year

SOLVING FOR CASH PAYMENT
(GENERAL ORDINARY ANNUITY)

Action	Press	Display
1. Clear calculator and select two-decimal display.	CLR 2nd CM 2nd FIX 2	0.00
2. Enter monthly interest rate (i).	18 ÷ 12 = %i	1.50
3. Calculate and enter mg/k.	12 × 40 ÷ 4 = N	120.00
4. Enter $1 as payment.	1 PMT	1.00
5. Calculate and store $(a\,\overline{n}|i)$.	CPT PV STO 0	55.50
6. Calculate and enter m/k.	12 ÷ 4 = N	3.00
7. Compute future value $(s\,\overline{m/k}|i)$.	CPT FV	3.05
8. Calculate cash payment amount (CP).	÷ RCL 0 ×	0.05
	10000 =	548.70

The necessary quarterly cash return is $548.70.

Example:
Future
Value
Given

Your firm wants to accumulate $50,000 in a sinking fund at the end of five years. Payments are to be made semiannually (at the end of each period) into an account paying 6.75% annual interest, compounded quarterly. How much should the semiannual deposit be?

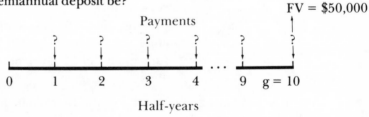

i = 6.75%/4 per quarter
m = 4 compounding periods per year
k = 2 payments per year

Action	Press	Display
1. Clear calculator and select two-decimal display.	CLR 2nd CM 2nd FIX 2	0.00
2. Enter quarterly interest rate (i).	6.75 ÷ 4 = %i	1.69
3. Calculate and enter mg/k.	4 × 10 ÷ 2 = N	20.00
4. Enter $1 as payment.	1 PMT	1.00
5. Calculate and store $s\,\overline{n}|i$.	CPT FV STO 0	23.56
6. Calculate and enter m/k.	4 ÷ 2 = N	2.00
7. Compute future value $(s\,\overline{m/k}|i)$.	CPT FV	2.02
8. Calculate cash payment amount.	× 50000 ÷	100843.75
	RCL 0 =	4281.12

The necessary semiannual payment is $4281.12

Present Value of a General Annuity Due

Knowing the payment amount and period, the interest rate and compounding period, and the life of a general annuity due, you can find the present value by using the formula

$$PV = \frac{CP}{a\,\overline{_{m/k}}\,|\,i}\left(a\,\overline{_{n}}\,|\,i\right)$$

where:
PV	=	present value
CP	=	general annuity cash payment
m	=	number of compounding periods per year
k	=	number of payments per year
i	=	interest rate per compounding period (m)
n	=	number of compounding periods per year × the total number of payments (g) ÷ the number of payments per year
$a\,\overline{_{m/k}}\,|\,i$	=	present value of $1 payments, compounded m/k periods at i%
$a\,\overline{_{n}}\,|\,i$	=	present value of $1 payments, compounded n periods at i%

Example: At the beginning of each quarter for the next 2½ years, your company will deposit $3000 in an account paying 8% annual interest, compounded monthly. What is the present value of the series of payments?

```
PV = ?                      Payments
$3000  $3000  $3000  $3000  $3000        $3000

0      1      2      3      4    . . .    9    g = 10
                    Quarters
```

i = 8%/12 monthly
m = 12 compounding periods per year
k = 4 payments per year

Action	Press	Display
1. Clear calculator and select two-decimal display.	CLR 2nd CM 2nd FIX 2	0.00
2. Enter $1 for payments.	1 PMT	1.00
3. Calculate and enter m/k.	12 ÷ 4 = N	3.00
4. Calculate and enter monthly interest rate.	8 ÷ 12 = %i	0.67
5. Calculate and store $a\,\overline{_{m/k}}\,|\,i$.	CPT PV STO 0	2.96
6. Calculate and enter mg/k.	12 × 10 ÷ 4 = N	30.00
7. Calculate present value $a\,\overline{_{n}}\,|\,i$.	CPT PV	27.11
8. Compute present value of the general annuity due.	× 3000 ÷	81326.55
	RCL 0 =	27471.10

The present value of the general annuity due is $27,471.10.

Future Value of a General Annuity Due

Given the payment amount and period, the interest rate and compounding period, and the life of a general annuity due, you can determine the future value of the annuity with the formula:

$$FV = \frac{CP}{a\,\overline{\underline{m/k}}|i} \left(s\,\overline{\underline{n}}|i \right)$$

where:

FV	=	future value
CP	=	general annuity due cash payment
m	=	number of compounding periods per year
k	=	number of payments per year
n	=	number of compounding periods per year (m) × the number of total payments (g) ÷ the number of payments per year (k)
$a\,\overline{\underline{m/k}}|i$	=	present value of $1 payments compounded m/k periods at i%
$s\,\overline{\underline{n}}|i$	=	future value of $1 payments compounded n periods at i%

Example: Your company will deposit $2000 in a savings account at the beginning of each quarter. The savings account pays 4% annual interest, compounded semiannually. What amount will be in the account at the end of three years?

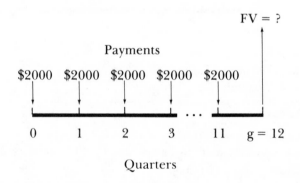

i = 4%/2 semiannually
m = 2 compounding periods per year
k = 4 payments per year

Action	Press	Display
1. Clear calculator and select two-decimal display.	CLR 2nd CM 2nd FIX 2	0.00
2. Enter $1 for payment.	1 PMT	1.00
3. Calculate and enter quarterly interest rate.	4 ÷ 2 = %i	2.00
4. Calculate and enter m/k.	2 ÷ 4 = N	0.50
5. Compute and store $a_{\overline{m/k}|i}$.	CPT PV STO 0	0.49
6. Calculate and enter n periods.	2 × 12 ÷ 4 = N	6.00
7. Calculate future value ($s_{\overline{n}|i}$).	CPT FV	6.31
8. Compute future value of general annuity due.	× 2000 ÷	12616.24
	RCL 0 =	25610.35

The future value is $25,610.35.

Finding the Annual Interest Rate (General Annuity Due)

Knowing the payment amount and period, the compounding period, the life of the annuity and either the present or future value, you can find the equivalent annual interest rate of a general annuity due with the same approach used in the general ordinary annuity:

$$\text{annual I} = m \left[(1 + r)^{k/m} - 1 \right] \times 100$$

where: k = number of payments per year

m = number of compounding periods per year

r = estimated periodic interest rate per period g (g = the total number of payments made throughout the life of the annuity)

Again, the first step in solving the problem will be to find r—the estimated periodic interest rate. This can easily be done using the simple annuity due keys on your calculator. Next, solve the equation to find the equivalent annual interest rate, using the same program given in the general ordinary annuity examples (listed here again for reference).

Program for solving $m \left[(1 + r)^{k/m} - 1 \right] \times 100$

Program Memory	Key Sequence	Program Memory	Key Sequence	Program Memory	Key Sequence
00 61	RCL	11 12	CPT	22 00	0
01 00	0	12 25	FV	23 00	0
02 45	÷	13 65	−	24 85	=
03 61	RCL	14 01	1	25 42	R/S
04 01	1	15 85	=	26 41	RST
05 85	=	16 55	×	27 00	
06 21	N	17 61	RCL	28 00	
07 00	0	18 01	1	29 00	
08 23	PMT	19 85	=	30 00	
09 01	1	20 55	×	31 00	
10 24	PV	21 01	1		

Example:
Present
Value
Known

You will receive payments of $2,300 at the beginning of each month for the next thirty-one months. These payments are being compounded semiannually, and have a present value of $64,000. What is the annual rate of interest?

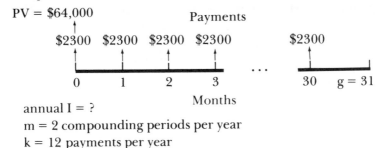

PV = $64,000

Payments

$2300 $2300 $2300 $2300 $2300

0   1   2   3   30   g = 31

Months

annual I = ?
m = 2 compounding periods per year
k = 12 payments per year

Action	Press	Display
1. Clear calculator and enter program.	2nd CA 2nd LRN	00 00
	Program 2nd LRN RST	0.
2. Select two-decimal display.	2nd FIX 2	0.00
3. Enter payment of general annuity due.	2300 PMT	2300.00
4. Enter present value.	64000 PV	64000.00
5. Enter total number of payments (g).	31 N	31.00
6. Calculate estimated periodic rate (r).	2nd DUE %i	0.74
7. Store number of payments per year (k) in memory 0.	12 STO 0	12.00
8. Store number of payments per year (m) in memory 1.	2 STO 1	2.00
9. Calculate equivalent annual interest rate (I).	R/S	9.01

The equivalent annual interest rate is 9.01%.

(Keep calculator on for next example.)

FINDING THE ANNUAL INTEREST RATE
(GENERAL ANNUITY DUE)

**Example:
Future
Value
Known**

Using the program still in your calculator, you can find the equivalent annual interest rate of a general annuity due when you know what the future value is. Assume that you are going to receive payments of $1500 twice a year, at the beginning of each six-month period. At the end of three years, you will have received $10,500. What is the annual interest rate, compounded quarterly?

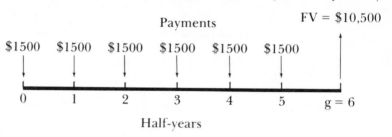

Payments   FV = $10,500

$1500 $1500 $1500 $1500 $1500 $1500

0   1   2   3   4   5   g = 6

Half-years

annual I = ?
m = 4 compounding periods per year
k = 2 payments per year

Action	Press	Display
1. Clear calculator and memories. (*Note:* This key sequence will not disturb your program.)	CLR 2nd **CM**	0.00
2. Enter payment.	1500 PMT	1500.00
3. Enter future value.	10500 FV	10500.00
4. Calculate and enter number of periods (g).	2 × 3 = N	6.00
5. Calculate estimated periodic rate (r).	2nd **DUE** %i	4.42
6. Store number of payments per year (k) in memory 0.	2 STO 0	2.00
7. Store number of compounding periods per year (m) in memory 1.	4 STO 1	4.00
8. Calculate equivalent annual interest rate.	R/S	8.75

The equivalent annual interest rate is 8.75%.

Solving for Cash Payment (General Annuity Due)

2

Given either the present value or future value of a general annuity due, plus the other information needed, you can compute the amount of the periodic cash payment with the formulas:

$$CP = \frac{PV}{a_{\overline{n}|i}} \left(a_{\overline{m/k}|i} \right)$$

or

$$CP = \frac{FV}{s_{\overline{n}|i}} \left(a_{\overline{m/k}|i} \right)$$

where:
CP	=	periodic cash payment
PV	=	present value
FV	=	future value
m	=	number of compounding periods per year
k	=	number of payments per year
i	=	interest rate per compounding period m
n	=	number of compounding periods per year (m) × the total number of payments (g) ÷ the number of payments per year (k)
$a_{\overline{m/k}|i}$	=	present value of $1 payments compounded m/k periods at rate i
$a_{\overline{n}|i}$	=	present value of $1 payments compounded n periods at rate i
$s_{\overline{n}|i}$	=	future value of $1 payments compounded for n periods at rate i

Example: Present Value Given

A tract of land has a present value of $100,000. The owner wants to lease it to a company for 25 years and earn an annual return of 18% annual interest compounded quarterly. The lease payments will be made annually at the beginning of the year. What is the annual payment?

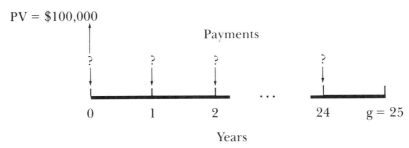

i = 18%/4 per quarter
m = 4 compounding periods per year
k = 1 payment per year

SOLVING FOR CASH PAYMENT (GENERAL ANNUITY DUE)

Action	Press	Display
1. Clear calculator and select two-decimal display.	CLR 2nd CM 2nd FIX 2	0.00
2. Calculate and enter quarterly interest rate.	18 ÷ 4 = %i	4.50
3. Calculate and enter mg/k.	4 × 25 ÷ 1 = N	100.00
4. Enter $1 for payment.	1 PMT	1.00
5. Compute and store $a_{\overline{n}|}i$.	CPT PV STO 0	21.95
6. Calculate and enter m/k.	4 ÷ 1 = N	4.00
7. Compute present value ($a_{\overline{m/k}|}i$).	CPT PV	3.59
8. Calculate cash payment (CP) amount.	× 100000 ÷ RCL 0 =	16344.19

The annual lease payment will be $16,344.19.

Example: Future Value Given

You want to accumulate $5000 in a savings account by making a weekly deposit (at the beginning of each week) for three years. The account draws 6.5% annual interest, compounded monthly. How much should the weekly deposit be?

i = 6.5%/ 12 per month
m = 12 compounding periods per year
k = 52 payments per year

Action	Press	Display
1. Clear calculator and select two-decimal display.	CLR 2nd CM 2nd FIX 2	0.00
2. Calculate and enter monthly interest rate.	6.5 ÷ 12 = %i	0.54
3. Calculate and enter mg/k.	12 × 156 ÷ 52 = N	36.00
4. Enter $1 for payment.	1 PMT	1.00
5. Calculate and store $s_{\overline{n}|}i$.	CPT FV STO 0	39.63
6. Calculate and enter m/k.	12 ÷ 52 = N	0.23
7. Compute present value ($a_{\overline{m/k}|}i$).	CPT PV	0.23
8. Calculate weekly cash payment.	× 5000 ÷ RCL 0 =	29.02

The required deposit at the first of each week is $29.02.

Finding the Total Number of Cash Payments (General Annuities)

You can calculate the total number of payments for a general annuity by finding an estimated rate of return per payment period and then solving for N in a simple annuity calculation. The relationship between the actual effective interest rate (i) and the estimated interest rate per payment period (r) is expressed by the formulas:

$$i = (1 + r)^{k/m} - 1$$

$$r = (1 + i)^{m/k} - 1$$

where:

i	=	compounding rate (expressed as a decimal) per period m
r	=	estimated interest rate (expressed as a decimal) per payment period
k	=	number of payments per year
m	=	number of compounding periods per year at i

In the examples that follow, use the following short program to find the estimated interest rate per payment period and then calculate the total number of payments for the annuity.

Program Memory	Key Sequence	Program Memory	Key Sequence	Program Memory	Key Sequence
00 01	1	11 01	1	22 00	
01 75	+	12 44	)	23 00	
02 61	RCL	13 85	=	24 00	
03 22	%i	14 65	−	25 00	
04 85	=	15 01	1	26 00	
05 37	2nd y^x	16 85	=	27 00	
06 43	(	17 51	STO	28 00	
07 61	RCL	18 22	%i	29 00	
08 00	0	19 42	R/S	30 00	
09 45	÷	20 41	RST	31 00	
10 61	RCL	21 00			

Finding the Total Number of Cash Payments (General Annuities)

Example:
General Ordinary Annuity with Future (or Present) Value Given

If your company pays $15,000 at the end of each quarter into a sinking fund paying 7% interest compounded monthly, how many payments are necessary to accumulate $1,000,000?

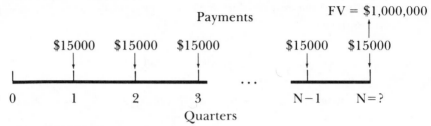

Payments

FV = $1,000,000

$15000 $15000 $15000 $15000 $15000

0   1   2   3   . . .   N−1   N=?

Quarters

$i = 7\%/12$ per month
$m = 12$ compounding periods per year
$k = 4$ payments per year

Action	Press	Display
1. Clear calculator and enter program.	2nd CA 2nd LRN	00 00
	Program 2nd LRN RST	0.
2. Select two-decimal display.	2nd FIX 2	0.00
3. Enter monthly interest rate.	7 ÷ 12 = %i	0.58
4. Enter payment amount.	15000 PMT	15000.00
5. Enter future value (amount you want to save).	1000000 FV	1000000.00
6. Store number of compounding periods per year (m) in memory 0.	12 STO 0	12.00
7. Store number of payments per year (k) in memory 1.	4 STO 1	4.00
8. **Calculate estimated interest rate per payment period** $r = (1 + i)^{m/k} - 1$.	R/S	0.02
9. **Compute total number of payments.**	CPT N	44.49

(Leave calculator on for next example.)

It will take approximately 49½ payments (one each quarter) to accumulate $1,000,000.

Note that if you know the present value of the cash payments, rather than the future value, you would enter that amount with the PV key in step 5, above, and omit the FV key sequence. The rest of the calculation is identical.

**Example:
General
Annuity
Due with
Future
(or Present)
Value
Given**

Calculating the number of payments for a general annuity due is done in the same way as the general ordinary annuity, with one exception. Instead of using the CPT key in the last step, use the 2nd **DUE** key sequence.

If you deposit $100 at the first of each month in a savings account paying 6% annual interest compounded quarterly, how many payments are necessary to accumulate $10,000? (Use the program already in your calculator.)

Payments   FV = $10,000

$100 $100 $100 $100 $100

0   1   2   3   ...   N−1   N=?

Months

i = 6%/4 per quarter
m = 4 compounding periods per year
k = 12 payments per year

Action	Press	Display
1. Clear calculator.	CLR 2nd **CM**	0.00
2. Enter quarterly interest rate.	6 ÷ 4 = %i	1.50
3. Enter payment amount.	100 PMT	100.00
4. Enter future value.	10000 FV	10000.00
5. Store number of compounding periods per year (m) in memory 0.	4 STO 0	4.00
6. Store number of payments per year (k) in memory 1.	12 STO 1	12.00
7. Calculate estimated interest rate per payment period $r = (1 + i)^{m/k} - 1$.	R/S	0.00
8. Compute total number of payments.	2nd **DUE** N	81.03

You will need to make about 81 monthly deposits of $100 to accumulate $10,000.

Note that the procedure is the same when the present value is known instead of the future value, except that you would enter present value with the PV key at step 4, rather than future value.

Solving for Final Payment Amount

General Ordinary Annuity with Present Value Given

When you calculate the total number of payments for a general ordinary annuity, you often find that there is a fractional final period, as in the two previous examples. This means that the final payment will be less than the preceding payments. Once you have solved for the number of payments (whole number plus fraction), you can easily compute the amount of the final payment using the annuity keys of your calculator. First enter the program to solve for the estimated interest rate per payment period (the program is listed here again for reference), and find the total number of payments. Then, you use the simple annuity routines built into your calculator to compute the partial payment, which is made at the end of period N + 1.

Program Memory	Key Sequence	Program Memory	Key Sequence	Program Memory	Key Sequence
00 01	1	11 01	1	22 00	
01 75	+	12 44	)	23 00	
02 61	RCL	13 85	=	24 00	
03 22	%i	14 65	−	25 00	
04 85	=	15 01	1	26 00	
05 37	2nd yˣ	16 85	=	27 00	
06 43	(	17 51	STO	28 00	
07 61	RCL	18 22	%i	29 00	
08 00	0	19 42	R/S	30 00	
09 45	÷	20 41	RST	31 00	
10 61	RCL	21 00			

Example:

John is purchasing a lot for $20,000, and he wants to pay off his loan by paying $400 a month at the end of each month. The interest rate on the loan is 8% annually, compounded quarterly. How many payments are necessary, and how much will the final payment be?

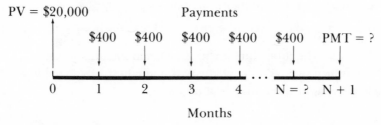

i = 8%/4 per quarter
m = 4 compounding periods per year
k = 12 payments per year

SOLVING FOR FINAL PAYMENT AMOUNT

2

Action	Press	Display
1. Clear calculator and enter program.	2nd CA 2nd LRN Program 2nd LRN RST	00 00 0.
2. Select two-decimal display.	2nd FIX 2	0.00
3. Enter quarterly interest rate.	8 ÷ 4 = %i	2.00
4. Enter payment.	400 PMT	400.00
5. Enter loan amount.	20000 PV	20000.00
6. Store number of compounding periods per year (m) in memory 0.	4 STO 0	4.00
7. Store number of payments per year (k) in memory 1.	12 STO 1	12.00
8. **Calculate estimated interest rate per payment period.**	R/S	0.01
9. **Calculate total number of payments.**	CPT N	60.93
10. Enter number of whole payments.	60 N	60.00
11. Compute present value.	CPT PV	19751.96
12. Subtract from original present value and reenter result as present value.	+/− + 20000 = PV	248.04
13. Clear PMT register and add 1 to N.	0 PMT 1 SUM N	1.00
14. **Compute final payment amount.**	CPT FV	371.02

The result, $371.02, is the amount of the last payment, made at the end of the 61st month.

Accounting

CHAPTER 3

Many financial calculations are required for the daily operation and maintenance of almost every company, large or small. These necessary calculations include the depreciation of various pieces of capital equipment, amortization schedules for leases, determining the number of outstanding shares of stock for earnings per share calculations and bond amortization.

Depreciation

The MBA Owner's Manual discusses the three most common types of depreciation but assumes that an asset is purchased at the beginning of a financial period. When depreciable assets are purchased during a year, the depreciation expense is allocated between periods. The following situation is used to demonstrate this allocation for assets purchased during a year, in this case an oven purchased on April 1st. The asset costs $5,000 and has a five-year life with a $750 salvage value. The company began its fiscal year January 1st. The three major depreciation methods (straight-line, sum-of-the-years'-digits and declining balance) are illustrated for the calculator using the above example.

Reference for these three methods: Kieso and Weygandt, *Intermediate Accounting*, pp. 487-490, 493-494.

Straight Line Depreciation

Straight line depreciation is computed using the formula

$$\text{Depreciation expense} = \frac{\text{Cost} - \text{Salvage}}{\text{Life}}$$

The annual expense is calculated first and then the fractional amount for the first year. This amount is then subtracted from the annual payment to determine the depreciation expense for the final period. The other periods have a depreciation expense equal to the amount computed above.

Calculating the straight line depreciation for our example, the annual depreciation expense is $\frac{\$5000 - \$750}{5} = \$850$ per year.

Year	Depreciation	Comments
1	(9/12) × $850 = $ 637.50	April 1 to Dec. 31 = 9 months
2	$ 850.00	or 9/12 years
3	$ 850.00	
4	$ 850.00	
5	$ 850.00	
6	(3/12) = $850 = $ 212.50	Jan. 1 to April 1 = 3 months
	Total Depreciation $4250.00	

To solve this problem on the MBA:

Action	Press	Display
1. Clear calculator and select two-decimal display.	CLR 2nd **CM** 2nd **FIX** 2	0.00
2. Calculate depreciable value.	5000 − 750 =	4250.00
3. Calculate annual depreciation.	÷ 5 =	850.00
4. Compute depreciation for year 1.	× 9 ÷ 12 =	637.50
5. Calculate depreciation for year 6.	850 × 3 ÷ 12 =	212.50

Sum-of-the-Year's-Digits (SYD) Method

3

The depreciation expense is computed by multiplying the depreciable value (original cost — salvage value) by the ratio of the number of remaining periods to the sum of all years in the life, N, of the asset.

$$\text{Depreciation Expense} = (\text{cost} - \text{salvage}) \times \frac{N + 1 - \text{Year Number}}{\text{Sum of Year's Numbers}}$$

The sum of five year numbers is $1 + 2 + 3 + 4 + 5 = 15$ or $\frac{N \times (N + 1)}{2} = \frac{5 \times 6}{2} = 15$. For each year of our example, the depreciation expense is $4250 \times \frac{6 - \text{year number}}{15}$.

A general program for calculating this type of depreciation follows.

Program Memory	Key Sequence	Program Memory	Key Sequence	Program Memory	Key Sequence
00 61	RCL	11 61	RCL	22 61	RCL
01 21	N	12 24	PV	23 25	FV
02 55	X	13 85	=	24 55	X
03 61	RCL	14 42	R/S	25 61	RCL
04 00	0	15 84	+/−	26 02	2
05 85	=	16 71	SUM	27 85	=
06 25	FV	17 23	PMT	28 24	PV
07 55	X	18 01	1	29 61	RCL
08 61	RCL	19 84	+/−	30 23	PMT
09 01	1	20 71	SUM	31 42	R/S
10 75	+	21 21	N		

Note:

The annuity keys, N , FV , PV , and PMT , are used in this program for data storage only. See the *Introduction* of this book for a list of the memory registers used by these keys.

Sum-of-the-Year's-Digits (SYD) Method

Example: Calculate the depreciation schedule using the $5000 oven depreciated to $750 in five years from its purchase date, April 1.

Action	Press	Display
1. Clear calculator and enter program.	2nd CA 2nd LRN **Program**	0
2. Select two-decimal display.	2nd FIX 2	0.00
3. Enter life of asset.	5 N	5.00
4. Enter cost of asset.	5000 PMT	5000.00
5. Store depreciable value in memory 0.	− 750 = STO 0	4250.00
6. Calculate the sum-of-the-	5 × (5 + 1)	6.00
years'-digits.	÷ 2 =	15.00
7. Divide depreciable value by SYD.	1/x 2nd PROD 0	0.07
8. Calculate fractional parts of	9 ÷ 12 = STO 1	0.75
first year for calculations.	+/− + 1 = STO 2	0.25
9. Calculate first year's depreciation.	RST R/S	1062.50
10. Calculate remaining depreciable value.	R/S	3937.50
Repeat *Steps 9-10* for each 2nd year	RST R/S	1204.17
year.	R/S	2733.33
3rd year	RST R/S	920.83
	R/S	1812.50
4th year	RST R/S	637.50
	R/S	1175.00
5th year	RST R/S	354.17
	R/S	820.83
6th year	RST R/S	70.83
Salvage value remains.	R/S	750.00

Note: You must stop executing the program at the end of the asset's life.

Declining Balance Method

This method of depreciation assumes the depreciation expense is a constant percentage of the net book value. The depreciation expense each year is computed by multiplying the net book value by a fixed percentage which is usually 150% or 200% of the straight-line depreciation rate. The depreciation expense is subtracted from the net book value and the cycle is repeated the following year. This method has some features which should be pointed out. First, unlike straight line or sum-of-the-years'-digits depreciation, the method does not stop depreciating at the end of the life. Rather, the process is stopped when the net book value equals the salvage value. This may occur before or after the asset's life. If it is fully depreciated before the end of the asset's life, you have no problems, but if it extends beyond the asset's life, then you should consider a switch to the straight-line method.

Program Memory	Key Sequence	Program Memory	Key Sequence	Program Memory	Key Sequence
00 61	RCL	11 55	✕	22 61	RCL
01 00	0	12 61	RCL	23 25	FV
02 55	✕	13 01	1	24 55	✕
03 61	RCL	14 75	+	25 61	RCL
04 22	%i	15 61	RCL	26 02	2
05 85	=	16 24	PV	27 85	=
06 25	FV	17 85	=	28 24	PV
07 84	+/−	18 42	R/S	29 61	RCL
08 71	SUM	19 84	+/−	30 23	PMT
09 00	0	20 71	SUM	31 42	R/S
10 84	+/−	21 23	PMT		

DECLINING BALANCE METHOD

Example: Calculate the declining balance depreciation schedule for the $5000 oven depreciated to $750 in five years beginning in April when it was purchased.

For this example, use a 200% factor. Note also that the depreciation stops in the fifth year while the SYD method continued until the sixth year.

Action	Press	Display
1. Clear calculator and enter program.	2nd **CA** 2nd **LRN** Program	0
2. Select two-decimal display.	2nd **FIX** 2	0.00
3. Enter cost of asset.	5000 STO 0 PMT	5000.00
4. Calculate $\frac{\text{Factor}}{\text{Life}}$.	200 ÷ 5 = %i	40.00
5. Calculate fractional parts of first years for calculations.	9 ÷ 12 = STO 1	0.75
	+/− + 1 = STO 2	0.25
6. Calculate first year's depreciation.	RST R/S	1500.00
7. Calculate net book value.	R/S	3500.00
Repeat *Step 6-7* for years 2 through 4.		
2nd year	RST R/S	1400.00
	R/S	2100.00
3rd year	RST R/S	840.00
	R/S	1260.00
4th year	RST R/S	504.00
	R/S	756.00
8. Calculate depreciation for fifth year.	− 750 =	6.00

The depreciation expense for the fifth year is the difference between the net book value at the end of the fourth year and the salvage value of the oven. Calculating the fifth year's depreciation with the program would result in a net book value below the salvage value.

Crossover Point from Declining Balance to Straight-Line Depreciation | 3

You can switch from the declining balance method of depreciation to the straight-line method during an asset's life. In some cases, the switch is unnecessary as shown in the previous declining balance example, but if the asset is not depreciated down to salvage value by the end of its life, then the switch allows you to fully depreciate the asset by the end of its life.

This technique compares the declining balance depreciation expense to what the straight-line expense would be if a crossover is made. Thus, for each year, the declining balance expense is compared to:

$$\frac{(\text{Beginning Net Book Value} - \text{Salvage})}{(\text{Life} + 1 - \text{Current Year})} = \text{Straight-Line expense}$$

When the comparison results in a negative number, then switch to straight-line depreciation in that period.

Program Memory	Key Sequence	Program Memory	Key Sequence	Program Memory	Key Sequence
00 21	N	11 61	RCL	22 61	RCL
01 12	CPT	12 25	FV	23 21	N
02 25	FV	13 65	−	24 85	=
03 55	×	14 61	RCL	25 42	R/S
04 61	RCL	15 01	1	26 84	+/−
05 22	%i	16 44	)	27 71	SUM
06 84	+/−	17 45	÷	28 02	2
07 85	=	18 43	(	29 61	RCL
08 51	STO	19 61	RCL	30 02	2
09 02	2	20 00	0	31 42	R/S
10 42	R/S	21 65	−		

CROSSOVER POINT FROM DECLINING BALANCE TO STRAIGHT-LINE DEPRECIATION

Example: A $98,000 asset has a life of 25 years and a salvage value of $10,000. If the declining balance method with a 150% factor is used to depreciate the asset, is there some point where a crossover to the straight-line method would be profitable?

Note: Data entry for this program must be adjusted by subtracting 1 from the intermediate year number *before* running the program. Otherwise, your results will be the *next* year's depreciation expenses.

Action	Press	Display
1. Clear calculator and enter program.	2nd CA 2nd LRN Program	0
2. Select two-decimal display.	2nd FIX 2	0.00
3. Enter life of asset. For partial first year, store life minus fractional depreciable portion of first year.	25 STO 0	25.00
4. Enter salvage value.	10000 STO 1	10000.00
5. Enter cost of asset. For partial first year, subtract depreciated net book value for that part of first year.	98000 PV	98000.00
6. Calculate declining balance rate $\frac{\text{Factor}}{\text{Life}}$ and enter as a negative value.	150 ÷ 25 = +/- %i	−6.00
7. Enter intermediate year number, subtract 1, and **calculate declining balance depreciation.**	11 − 1 = RST R/S	3167.06
8. **Calculate straight-line depreciation.**	R/S	2852.29
9. **Calculate difference.**	R/S	314.77
If difference is positive, repeat	12 − 1 = RST R/S	2977.03
Steps 7-9 with a later year than	R/S	2829.80
just used.	R/S	147.23
If difference is negative, repeat	13 − 1 = RST R/S	2798.41
Steps 7-9 with an earlier year	R/S	2818.48
than just used.	R/S	−20.06

The year to cross over from declining balance depreciation to the straight-line method is the earliest year which gives a negative result. In this case the crossover point is year 13.

Two Compound Interest Methods of Depreciation

3

Two depreciation methods which are discussed in most advanced accounting textbooks and used by many public utilities are the Sinking Fund and Annuity Methods. Both of these use the same compound interest assumptions as simple annuities.

Each method assumes that the depreciation expense for the period is the sum of the allocation of the asset's cost and the imputed interest for that period. The difference between the two methods is the treatment of the imputed interest.

Reference for these methods is Welsch, Zlatkovich, and White, *Intermediate Accounting,* pp. 570-573. For a historical view of the development of these methods, see W.A. Paton, *Accountant's Handbook,* pp. 629-634.

SINKING FUND METHOD

This method *assumes* that a fund is established which will equal the accumulated depreciation at the end of the depreciable asset's life. The depreciation expense is the sum of the assumed annual investment and the implicit interest earned on the accumulating fund. Accumulated depreciation is increased each period by the amount of the depreciation expense, which also increases each period under this method.

The following program computes the depreciation expense, imputed interest income, accumulated depreciation and net book value when the period is entered.

Program Memory	Key Sequence	Program Memory	Key Sequence	Program Memory	Key Sequence
00 51	STO	11 61	RCL	22 00	
01 01	1	12 00	0	23 00	
02 26	2nd P/I	13 85	=	24 00	
03 42	R/S	14 42	R/S	25 00	
04 34	x:y	15 41	RST	26 00	
05 42	R/S	16 00		27 00	
06 61	RCL	17 00		28 00	
07 01	1	18 00		29 00	
08 20	2nd BAL	19 00		30 00	
09 42	R/S	20 00		31 00	
10 75	+	21 00			

Two Compound Interest Methods
of Depreciation

Example: A utility company purchases a delivery van for $9000 and expects to sell it in four years for $1000. With a 7% rate assumed to depreciate the value of the van with the sinking fund method, calculate the assumed annual payment and the depreciation expense, imputed interest earned, accumulated depreciation and net book value for each period.

Action	Press	Display
1. Clear calculator and enter program.	2nd CA 2nd LRN	00 00
	Program 2nd LRN RST	0.
2. Select two-decimal display.	2nd FIX 2	0.00
3. Enter life of asset.	4 N	4.00
4. Enter interest rate.	7 %i	7.00
5. Calculate cost — salvage.	9000 STO 0	9000.00
	− 1000 = FV	8000.00
6. Compute payment.	CPT PMT	1801.82
7. Enter period number and calculate depreciation expense.	1 R/S	1801.82
8. Calculate imputed interest.	R/S	0.00
9. Calculate accumulated depreciation.	R/S	−1801.82
10. Calculate net book value.	R/S	7198.18
Repeat *Steps 7-10* for each period.	2 R/S	1927.95
	R/S	−126.13
	R/S	−3729.78
	R/S	5270.22
	3 R/S	2062.91
	R/S	−261.08
	R/S	−5792.69
	R/S	3207.31
	4 R/S	2207.31
	R/S	−405.49
	R/S	−8000.00
	R/S	1000.00

The interest earned on the balance and accumulated depreciation are shown as negative numbers. Think of these as the credit entry for interest and the credit balance for accumulated depreciation. Here, the assumed constant investment is $1801.82 each period. Thus, for period 2 the depreciation expense is the sum of the assumed payment and the imputed interest earned, i.e.:

Period 2

Payment	$1801.82
Imputed interest	126.13
Depreciation Expense	$1927.95

ANNUITY METHOD

The annuity method of depreciation assumes the purchase price of a fixed asset is an investment of capital which would earn an annual (or periodic) return if it were invested at some given interest rate. The annual depreciation expense is a constant amount equal to the annual return on an assumed capital investment of an amount equal to the net purchase price of the asset. Interest is computed each period on the net book value of the asset and is deducted from the periodic depreciation expense to determine the credit to accumulated depreciation. In other words, accumulated depreciation increases each period by the depreciation expense *less* the imputed interest amount.

Under this method, the net purchase price of the asset, plus periodic interest on net book value, is allocated over the life of the asset.

After determining the annual depreciation expense, the following program can be used to compute the credit to accumulated depreciation, the interest earned, and the net book value for each period.

Program Memory	Key Sequence	Program Memory	Key Sequence	Program Memory	Key Sequence
00 51	STO	11 00		22 00	
01 00	0	12 00		23 00	
02 26	2nd P/I	13 00		24 00	
03 42	R/S	14 00		25 00	
04 34	x:y	15 00		26 00	
05 42	R/S	16 00		27 00	
06 61	RCL	17 00		28 00	
07 00	0	18 00		29 00	
08 20	2nd BAL	19 00		30 00	
09 42	R/S	20 00		31 00	
10 41	RST	21 00			

TWO COMPOUND INTEREST METHODS
OF DEPRECIATION

Example: A transformer sub-station costs $800,000 with an estimated salvage value of $100,000 in ten years. Calculate the annual depreciation expense and the credit to accumulated depreciation, interest earned, and net book value for each year. A 6% interest rate is assumed.

Action	Press	Display
1. Clear calculator and enter program.	2nd CA 2nd LRN	00 00
	Program 2nd LRN RST	0.
2. Select two-decimal display.	2nd FIX 2	0.00
3. Enter life of asset.	10 N	10.00
4. Enter interest rate.	6 %i	6.00
5. Enter salvage value.	100000 FV	100000.00
6. Compute present value.	CPT PV	55839.48
7. Calculate net book value.	+/− + 800000 =	744160.52
8. Compute annual depreciation expense.	PV CPT PMT	101107.57
9. Enter cost of asset.	800000 PV	800000.00
10. Enter period number and calculate credit to accumulated depreciation.	1 R/S	53107.57
11. Calculate imputed interest.	R/S	48000.00
12. Calculate net book value at end of period.	R/S	746892.43
Repeat *Steps 10-12* for each period to find full depreciation schedule.		
2nd year	2 R/S	56294.02
	R/S	44813.55
	R/S	690598.40
3rd year	3 R/S	59671.67
⋮	R/S	41435.90
	R/S	630926.74
10th year	10 R/S	89724.12
	R/S	11383.45
(salvage value)	R/S	100000.00

Leasehold Amortization

3

Leasehold amortization requires determining the present value of the lease payments using an appropriate discount rate. This lease obligation is then amortized over the life of the lease with the annual lease payment being separated into two components—interest on the unpaid obligation and reduction of the lease obligation. The schedules can differ depending on the timing of the payments. The solutions for leases with payments made at the beginning of the period and for leases with payments made at the end of the period are shown below.

Program Memory	Key Sequence	Program Memory	Key Sequence	Program Memory	Key Sequence
00 51	STO	11 00		22 00	
01 00	0	12 00		23 00	
02 26	2nd P/I	13 00		24 00	
03 42	R/S	14 00		25 00	
04 34	x:y	15 00		26 00	
05 42	R/S	16 00		27 00	
06 61	RCL	17 00		28 00	
07 00	0	18 00		29 00	
08 20	2nd BAL	19 00		30 00	
09 42	R/S	20 00		31 00	
10 41	RST	21 00			

Example: A firm has leased some equipment for four years and has agreed to pay the annual $5000 lease at the beginning of each yearly period. Assuming an annual effective discount rate of 6%, prepare a leasehold amortization schedule for this equipment.

Note: Because the 2nd P/I and 2nd BAL routines are set up to handle payments at the *end* of the period, while the payments in this example are made at the *beginning* of each year, you'll need to make certain adjustments in your imput data. Also, if you want the results for some intermediate period, simply enter the period number, adjust for the annuity due situation, and execute the program. It is not necessary to compute the complete amortization schedule in sequence.

Calculating Leasehold Amortization Schedule (Payments at beginning of period)

Action	Press	Display
1. Clear calculator and enter program.	[2nd] CA [2nd] LRN	00 00
	Program [2nd] LRN [RST]	0.
2. Select two-decimal display.	[2nd] FIX 2	0.00
3. Enter life of asset.	4 [N]	4.00
4. Enter discount rate.	6 [%i]	6.00
5. Enter lease payment.	5000 [PMT]	5000.00
6. Calculate discounted lease balance.	[2nd] DUE [PV]	18365.06
7. Calculate balance after payment at start of first period and reenter as present value.	[−] [RCL] [PMT] [=] [PV]	13365.06
8. Enter next period number and adjust for annuity due situation.	2 [−] 1 [=]	1.00
9. Calculate reduction in lease balance.	[R/S]	4198.10
10. Calculate interest.	[R/S]	801.90
11. Calculate balance after payment.	[R/S]	9166.96
Repeat *Steps 8-11* for each period.	3 [−] 1 [=] [R/S]	4449.98
	[R/S]	550.02
	[R/S]	4716.98
	4 [−] 1 [=] [R/S]	4716.98
	[R/S]	283.02
	[R/S]	−0.00

The same program can be used to solve for payments at the end of each period as was used for payments at the beginning of a period. So, press [CLR] [2nd] CM instead of [2nd] CA when you start to work the example.

3

Example:	Design a leasehold amortization schedule for the previous example assuming now that payments are made at the end of each period.	

	Action	Press	Display
Calculating Leasehold Amortization Schedule (Payment at end of period)	1. Clear calculator and reset program counter.	CLR 2nd CM RST	0.00
	2. Enter life.	4 N	4.00
	3. Enter discount rate.	6 %i	6.00
	4. Enter lease payment.	5000 PMT	5000.00
	5. Calculate discounted lease balance.	CPT PV	17325.53
	6. Enter period number and calculate reduction in lease balance.	1 R/S	3960.47
	7. Calculate interest.	R/S	1039.53
	8. Calculate balance after payment.	R/S	13365.06
	Repeat *Steps 6-8* for each period.	2 R/S	4198.10
		R/S	801.90
		R/S	9166.96
		3 R/S	4449.98
		R/S	550.02
		R/S	4716.98
		4 R/S	4716.98
		R/S	283.02
		R/S	0.00

Reference:	Kieso and Weygandt, *Intermediate Accounting,* pp. 928-930.

Weighted Average Number of Shares

In order to compute earnings per share, the weighted average number of shares outstanding during the period must be computed. The program below computes the weighted average number of shares outstanding based on actual days held. Stock dividends and splits are not considered in this program.

Program Memory	Key Sequence	Program Memory	Key Sequence	Program Memory	Key Sequence
00 23	PMT	11 42	R/S	22 61	RCL
01 61	RCL	12 24	PV	23 24	PV
02 21	N	13 61	RCL	24 51	STO
03 33	DBD	14 01	1	25 01	1
04 61	RCL	15 55	X	26 61	RCL
05 23	PMT	16 61	RCL	27 25	FV
06 21	N	17 23	PMT	28 42	R/S
07 85	=	18 85	=	29 41	RST
08 23	PMT	19 25	FV	30 00	
09 71	SUM	20 71	SUM	31 00	
10 00	0	21 02	2		

Example: Calculate the weighted average number of shares for 1976 for a printing company if it entered the year with 50,000 shares and ended the year with 59,300 shares. The following transactions took place during the year.

Date	Shares Issued (Purchased)	Outstanding Shares
1-25-76	2500	52500
5-3-76	8000	60500
10-15-76	(1200)	59300

3

Action	Press	Display
1. Clear calculator and enter program.	2nd CA 2nd LRN	00 00
	Program 2nd LRN RST	0.
2. Select two-decimal display.	2nd FIX 2	0.00
3. Enter date for first day of period in MM. DDYYYY format.	1.011976 N	1.01
4. Enter number of shares outstanding at first of period.	50000 STO 1	50000.00
5. Enter transaction date in MM.DDYYYY format and calculate number of days shares held.	1.251976 R/S	24.00
6. Enter number of shares held after transaction.	52500 R/S	1200000.00
Repeat *Steps 5-6* for each transaction in order of occurrence.	5.031976 R/S	99.00
	60500 R/S	5197500.00
	10.151976 R/S	165.00
	59300 R/S	9982500.00
7. Enter date of last day of period in MM.DDYYYY format.	12.311976 R/S	77.00
8. Enter number of shares held at end of period.	59300 R/S	4566100.00
9. Recall total share days.	RCL 2 ÷	20946100.00
10. Recall total days.	RCL 0	365.00
11. Calculate weighted average number of shares outstanding during year.	=	57386.58

Reference: Kieso and Weygandt, *Intermediate Accounting*, pp. 672-675.

Amortizing Bond Premium or Discount (Effective Interest Method)

This method assumes bond interest expense is computed using the effective interest rate times the bond book value rather than the nominal rate times the par value. The cash paid out, however, is computed using the nominal interest rate times the par value. The difference between the interest expense and cash payment is the bond premium or discount. This amount is added to the bond book value if it is a discount and subtracted if it is a premium. The adjusted book value is used for the interest expense computation for the next period.

Program

Program Memory	Key Sequence	Program Memory	Key Sequence	Program Memory	Key Sequence
00 51	STO	11 00		22 00	
01 00	0	12 00		23 00	
02 26	2nd P/I	13 00		24 00	
03 42	R/S	14 00		25 00	
04 34	x:y	15 00		26 00	
05 42	R/S	16 00		27 00	
06 61	RCL	17 00		28 00	
07 00	0	18 00		29 00	
08 20	2nd BAL	19 00		30 00	
09 42	R/S	20 00		31 00	
10 41	RST	21 00			

Example:

The LB Tennis Ranch has issued $100,000 worth of bonds for $93,204.84. The bonds mature in ten years and have a nominal rate of 7% with a semiannual coupon. The effective interest rate or yield is 8%. Calculate the bond discount, interest, and balance after interest for period 1 and 10.

Action	Press	Display
1. Clear calculator and enter program.	2nd CA 2nd LRN	00 00
	Program 2nd LRN RST	0.
2. Select two-decimal display.	2nd FIX 2	0.00
3. Enter number of periods.	20 N	20.00
4. Calculate and enter coupon	7 % × 100000	
payment per period.	÷ 2 = PMT	3500.00
5. Enter interest rate per period.	8 ÷ 2 = %i	4.00
6. Enter cost of bond.	93204.84 PV	93204.84
7. Enter period number and		
calculate bond discount.	1 R/S	−228.19
8. Calculate bond interest expense.	R/S	3728.19
9. Calculate adjusted book value.	R/S	93433.03
Repeat *Steps 7-9* for each period.	10 R/S	−324.79
	R/S	3824.79
	R/S	95944.56

Reference: Kieso and Weygandt, *Intermediate Accounting*, pp. 560-562.

Installment Contracts (U.S. and European Methods)   3

The method used in the U.S. to determine the periodic interest rate (from a given nominal annual interest rate) differs from the method used in European countries. This application shows you how to compute the payment and the principal, interest, and remaining balance, using both methods. (In our model, we assume that payments are made at the end of each payment period.)

First, the U.S. method is shown and then the European method.

Use the following program to compute a complete amortization schedule in each example:

Program Memory	Key Sequence	Program Memory	Key Sequence	Program Memory	Key Sequence
00 01	1	11 61	RCL	22 00	
01 71	SUM	12 00	0	23 00	
02 00	0	13 20	2nd BAL	24 00	
03 61	RCL	14 42	R/S	25 00	
04 00	0	15 41	RST	26 00	
05 42	R/S	16 00		27 00	
06 26	2nd P/I	17 00		28 00	
07 34	x:y	18 00		29 00	
08 42	R/S	19 00		30 00	
09 34	x:y	20 00		31 00	
10 42	R/S	21 00			

U.S. Method

In the U.S., the normal practice is to give the nominal annual interest rate. This means that a 6% annual rate compounded monthly is computed as 6% ÷ 12 = 0.5% per month. This procedure has been followed in the examples in this book.

Example:

A company is buying a machine and will pay off the loan in six monthly installments. The machine costs $18,000, and the nominal annual interest rate on the loan is 11.5%, compounded monthly. How much is the payment, what will the principal, interest, and remaining balance be after the third payment, and what is the complete amortization schedule?

INSTALLMENT CONTRACTS
(U.S. AND EUROPEAN METHODS)

Action	Press	Display
1. Clear calculator and enter program.	2nd CA 2nd LRN	00 00
	Program 2nd LRN RST	0.
2. Select two-decimal display.	2nd FIX 2	0.00
3. Enter number of periods.	6 N	6.00
4. Enter amount of loan.	18000 PV	18000.00
5. Enter monthly interest.	11.5 ÷ 12 = %i	0.96
6. Compute monthly payment.	CPT PMT	3101.42
7. Enter 3rd period and compute		
principal.	3 2nd P/I	2985.33
8. Compute interest.	x:y	116.09
9. Enter 3rd period and compute		
remaining balance.	3 2nd BAL	9128.75
10. Calculate complete amortization		
schedule.		
period	R/S	1.00
interest	R/S	172.50
principal	R/S	2928.92
balance	R/S	15071.08
period	R/S	2.00
interest	R/S	144.43
principal	R/S	2956.99
balance	R/S	12114.08
period	R/S	3.00
interest	R/S	116.09
principal	R/S	2985.33
balance	R/S	9128.75
period	R/S	4.00
interest	R/S	87.48
principal	R/S	3013.94
balance	R/S	6114.81
period	R/S	5.00
interest	R/S	58.60
principal	R/S	3042.82
balance	R/S	3071.98
period	R/S	6.00
interest	R/S	29.44
principal	R/S	3071.98
balance	R/S	−0.00

Note: If you re-entered your data (payment amount, interest rate, etc.) before running the amortization program, you would have a final balance of $0.03, rather than zero. The reason is that the payment amount, 3101.42, is actually 3101.424736, rounded to two places. Whenever you want to check the results of one calculation by running your data through another calculation, be sure that you enter all the significant digits of any calculated result; otherwise, small variances may show up. Remember, you can at any point obtain the full calculated answer by pressing 2nd FIX **9.** This key sequence will not interrupt any calculation you may have in progress.

European (or Effective Interest) Method   The European or Effective Interest Method of computing a loan amortization schedule differs only in how the periodic interest is determined. Annual interest is stated as an effective, rather than nominal, rate; therefore, it is incorrect to divide the annual rate by the number of compounding periods per year to find the periodic compounding rate. Instead, the periodic rate must be calculated. The relationship is expressed as

$$(1 + PE_i)^n = 1 + AE_i$$

where PE_i = periodic effective interest rate, expressed as a decimal.
   AE_i = annual effective interest rate, expressed as a decimal.
   n = number of compounding periods per year.

If you know the annual effective rate, you can solve for the periodic rate with the formula

$$PE_i = (1 + AE_i)^{1/n} - 1$$

If you know the periodic effective rate, you can solve for the annual rate by using

$$AE_i = (1 + PE_i)^n - 1$$

You can use the annuity routines built into your calculator to solve for the periodic effective interest. The procedure is:

- Enter the number of periods, and press N .
- Enter $1 and press PV .
- Enter 1 + AE_i (expressed as a decimal), and press FV .
- Press CPT %i .

Note: The result is expressed as a percent rather than a decimal.

INSTALLMENT CONTRACTS
(U.S. AND EUROPEAN METHODS)

Example: (Using the same values as in the previous example, so that you can compare the results): A company is taking out a loan for $18,000, which it will repay in six monthly installments. The effective annual interest rate is 11.5%, compounded monthly. What is the monthly payment amount, what will be the interest, principal, and remaining balance after the third payment, and what is the complete amortization schedule?

Since the only difference between the U.S. and European methods is the way the periodic effective interest rate is calculated, we'll use the same amortization schedule program listed above.

Action	Press	Display
1. Clear calculator and enter program.	2nd CA 2nd LRN	00 00
	Program 2nd LRN RST	0.
2. Select two-decimal display.	2nd FIX 2	0.00
3. Enter data and **calculate periodic effective interest rate (PE$_i$).**	12 N 1 PV	1.00
	1 + 11.5 % = FV	1.12
	CPT %i 2nd FIX 9	0.91124684
The periodic interest rate is 0.911%. Remember, the key sequence gives you your answer as a percent, while the formula expresses the rate as a decimal.		
4. **Calculate the monthly payment on the loan.**	2nd FIX 2	0.91
	0 FV 6 N	6.00
	18000 PV	18000.00
	CPT PMT	3096.40
5. **Enter 3rd period and compute principal.**	3 2nd P/I	2986.07
6. **Compute interest.**	x:y	110.34
7. **Enter 3rd period, and compute remaining balance.**	3 2nd BAL	9122.45

Action	Press	Display
8. Calculate amortization schedule.		
period	R/S	1.00
interest	R/S	164.02
principal	R/S	2932.38
balance	R/S	15067.62
period	R/S	2.00
interest	R/S	137.30
principal	R/S	2959.10
balance	R/S	12108.52
period	R/S	3.00
interest	R/S	110.34
principal	R/S	2986.07
balance	R/S	9122.45
period	R/S	4.00
interest	R/S	83.13
principal	R/S	3013.28
balance	R/S	6109.18
period	R/S	5.00
interest	R/S	55.67
principal	R/S	3040.73
balance	R/S	3068.44
period	R/S	6.00
interest	R/S	27.96
principal	R/S	3068.44
balance	R/S	0.00

Finance

CHAPTER 4

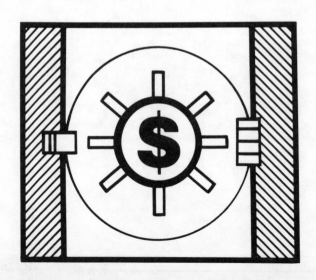

Finance is a subject that involves everyone, whether you are setting up a personal budget or managing a multimillion-dollar corporation. Without an understanding of the way financial transactions work, you are seriously handicapped when it comes to sound financial decision-making. Your calculator and the applications offered in this chapter can help you answer the questions posed today by real-life money management: Should you buy on credit or save toward a purchase? How much will you pay for a loan? Will stock A or stock B offer the best return on your money? Which financial alternative should your firm choose?

This chapter is divided into two major sections. The first section covers personal financial situations, and the second section deals with business finance. Each section begins with basic examples and moves on to more advanced problems. You'll find problems about the total cost of interest on a loan, life insurance, installment schedules, corporate cash management, growth stocks, capital budgeting, and many more. Of course, not every financial situation is covered in this chapter, but remember that many of the applications and programs contained here can be adapted by minor changes to fit other situations.

Doubling Period for a Compounded Annual Growth Rate

You may sometimes find it necessary to determine how long it will take for an amount of money to double, if compounded at an annual interest or growth rate.

Example: If the annual rate of inflation is 7%, how long will it take for the cost of living to double? To answer this question, take $1 and move it forward in time until it grows to $2.

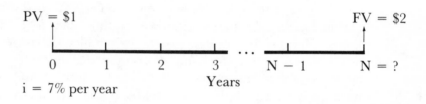

Action	Press	Display
1. Clear calculator and select two-decimal display.	CLR 2nd CM 2nd FIX 2	0.00
2. Enter $1 as present value and $2 as future value.	1 PV 2 FV	2.00
3. Enter annual growth rate.	7 %i	7.00
4. Calculate the number of periods.	CPT N	10.24

If the 7% inflation rate continues, it will take a little over 10 years for the cost of living to double. Try the same situation at a 12% inflation rate.

Average Yield on an Investment

4

Yield rates on investments are figured in a variety of ways, so you need to be careful when comparing claims concerning yields. One way to analyze yield claims and to be sure that you're comparing "apples with apples" is to compute the average annual return of the investment.

Example: Last year you bought several shares of stock in a corporation at $98 per share. This year the stock is selling at $122 per share. The stock has paid no dividends. What is the percentage increase in value that you could collect if you sold the stock? Ignore any sales fees to sell the stock.

Calculating Average Yield on an Investment *Without* Dividends

Action	Press	Display
1. Clear calculator and select two-decimal display.	CLR 2nd CM 2nd FIX 2	0.00
2. Enter the original value of the stock.	98 PV	98.00
3. Enter the new value.	122 FV	122.00
4. Enter number of periods.	1 N	1.00
5. **Calculate average annual yield.**	CPT %i	24.49

The yield is about 24.5%.

As another example, consider the stock you bought two years ago for $22.50 a share. You have received dividends amounting to $2.00 per share since you bought it, and it's now selling for $30.00 per share. What is its average annual yield?

Calculating Average Yield on an Investment *With* Dividends

Action	Press	Display
1. Clear calculator and select two-decimal display.	CLR 2nd CM 2nd FIX 2	0.00
2. Enter the original value.	22.5 PV	22.50
3. Calculate and enter the new value (present selling price plus dividends).	30 + 2 = FV	32.00
4. Enter number of periods that you've owned the stock.	2 N	2.00
5. **Calculate average annual yield.**	CPT %i	19.26

The yield is approximately 19.26%.

Equivalent Yields on Tax-Free and Taxable Bonds

Some municipal and state governments issue tax-free bonds; that is, you receive dividends which are exempt from federal income tax. These bonds usually don't pay a high rate of interest, but the income tax savings could result in a higher yield for you than some taxable investments.

For example, you're currently in a 45% income tax bracket and are considering buying a 6% tax-free yield municipal bond. What taxable yield would you have to earn to get the same amount after taxes?

Formula

$$\text{Equivalent taxable yield} = \frac{\text{tax-free yield}}{(100\% - \text{income tax percentage})}$$

Calculating equivalent taxable yield

Action	Press	Display
1. Clear calculator and select two-decimal display.	CLR 2nd CM 2nd FIX 2	0.00
2. Enter tax-free yield.	6 ÷	6.00
3. Calculate equivalent taxable yield.	(1 − 45 % =	10.91

Note:

100 % − 45 % is the same as 1 − 45 % . A shorter key sequence has been used for keystroke economy. Also, note that the = key automatically completes the open parenthesis before performing the pending operation, division in this case.

The equivalent taxable yield would be 10.91%.

Another example:

You currently own a taxable bond that pays 10% dividends and you are in a 38% income tax bracket. What dividend rate would you need to earn in a tax-free bond to get the same return?

Formula

Equivalent tax-free yield = Taxable yield (100% − income tax percentage)

Calculating equivalent tax-free yield

Action	Press	Display
1. Clear calculator and select two-decimal display.	CLR 2nd CM 2nd FIX 2	0.00
2. Enter taxable yield.	10 ×	10.00
3. Calculate equivalent tax-free yield.	(1 − 38 % =	6.20

You would need to earn a 6.2% annual dividend rate on a tax-free bond.

Cost of Whole Life Versus Term Insurance

4

Most term life insurance policies offer you coverage at a relatively low premium rate, but do not build any cash value. Whole life insurance policies, on the other hand, usually have a certain cash value at the end of a specified period, but their premiums are generally higher.

Example: You have decided that you need $20,000 of life insurance coverage. You can get that coverage with term insurance for a $4.20 premium payment each month. An insurance salesman offers you a whole life policy which will have a cash value of $5000 after 25 years, but the monthly premiums for this policy are $18. Which policy should you buy?

One way to decide is to calculate the difference in monthly premiums (18 − $4.20 = $13.80). You know that you can earn 6% annual interest compounded monthly if you deposit this amount in a savings account at the first of each month. At the end of 25 years, will this monthly saving be worth more or less than the $5000 cash value of the second policy?

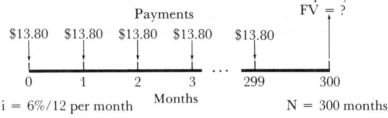

Action	Press	Display
1. Clear calculator and select two-decimal display.	CLR 2nd CM 2nd FIX 2	0.00
2. Calculate and enter extra premium amount per month.	18 − 4.2 = PMT	13.80
3. Calculate and enter number of monthly payments.	25 × 12 = N	300.00
4. Calculate and enter monthly interest rate.	6 ÷ 12 = %i	0.50
5. **Calculate the value of the payments at the end of 25 years.**	2nd DUE FV	9611.13
6. **Compare this amount to the cash value of the whole life policy.**	− 5000 =	4611.13

Buying the term insurance and depositing the premium difference in savings each month will result in an additional $4611.13 over the 25 years.

Note: This solution assumes that the price of term insurance and the interest rate remain the same and that you deposit the premium difference in a savings account faithfully each month.

Comparing Time Payments to Price

Products are often purchased on a time payment, or credit, plan. One way to evaluate a time payment purchase is to compute the present value of the series of payments at the interest rate quoted by the seller and compare that amount to the sale price of the item.

Example: A salesman tells you he will sell you the latest vacuum cleaner for payments of only $15 a month for three years at 1¾% interest a month. A store has advertised the same vacuum cleaner for $325. Which deal is best?

This situation is a simple matter of finding the present value of the monthly payments.

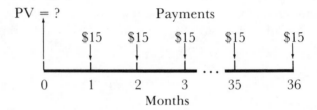

Action	Press	Display
1. Clear calculator and select two-decimal display.	CLR 2nd CM 2nd FIX 2	0.00
2. Calculate and enter number of payments	3 × 12 = N	36.00
3. Enter monthly interest rate.	1.75 %i	1.75
4. Enter monthly payment.	15 PMT	15.00
5. **Calculate present value.**	CPT PV	398.14

Compare this amount to the store's advertised price. The salesman's "deal" is not really a good one. The rate of interest is too high.

Total Amount of Interest Paid

When you borrow, you may want to determine exactly how much money the loan is costing you.

xample: You borrow $4400 from your credit union to buy a new car. The credit union charges 10.5% annual interest, compounded monthly, and you will repay the loan in 36 monthly payments. How much will it cost to borrow the $4400?

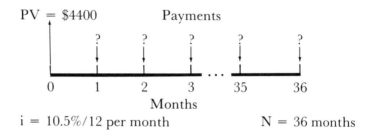

PV = $4400   Payments

0   1   2   3   35   36

Months

i = 10.5%/12 per month   N = 36 months

Action	Press	Display
1. Clear calculator and select two-decimal display.	CLR 2nd CM 2nd FIX 2	0.00
2. Enter number of periods.	36 N	36.00
3. Enter monthly interest rate.	10.5 ÷ 12 = %i	0.88
4. Enter loan amount as present value.	4400 PV	4400.00
5. Compute monthly payment amount.	CPT PMT	143.01
6. **Calculate the total amount you will repay on the loan.**	× 36 =	5148.39
7. **Subtract the principal to find the total interest paid.**	− 4400 =	748.39

Savings that Result from a Down Payment

There is often a need to examine a loan from several angles to find the best option for you.

Example: You need to buy a new refrigerator ($895) and can afford a monthly payment of $50 a month. The finance company charges 18% annual interest compounded monthly. How would it affect the loan if you made a $300 down payment, rather than financing the entire purchase?

Time line for purchase *without* down payment

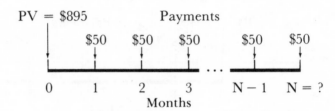

$i = 18\%/12$ per month

Time line for purchase *with* $300 down payment

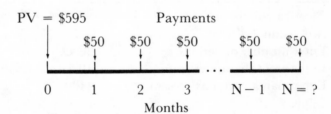

$i = 18\%/12$ per month

Savings that Result from a Down Payment

Calculating the interest paid without a down payment

Action	Press	Display
1. Clear calculator and select two-decimal display.	CLR 2nd CM 2nd FIX 2	0.00
2. Enter purchase price.	895 PV	895.00
3. Enter payment.	50 PMT	50.00
4. Calculate and enter monthly interest rate.	18 ÷ 12 = %i	1.50
5. Calculate the number of payments needed to pay off the loan.	CPT N	21.00
6. Compute total amount you will pay (principal plus interest).	50 × 21 =	1050.00
7. **Calculate the total amount of interest paid without a down payment.** (Leave your calculator on.)	− RCL PV = STO 0	155.00

Calculating the interest paid with a $300 down payment

Action	Press	Display
8. Deduct down payment from purchase price and enter new present value.	RCL PV − 300 = PV	595.00
9. Calculate the number of payments needed to pay off this loan.	CPT N	13.21
10. Compute total amount.	× 50 =	660.31
11. **Calculate total interest.**	− RCL PV =	65.31
12. **Compare this amount to total interest paid without a down payment.**	+/− + RCL 0 =	89.69

Almost $90 in interest is saved by making the $300 down payment.

Converting Add-on Interest to an Annual Rate

To figure "add-on" interest, multiply the total amount financed by the annual add-on rate, then multiply this result by the number of years of the loan. This gives you the total amount of the interest you pay for the loan. To figure your payments, add the interest to the principal and divide the total by the number of payments. In other words, a fixed part of each payment is interest and the rest goes to pay back the principal.

Example:

During a recent storm, you discovered that your roof leaks. A repairman offers to give you a whole new roof for $2500. He will finance the work for you at 6% add-on interest, with payments to be made at the end of each month for two years (24 months). What would your payments be and what is the equivalent annual interest rate compounded monthly?

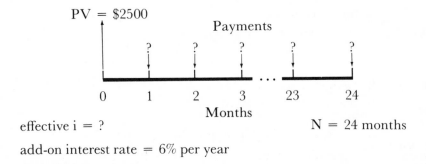

effective i = ?

N = 24 months

add-on interest rate = 6% per year

Action	Press	Display
1. Clear calculator and select two-decimal display.	CLR 2nd CM 2nd FIX 2	0.00
2. Enter total amount financed.	2500 PV	2500.00
3. Calculate add-on interest.	× 6 % × 2 =	300.00
4. Calculate and enter monthly payment.	+ RCL PV =	2800.00
	÷ 24 = PMT	116.67
5. Enter number of periods.	24 N	24.00
6. **Compute monthly nominal interest rate.**	CPT %i	0.93
7. **Convert to annual interest.**	× 12 =	11.13

Notice that add-on interest rates often appear to be very low, but the equivalent annual rate is quite high. If you're ever considering a loan at an add-on rate, you should always ask for or compute the equivalent annual rate and compare that percentage to the annual rate you could get on the same loan from other sources.

Computation of Rebate Due (Rule of 78's)

4

When you decide to pay off a loan before the end of its original life, you need to know two things: how much of an interest rebate you will receive and how much will be needed to pay off the loan.

A formula called "the rule of 78's" is commonly used to calculate the rebate due. Once you determine this amount you can easily find the payoff amount.

The rule of 78's formula

$$\frac{(n - k + 1)(n - k)}{n^2 + n} \times \text{total interest cost of the loan}$$

where: n = original number of loan payments
k = number of payment periods that will have elapsed when loan is paid off

The problem can be solved in three stages. First, calculate the total interest due on the original loan. Next, compute the rebate received for early payoff, using the rule of 78's. Finally, determine the payoff amount by multiplying the number of payments left by the payment amount and then subtracting the rebate. The result is the amount that must be paid.

Use the following rule of 78's program to calculate the rebate, and to compute the payoff amount.

Program Memory	Key Sequence	Program Memory	Key Sequence	Program Memory	Key Sequence
00 55	×	11 43	(	22 55	×
01 43	(	12 61	RCL	23 43	(
02 61	RCL	13 00	0	24 61	RCL
03 01	1	14 75	+	25 01	1
04 75	+	15 14	x²	26 75	+
05 01	1	16 85	=	27 01	1
06 44	)	17 42	R/S	28 85	=
07 55	×	18 84	+/−	29 42	R/S
08 61	RCL	19 75	+	30 41	RST
09 01	1	20 61	RCL	31 00	
10 45	÷	21 02	2		

COMPUTATION OF REBATE DUE
(RULE OF 78's)

Example: You want to pay off your three-year (36 month) car loan after the eighteenth payment. You originally borrowed $5000 at 5% add-on annual interest, and your monthly payments are $159.72. How much interest will be rebated, and what amount will pay off the loan?

Rebate due = ?
Payoff amount = ?

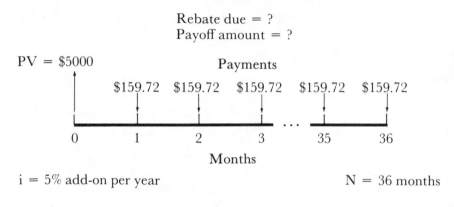

PV = $5000

Payments

$159.72 $159.72 $159.72 $159.72 $159.72

0   1   2   3   35   36

Months

i = 5% add-on per year

N = 36 months

Action	Press	Display
1. Clear calculator and enter program.	2nd CA 2nd LRN Program 2nd LRN RST	00 00 0.
2. Select two-decimal display.	2nd FIX 2	0.00
3. Store original number of payment periods in memory 0.	36 STO 0	36.00
4. Subtract current period number and store result in memory 1.	– 19 = STO 1	17.00
5. Store payment amount in memory 2.	159.72 STO 2	159.72
6. Calculate total (add-on) interest on loan.	5000 × 5 % × 3 =	750.00
7. Calculate rebate due using the rule of 78's.	R/S	172.30
8. Calculate payoff amount.	R/S	2702.66

Your interest rebate will be $172.30 and the payoff amount will be $2702.66.

A Personal Lease-or-Purchase Decision

4

Sometimes you need to decide whether to lease or buy an item on credit. One way to evaluate these alternatives is to compute the present values of both series of cash flows (payments and expenses) and to compare these amounts, ignoring taxes.

Example: The sale price of a car is $5000. You can purchase the car by making a $1000 down payment and financing the balance at 1% per month for three years (36 months). You figure that your maintenance costs will be $15 a month and that you can sell the car for $2500 at the end of the three years. Alternatively, you can lease a similar car for three years at $115 a month with the leasing company taking care of maintenance. Which alternative would save you money in the long run?

Your bank currently pays 5% annual interest, compounded monthly, so use that rate in calculating the two present values. The problem can be solved in the following steps.

1. Calculate the monthly payments on the car loan.
2. Add the monthly maintenance cost to the payment and compute the present value.
3. Add the down payment to the present value of the monthly expenses of purchasing the car.
4. Calculate the present value of the $2500 resale value of the car and subtract it from the amount in *step 3* above, since it is a cash return. The result is the present value of the cost of purchasing the car.
5. Compute the present value of the lease payments and compare this amount to the present value of the purchase option.

Time line for purchase option

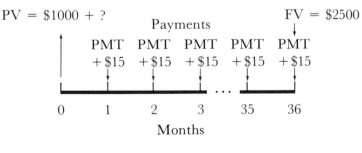

$$PV = \$1000 + ?$$

Payments

PMT PMT PMT PMT PMT
+ $15 + $15 + $15 + $15 + $15

$$FV = \$2500$$

0   1   2   3   35   36

Months

%i = 5%/12 per month   N = 36 months

A Personal Lease-or-Purchase Decision

Time line for lease option

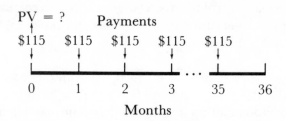

$$PV = ?$$ Payments

$115 $115 $115 $115 $115

0   1   2   3   35   36

Months

%i = 5%/12 per month   N = 36 months

Action	Press	Display
1. Clear calculator and select two-decimal display.	CLR 2nd CM 2nd FIX 2	0.00
2. Enter loan amount.	4000 PV	4000.00
3. Enter number of periods.	36 N	36.00
4. Enter loan interest rate.	1 %i	1.00
5. Compute monthly loan payment.	CPT PMT	132.86
6. Add monthly maintenance cost.	15 SUM PMT	15.00
7. Enter current interest rate.	5 ÷ 12 = %i	0.42
8. Calculate present value of monthly expenses.	CPT PV STO 0	4933.36
9. Add down payment.	1000 SUM 0	1000.00
10. Clear PMT register.	0 PMT	0.00
11. Enter resale value.	2500 FV	2500.00
12. Compute present value.	CPT PV	2152.44
13. **Calculate present value of the total cost of purchasing the car.**	+/− + RCL 0 = STO 0	3780.92
14. Enter monthly lease payments.	115 PMT	115.00
15. **Calculate present value.**	2nd DUE PV	3853.04
16. **Compare present value of lease payments to present value of the cost of the car.**	− RCL 0 =	72.12

Based on these calculations, it costs $72.12 more to lease the car. Since this is a rather small difference, you can go on and weigh other reasons in favor of one decision or the other.

A Credit Installment Plan Schedule

4

Some businesses offer a type of installment plan for credit purchases in which you are billed each month for a varying payment. The payment consists of a set amount, *plus* interest on the unpaid balance of the loan. With your calculator and the following program, you can easily work out each month's payment and the unpaid balance.

Program Memory		Key Sequence	Program Memory		Key Sequence	Program Memory		Key Sequence
00	55	$\times$	11	61	RCL	22	61	RCL
01	61	RCL	12	23	PMT	23	00	0
02	23	PMT	13	85	=	24	42	R/S
03	84	+/−	14	55	$\times$	25	41	RST
04	75	+	15	61	RCL	26	00	
05	61	RCL	16	22	%i	27	00	
06	24	PV	17	75	+	28	00	
07	85	=	18	61	RCL	29	00	
08	51	STO	19	23	PMT	30	00	
09	00	0	20	85	=	31	00	
10	75	+	21	42	R/S			

Notice that, in this program, the keys %i , PMT and PV are used only for memory storage. %i stores in memory 4, PMT in memory 5 and PV stores in memory 6.

Example: A lounge chair you want to buy is priced at $120. The store will let you have the chair on terms and apply its six-month installment plan at 1½% interest on the unpaid balance each month. This means that the unpaid balance will decrease by $20 (120 ÷ 6) each month, while your monthly payment will be $20 *plus* 1½% interest on that month's unpaid balance. How much will each month's payments and unpaid balance be?

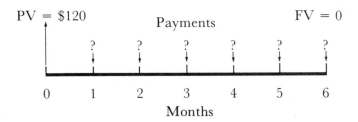

$i = 1½\%$ per month on unpaid balance $N = 6$ months

A Credit Installment Plan Schedule

Action	Press	Display
1. Clear calculator and enter program.	2nd CA 2nd LRN	00 00
	Program 2nd LRN RST	0.
2. Select two-decimal display.	2nd FIX 2	0.00
3. Enter cost of item.	120 PV	120.00
4. Enter interest rate.	1.5 %i	1.50
5. Calculate and enter fixed payment amount.	120 ÷ 6 = PMT	20.00
6. Enter any period number and press R/S to **calculate the payment** (fixed payment + interest) for that period.	1 R/S	21.80
7. **Calculate unpaid balance at end of that period.**	R/S	100.00
8. Repeat steps 6 and 7 for any period. (You can work out a complete schedule by entering the periods in sequential order.)	5 R/S	20.60
	R/S	20.00
	6 R/S	20.30
	R/S	0.00

Financing or Saving for a Purchase

4

In business, acquiring new equipment is a major expense, and the cost of the equipment may exceed the cash you have on hand. In this case you must decide if you should borrow the balance of the money you need or buy what you can afford now and save for the rest. Your calculator can help you evaluate the alternatives.

Example: If you are starting a new business, you need to purchase a dictation transcriber ($285), an electric typewriter ($995), and some office furniture ($1500). But you have only $1000 set aside for office equipment. You decide to use this for a down payment and finance the rest at 15% compounded monthly for three years. What will your monthly payments be and what would the total cost of the equipment be (including financing)? For this example, disregard tax effects.

$$PV = \$1780 \qquad \text{Payments}$$

0   1   2   3 ... 35   36

Months

$$i = 15\%/12 \text{ per month} \qquad N = 36 \text{ months}$$

Action	Press	Display
1. Clear calculator and select two-decimal display.	CLR 2nd CM 2nd FIX 2	0.00
2. Calculate amount of cash you need and deduct down payment.	285 + 995 + 1500 = − 1000 = PV	2780.00 1780.00
3. Compute and enter monthly interest rate.	15 ÷ 12 = %i	1.25
4. Calculate and enter number of payments.	3 × 12 = N	36.00
5. Compute payment.	CPT PMT	61.70
6. Compute total cost of the three items, including interest and down payment. (Leave your calculator on.)	× 36 + 1000 = STO 0	3221.35

You decide you could really get by if you only purchased the typewriter now, paying cash, and saved for the rest. You plan to deposit each month the amount you would have made in payments, and your saving account pays 6% annual interest, compounded monthly. How long will it take you to accumulate the money you need, and how much of a savings will this plan give you?

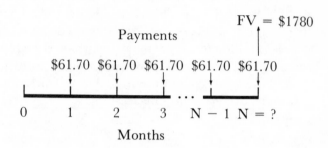

$i = 6\%/12$ per month

Action	Press	Display
7. Eliminate present value from previous calculation.	0 [PV]	0.00
8. Calculate and enter amount you need to save.	285 [+] 1500 [−] [(] 1000 [−] 995 [)] [=] [FV]	1780.00
9. Calculate and enter periodic interest rate on savings account.	6 [÷] 12 [=] [%i]	0.50
10. **Compute number of months it will take you to save the amount you need.**	[CPT] [N]	27.01
11. Calculate total cost of the three items.	[×] [RCL] [PMT] [+] 1000 [=]	2666.93
12. **Compute savings generated by this plan.**	[+/−] [+] [RCL] 0 [=]	554.43

You would save $554.43 by waiting and saving. Now, with this in mind, you can decide whether to wait or buy all of your equipment now.

Capital Asset Pricing Model

4

The Capital Asset Pricing Model gives the expected rate of return in equilibrium for assumed stock return volatility, risk-free returns, and expected market return. An analyst can use the model to derive the expected future return on a security.

Formula

$$E(R_i) = R_F + [E(R_M) - R_F]\beta$$

where: $E(R_i)$ = expected future return on the security
R_F = risk-free rate of interest
$E(R_M)$ = expected return on the market portfolio of securities
β = volatility of stock return (degree of responsiveness relative to that of the market portfolio)

Example:

Suppose an analyst wants to use the Capital Asset Pricing model to determine the expected return on a certain security for the coming period. Assume that:

R_F = 6%
$E(R_M)$ = 9%
β = 1.5

Action	Press	Display
1. Clear calculator and select two-decimal display.	CLR 2nd CM. 2nd FIX 2	0.00
2. **Calculate expected return on the security.**	6 + (9 − 6) × 1.5 =	10.50

The expected return rate is 10.5%.

Reference: Weston and Brigham, *Managerial Finance,* pp. 657-660, 686.

A Cash Management Model

The cash management model developed by Miller and Orr (see reference at the end of this problem) minimizes the total of the expected cost of transfers between the investment and the cash accounts of a company, along with the opportunity cost of holding cash. It computes a return point (Z) to which the cash balance is returned if cash is either transferred into the investment account or obtained from the investment account. The formula for determining the return point is:

$$Z = \left(\frac{3b\sigma^2}{4i}\right)^{1/3} \text{, and}$$

the formula for finding the upper allowable limit for the cash balance is:

$$h = 3Z$$

where: Z = point to which the balance is returned
       b = cost per transfer between the cash account and the investment account
      σ^2 = variance of daily changes in the cash balance
      i = daily rate of interest earned on investment
      h = upper allowable limit for the cash balance.
                Cash in excess of h should be transferred into the investment account.

When the cash balance hits zero, cash in the amount of Z is transferred from the investment account.

The lower allowable limit is assumed to be zero in this model. A statement at the end of the following example shows you how to adjust your calculations for other lower limits.

A Cash Management Model

Example: Your company wants to find the return point for its cash account and the upper allowable limit for the cash balance. You know that it costs $30 to transfer money between the cash and investment accounts and that the variance of the daily changes in the cash balance is $200,000. The interest rate on your investment account is 9% annually, compounded daily.

Therefore: b = $30
σ^2 = $200,000
i = 9%/365 per day

Action	Press	Display
1. Clear calculator and select two-decimal display.	CLR 2nd CM 2nd FIX 2	0.00
2. Calculate return point.	3 ✕ 30 ✕	90.00
	200000 ÷	18000000.00
	(4 ✕ (.09 ÷	0.09
	365 =	1.83 10
	2nd y^x 3 1/x =	2632.82
3. Calculate upper allowable limit for cash balance.	✕ 3 =	7898.46

If a positive minimum cash level is required in the account — for example, if your bank requires a minimum of $5000 in the account — that amount should be added to both the above results. The return point would become $7632.82 and the upper limit $12,898.46.

References: Miller and Orr, "A Model of the Demand for Money by Firms," pp. 413-435. Weston and Brigham, *Managerial Finance,* pp. 189-192.

Variable Periodic Cash Flows

Often a businessman must deal with annuity-like situations in which the periodic cash flows are unequal amounts. Because the built-in annuity routines in your calculator are designed to handle equal payments only, other keys must be utilized to take care of these variable periodic cash flows.

- n [x⤄y] , n [2nd] [NPV]

  Enters the number of the period and the amount of the cash flow and calculates the net present value.

- [STO] n

  Enters data (cash flows) so that the rate of return or the "break even" interest rate for a series of unequal payments can be calculated. Up to 12 cash flows can be entered, one in each memory.

- [2nd] [IRR]

  Computes the periodic interest rate (Internal Rate of Return) which will make the net present value of a series of cash flows equal to zero (the "break-even" rate). It can also be used to find the internal rate of return needed for several unequal cash flows to amount to a set future value.

Keep these things in mind when using calculations dealing with variable cash flows.

- Cash *outflows* (expenses or losses) must be entered as negative quantities, *except* for one specific case. The IRR routine assumes that any quantity stored in memory 0 is negative. If you want to store a cash *inflow* in memory zero, enter it as a negative value to offset the IRR conversion.

- The IRR routine uses an iterative process, and there is some probability that more than one answer may exist to certain problems. In this case the calculator will, in general, find the smallest rate of return satisfying the conditions you entered. It can also be possible that no solution exists for a problem you enter. In this case the calculator will keep on trying to find a solution until you stop it by turning the machine OFF.

- Because the IRR routine uses almost all the memories of the calculator, you can't do other financial or statistical routines or retain a stored program while computing IRR. You should clear the entire claculator before beginning an IRR calculation (either by turning the unit OFF, then ON, or by pressing [2nd] [CA]), to be sure that previously stored data won't interfere or cause an incorrect result.

4

CASH FLOWS OCCURRING AT THE END OF EACH PERIOD

Variable cash flow and IRR calculations are traditionally complex and time-consuming computations, but they play an important role in business and finance. You can handle them quickly and easily on your calculator. Examine the following situations involving variable cash flows.

**Example:
Find
Present
and Future
Value**

Your company has bought a new machine. Its projected savings at the end of each year for the next five years are:

Year	1	2	3	4	5
Savings	$500	$9,400	$10,500	$10,000	$9,800

You want to know the net present value and the expected future value (ignoring taxes) of the savings. Your company expects a 15% annual return on all investments.

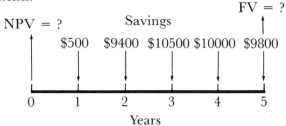

$i = 15\%$ per year $N = 5$ years

Action	Press	Display
1. Clear calculator and select two-decimal display.	[CLR] [2nd] [CM] [2nd] [FIX] 2	0.00
2. Enter interest rate.	15 [%i]	15.00
3. Enter first period number and cash flow and compute present value.	1 [x:y] 500 [2nd] [NPV]	434.78
4. Repeat *Step 3* for each cash flow.	2 [x:y] 9400 [2nd] [NPV]	7542.53
	3 [x:y] 10500 [2nd] [NPV]	14446.45
	4 [x:y] 10000 [2nd] [NPV]	20163.99
	5 [x:y] 9800 [2nd] [NPV]	25036.32
(The net present value of the series of cash savings is $25,036.32. Now you are ready to find the future value.)		
5. Enter number of periods involved.	5 [N]	5.00
6. Compute future value.	[CPT] [FV]	50356.98

Variable Periodic Cash Flows

Example: Calculating Internal Rate of Return (Present Value Known)

You must evaluate the proposed purchase of a new machine. It costs $40,200 and will generate the following savings at the end of each year:

Year	1	2	3	4	5
Savings	$400	$9200	$11,560	$17,048	$24,000

Ignoring tax effects, what is the internal rate of return?

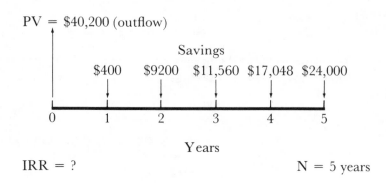

IRR = ?   N = 5 years

Action	Press	Display
1. Clear calculator and select two-decimal display.	2nd CA 2nd FIX 2	0.00
2. Enter purchase price.	40200 STO 0	40200.00
3. Enter each cash flow.	400 STO 1	400.00
	9200 STO 2	9200.00
	11560 STO 3	11560.00
	17048 STO 4	17048.00
	24000 STO 5	24000.00
4. Compute internal rate of return.	2nd IRR	12.13

The return rate is 12.13%.

Note: The IRR routine automatically converted the cash outflow (purchase price) stored in memory 0 to a negative value, so you did not have to change the sign of the initial expense before storing it.

**Example:
Calculating
Internal
Rate of
Return
(Future
Value
Known)**

Your company has made the following deposits in an account at the end of each month:

Month	1	2	3	4	5
Savings	$500	$800	$1000	$1200	$1500

At the end of the fifth month, the amount in the account is $5564.33. What return rate are you earning?

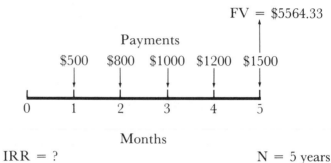

To calculate IRR, given the future value of a series of variable cash flows occurring at the end of each period, you must subtract the future value from the last period's cash flow and use that negative value as your last entry.

1. Clear calculator and select two-decimal display.

    [2nd] [CA] [2nd] [FIX] 2   0.00

2. Enter all but the last cash flow.

    500 [STO] 1   500.00
    800 [STO] 2   800.00
    1000 [STO] 3   1000.00
    1200 [STO] 4   1200.00

3. Net future value against last cash flow and enter.

    1500 [−] 5564.33 [=]   −4064.33
    [STO] 5   −4064.33

4. Compute return rate.

    [2nd] [IRR]   7.00

The account pays 7% interest.

CASH FLOWS OCCURRING AT THE BEGINNING OF EACH PERIOD

Example:
Finding
Present
Value

Your company has the option of leasing a machine for six years or buying it, with the purchase price being equal to the present value of the lease payments discounted by an 11% annual rate. The payments would be the following amounts, payable at the beginning of each year.

Year	1	2	3	4	5	6
Lease Payments	$16,000	$15,500	$14,500	$13,500	$12,500	$11,000

Ignoring tax effects, what is the purchase price (the net present value of the lease payments)?

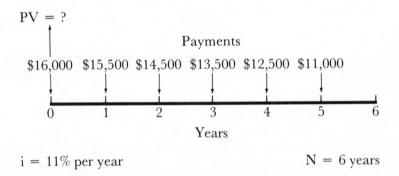

$i = 11\%$ per year $N = 6$ years

Because the NPV routine assumes that the cash flows occur at the *end* of each period, you have to adjust your calculations by finding the net present value in the usual way and then moving the result *forward* one period. This procedure "tricks" the calculator into giving you the net present value of a series of payments made at the beginning of the period.

Action	Press	Display
1. Clear calculator and select two-decimal display.	CLR 2nd CM 2nd FIX 2	0.00
2. Enter interest rate.	11 %i	11.00
3. Enter cash flows and calculate net present value.	1 x:y 16000 2nd NPV	14414.41
	2 x:y 15500 2nd NPV	26994.56
	3 x:y 14500 2nd NPV	37596.84
	4 x:y 13500 2nd NPV	46489.71
	5 x:y 12500 2nd NPV	53907.85
	6 x:y 11000 2nd NPV	59788.90
4. Move result forward one period.	1 N CPT FV	66365.67

The net present value of the series of lease payments is $66365.67.

**Example:
Finding
Future
Value**

At the *beginning* of each month, your company wants to deposit the following amounts in a fund paying 6.5% annually, compounded monthly:

Month	1	2	3	4
Deposits	$1000	$500	$2000	$1500

What will the balance be at the end of the fourth month?

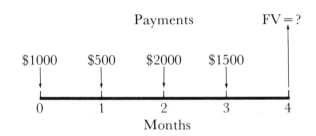

$$i = 6.5\%/12 \text{ per month} \qquad N = 4 \text{ months}$$

Again, to calculate the future value of a series of cash flows occurring at the *start* of each period, you have to adjust the built-in NPV routine. Enter your cash flows in the usual way, find the net present value; then compute future value for $n + 1$ periods. This procedure allows for the fact that the cash flows happen at the beginning of the period rather than the end.

Action	Press	Display
1. Clear calculator and select two-decimal display.	CLR 2nd CM 2nd FIX 2	0.00
2. Enter interest rate.	6.5 ÷ 12 = %i	0.54
3. Enter cash flows and find NPV.	1 x:y 1000 2nd NPV	994.61
	2 x:y 500 2nd NPV	1489.24
	3 x:y 2000 2nd NPV	3457.09
	4 x:y 1500 2nd NPV	4925.02
4. Enter number of periods *plus one,* and compute future value.	5 N CPT FV	5059.86

At the end of the fourth month the amount in the account will be $5059.86.

Example: Calculating Internal Rate of Return (Present Value Known)

A manufacturer has offered to sell you a machine for $50,000 or to lease it to you for five years, with payments to be made at the beginning of each year. The lease payments would be:

Year	1	2	3	4	5
Payment	$14,500	$13,500	$12,500	$11,000	$10,000

What interest rate is implied in the lease?

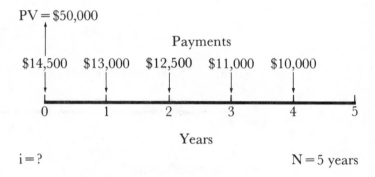

Because the IRR routine is designed for cash flows occurring at the *end* of each period, rather than the beginning, you have to compensate by moving each payment number back by one. Therefore, cash flow 1 becomes payment 0, cash flow 2 becomes payment 1, etc. You also net the first year's payment against the purchase price of the machine. You are really looking at this problem from the viewpoint of the leasing company, and this is money they stand to lose the first year if they lease, rather than sell, the machine to you.

Action	Press	Display
1. Clear calculator and select two-decimal display.	[2nd] CA [2nd] FIX 2	0.00
2. Enter cash flows.	50000 [−] 14500 [=]	35500.00
	STO 0	35500.00
	13500 STO 1	13500.00
	12500 STO 2	12500.00
	11000 STO 3	11000.00
	10000 STO 4	10000.00
3. Calculate interest rate.	[2nd] IRR	12.99

The annual rate of interest on the lease is almost 13%.

**Example:
Calculating
Internal
Rate of
Return
(Future
Value
Known)**

An investment project has been proposed to your company, with a projected return of $5,059.86 at the end of four months. The following amounts will have to be invested at the beginning of each month.

Month	1	2	3	4
Investment	$1000	$500	$2000	$1500

Ignoring tax effects, what is the rate of return on the project?

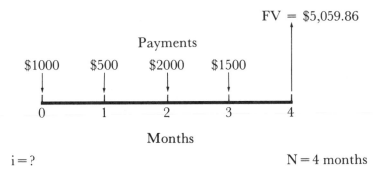

$$FV = \$5,059.86$$

Payments

$1000 $500 $2000 $1500

0   1   2   3   4

Months

$i = ?$ $N = 4$ months

Since the cash return occurs at the end of the four months, while the payments are made at the *beginning* of each month, enter $5,059.86 as your last cash flow; actually, five cash flows, rather than four, are involved here. Also, the $5,059.86 must be entered as a negative value, because it is a cash return and the other cash flows are costs.

Action	Press	Display
1. Clear calculator and select two-decimal display.	[2nd] [CA] [2nd] [FIX] 2	0.00
2. Enter cash flows.	1000 [STO] 1	1000.00
	500 [STO] 2	500.00
	2000 [STO] 3	2000.00
	1500 [STO] 4	1500.00
	5059.86 [+/−] [STO] 5	− 5059.86
3. Calculate monthly return rate.	[2nd] [IRR]	0.54
4. Calculate annual return rate.	[×] 12 [=]	6.50

The annual return rate on the project is 6.5%.

Cost of Capital

One way to minimize the cost of capital is to group all capital into *debt* and *equity* classes and determine the average cost of debt capital, the proportion of equity remaining in the capital structure, and the average cost of equity capital for various proportions of debt in the capital structure. These factors can then be used to compute the average cost of capital for each mix of capital structure, and these costs can be plotted on a curve for analysis and projection. The formula used is:

$$W_c = P_d C_d + P_e C_e$$

where: W_c = average cost of capital
P_d = proportion of debt in capital structure
C_d = average cost of debt capital
P_e = proportion of equity in capital structure
C_e = average cost of equity capital

A short program in your calculator allows you to enter each factor sequentially and compute the average cost of capital for each assumed condition. In this way, you can evaluate the average cost of capital for each of your situations without repetitive keystrokes.

Program Memory	Key Sequence	Program Memory	Key Sequence	Program Memory	Key Sequence
00 55	☒	11 00		22 00	
01 42	R/S	12 00		23 00	
02 75	＋	13 00		24 00	
03 42	R/S	14 00		25 00	
04 55	☒	15 00		26 00	
05 42	R/S	16 00		27 00	
06 85	＝	17 00		28 00	
07 42	R/S	18 00		29 00	
08 41	RST	19 00		30 00	
09 00		20 00		31 00	
10 00		21 00			

COST OF CAPITAL

Example: Your company has projected data regarding the cost of capital for seven conditions. Find the average cost of capital for each situation.

Data:

Condition	Debt		Equity		Average Cost of Capital (to be computed)
	P_d	C_d	P_e	C_e	
A	0	3.5	1.00	11	11.00
B	.10	3.7	.90	11	10.27
C	.20	4.0	.80	11.5	10.00
D	.30	4.5	.70	13	10.45
E	.40	5.0	.60	15	11.00
F	.50	5.5	.50	17	11.25
G	.60	7.5	.40	20	12.50

Action	Press	Display
1. Clear calculator and enter program.	[2nd] CA [2nd] LRN	00 00
	Program [2nd] LRN [RST]	0.
2. Select two-decimal display.	[2nd] FIX 2	0.00
3. Enter the proportion of debt for the period.	0 [R/S]	0.00
4. Enter the average cost of debt capital for the period.	3.5 [R/S]	0.00
5. Enter the proportion of equity for the period.	1 [R/S]	1.00
6. Enter the average cost of equity capital for the period and **calculate the average cost of capital.**	11 [R/S]	11.00

7. Repeat *Steps 3–6* for each time period.

Repeating this procedure for each set of data given in the example will allow computation of the average cost of capital for each situation. Capital costs are lowest where debt makes up 20% of the capital structure.

Reference: Weston and Brigham, *Managerial Finance,* pp. 609–611.

Investment Returns under Uncertainty

The estimated returns on certain projects must be based on assumptions about the economy. To estimate a return in this situation, probability factors must be assigned to the various conditions that could affect the value of the return. The formulas used to estimate investment returns under uncertainty are:

$$E(R) = \sum_{i=1}^{n} R_i P_i$$

$$\sigma_R = \sqrt{\sum_{i=1}^{n} [R_i - E(R_i)]^2 P_i}$$

where: $E(R)$ = expected value of project return
R_i = return for project if condition in period i exists
P_i = probability that condition in period i will occur
σ_R = standard deviation of expected value of return

Note that:

$$\sqrt{\sum_{i=1}^{n} [R_i - E(R)]^2 P_i} = \sqrt{\sum_{i=1}^{n} R_i^2 P_i - \left(\sum_{i=1}^{n} P_i R_i\right)^2}$$

Since the estimated return has to be evaluated under several sets of circumstances, use a program for the repetitive keystrokes.

Program for estimating investment returns under uncertainty

Program Memory	Key Sequence	Program Memory	Key Sequence	Program Memory	Key Sequence
00 51	STO	11 71	SUM	22 42	R/S
01 00	0	12 02	2	23 61	RCL
02 55	×	13 42	R/S	24 01	1
03 42	R/S	14 61	RCL	25 42	R/S
04 85	=	15 02	2	26 41	RST
05 71	SUM	16 65	−	27 00	
06 01	1	17 61	RCL	28 00	
07 55	×	18 01	1	29 00	
08 61	RCL	19 14	x^2	30 00	
09 00	0	20 85	=	31 00	
10 85	=	21 19	2nd $\sqrt{x}$		

Reference: Weston and Brigham, *Managerial Finance*, pp. 309–316.

4

Example: Your company is considering a project which will yield the following returns based on certain assumptions about the economy. The returns and the probability of each state of the economy are estimated as follows:

Future State of the Economy	Project Return as Percent	Probability of Economic State Occurring
Depression	− 10%	.1
Recession	− 1%	.2
Normal	8%	.4
Above Average	15%	.2
Boom	25%	.1

What is the expected value of the project and its standard deviation?

Action	Press	Display
1. Clear calculator and enter program.	2nd CA 2nd LRN	00 00
	Program 2nd LRN RST	0.
2. Select three-decimal display.	2nd FIX 3	0.000
3. Enter first project return percentage.	10 % +/− R/S	−0.100
4. Enter first probability factor and calculate first estimated return.	.1 R/S	0.001
5. Reset program counter to step 00 and enter second project return percentage.	RST 1 % +/− R/S	−0.010
6. Enter second probability factor and calculate second estimated return.	.2 R/S	0.000
7. Repeat *Steps 5 and 6* for each set of data.	RST 8 % R/S	0.080
third estimated return	.4 R/S	0.003
	RST 15 % R/S	0.150
fourth estimated return	.2 R/S	0.005
	RST 25 % R/S	0.250
fifth estimated return	.1 R/S	0.006
8. Once returns have been estimated under each condition, **calculate the standard deviation of the returns.** (Do *not* reset program counter at this stage.)	R/S	0.093
9. **Find the expected value of the project.**	R/S	0.075

The estimated return of the project is 7.5%, and its standard deviation is .093.

Value of a Growth Stock

Sometimes a particular stock will be expected to experience "supernormal growth." That is, for a limited, predictable period, it will grow at a much faster rate than the economy as a whole, then drop back to a lower growth rate. The value of such a stock can be determined by the formula:

$$\text{Stock Value} = \sum_{t=1}^{n} \frac{D\,(1+g)^t}{(1+k)^t} + \left[\frac{D_{n+1}}{(k-r)} \times \frac{1}{(1+k)^n} \right]$$

where:
D = present dividend level
g = high "supernormal" growth rate
n = number of years high growth rate is expected to occur
t = successive time periods between 1 and n
k = investor's required annual rate of return
r = normal growth rate of dividends expected after supernormal growth ends
D_{n+1} = dividend level at end of year after supernormal growth ends

Note: $\frac{1+g}{1+k} = 1+i$, for equivalent interest rate in the annuity due calculation used in our solution.

This formula discounts and sums a growing dividend stream for a number of years and then adds in the extra, terminal value of a slower-growing dividend stream in perpetuity.

Example: You are investigating a stock that currently pays a dividend of $2.20 annually, but is expected to grow at a rate of 25% per year for the next eight years. Then it will drop back to a growth rate of 5% per year. What is the value of the stock? (Your company requires an annual rate of return of 11% per year on all investments.)

4

Action	Press	Display
1. Clear calculator and select two-decimal display.	CLR 2nd CM 2nd FIX 2	0.00
2. Calculate and enter equivalent interest rate: $$i = \frac{1+g}{1+k} - 1$$	1 + 25 % = ÷	1.25
	(1 + 11 %) =	1.13
	− 1 = × 100 =	12.61
	%i	12.61
3. Enter number of periods rapid growth is expected.	8 N	8.00
4. Enter dividend.	2.2 PMT	2.20
5. Compute present value of first eight years' dividends (will be handled as the future value of an annuity due situation at the equivalent interest rate).	2nd DUE FV	31.16
	STO 2	31.16
6. Enter high growth rate and calculate future value of present dividend at end of 8 years' supernormal growth.	25 %i RCL PMT	2.20
	PV 0 PMT	0.00
	2nd DUE FV	13.11
7. Calculate and enter value of stock at the end of the 9th year (n + 1).	× (1 + 5 %)	1.05
	÷ (11 − 5) %	0.06
	= FV	229.48
8. Enter investor's required rate and **compute present value.**	11 %i CPT PV	99.58
9. **Add present value of dividends for total current stock value.**	+ RCL 2 =	130.74

The value of the stock is $130.74.

Reference: Weston and Brigham, *Managerial Finance,* pp. 554–558.

A Two-Investment Security Portfolio Model

This model is used to determine the return and risks of two investment securities, given the expected return of each security, the standard deviation of the return for each security, and the correlation between their returns. First, calculate the expected return of the portfolio and its standard deviation, given various mixes of the two securities. Then, inspect the results to determine the optimal mix. The mix selected for investment depends on the investor's risk preference.

The expected return and standard deviation are computed using these formulas:

$$E(P) = ZS_A + (1-Z) S_B$$

$$\sigma_P = \sqrt{Z^2\sigma_A{}^2 + (1-Z)^2\sigma_B{}^2 + 2Z(1-Z) R_{AB}\sigma_A\sigma_B}$$

where:
$E(P)$	=	expected return on portfolio with mix of Z% A and (1–Z%) B proportion
Z	=	proportion of portfolio invested in security A
$(1-Z)$	=	proportion of portfolio invested in security B
S_A	=	expected return on security A
S_B	=	expected return on security B
σ_A	=	standard deviation of return on security A
σ_B	=	standard deviation of return on security B
R_{AB}	=	correlation coefficient between returns on securities A and B
σ_P	=	standard deviation of portfolio return

Two programs are needed here, one to find the expected returns [E(P)] on the various mixes and one to compute the standard deviation of the portfolio returns for various mixes and correlation coefficients, so that the necessary information can be obtained to evaluate the portfolio mixes.

A Two-Investment Security Portfolio Model

4

Program for expected return on various mixes of securities A and B

Program Memory	Key Sequence	Program Memory	Key Sequence	Program Memory	Key Sequence
00 51	STO	11 05	5	22 00	
01 05	5	12 55	×	23 00	
02 84	+/−	13 61	RCL	24 00	
03 75	+	14 00	0	25 00	
04 01	1	15 85	=	26 00	
05 85	=	16 42	R/S	27 00	
06 55	×	17 41	RST	28 00	
07 61	RCL	18 00		29 00	
08 01	1	19 00		30 00	
09 75	+	20 00		31 00	
10 61	RCL	21 00			

Program for the standard deviation of the portfolio return for various mixes of securities A and B

Program Memory	Key Sequence	Program Memory	Key Sequence	Program Memory	Key Sequence
00 55	×	11 75	+	22 14	x^2
01 02	2	12 61	RCL	23 55	×
02 55	×	13 05	5	24 61	RCL
03 61	RCL	14 14	x^2	25 03	3
04 05	5	15 55	×	26 14	x^2
05 55	×	16 61	RCL	27 85	=
06 61	RCL	17 02	2	28 19	2nd √x
07 06	6	18 14	x^2	29 42	R/S
08 55	×	19 75	+	30 41	RST
09 61	RCL	20 61	RCL	31 00	
10 04	4	21 06	6		

A TWO-INVESTMENT SECURITY
PORTFOLIO MODEL

Example: An investor has two securities with the following returns and standard deviations.

	Expected Return (S_i)	Standard Deviation (σ_i)
Security A	10%	4%
Security B	11%	6%

He is comtemplating investing with the following mixes.

1) 100% A,
2) 50% A and 50% B, or
3) 100% B.

Also, he expects that the correlation coefficient between the two securities will be either 1 or 0, so he must evaluate both possible situations.

Action	Press	Display
1. Clear calculator and enter program for expected returns.	[2nd] [CA] [2nd] [LRN] Program [2nd] [LRN] [RST]	00 00 0.
2. Select three-decimal display.	[2nd] [FIX] 3	0.000
3. Enter return on security A and store in memory 0.	10 [%] [STO] 0	0.100
4. Enter return on security B and store in memory 1.	11 [%] [STO] 1	0.110
5. Enter proportion of security A in first mix and calculate portfolio return for that mix.	100 [%] [R/S]	0.100
6. Repeat *Step 5* for each mix.	50 [%] [R/S] 0 [%] [R/S]	0.105 0.110
7. After expected returns for each mix have been calculated and recorded, clear calculator and enter program for the standard deviation calculation.	[2nd] [CA] [2nd] [LRN] Program [2nd] [LRN] [RST]	00 00 0.
8. Select three-decimal display	[2nd] [FIX] 3	0.000
9. Store the standard deviation of returns on security A in memory 2.	4 [%] [STO] 2	0.040
10. Store the standard deviation of returns on security B in memory 3.	6 [%] [STO] 3	0.060
11. Calculate $\sigma_A \times \sigma_B$ and store in memory 4.	[RCL] 2 [×] [RCL] 3 [=] [STO] 4	0.002

Action	Press	Display
12. Store the proportion of security A in the mix in memory 5.	100 % STO 5	1.000
13. Store the proportion of security B in the mix in memory 6.	0 % STO 6	0.000
14. Enter first correlation coefficient and **calculate standard deviation,** where $R_{AB} = 1$ and $Z = 100\%$.	1 R/S	0.040
15. Enter second correlation coefficient and **calculate standard deviation,** where $R_{AB} = 0$ and $Z = 100\%$.	0 R/S	0.040
16. Repeat *Steps 12* through *15* for each mix.	50 % STO 5	0.500
	50 % STO 6	0.500
$(R_{AB}=1, Z=50\%)$	1 R/S	0.050
$(R_{AB}=0, Z=50\%)$	0 R/S	0.036
	0 % STO 5	0.000
	100 % STO 6	1.000
$(R_{AB}=1, Z=0\%)$	1 R/S	0.060
$(R_{AB}=0, Z=0\%)$	0 R/S	0.060

Summarizing, we now have the following information.

Portfolio	Proportion of Stock A (Z)	Proportion of Stock B (1 − Z)	Correlation Coefficients			
			$R_{AB} = 1$		$R_{AB} = 0$	
			E (P)	σ_p	E (P)	σ_p
1	100%	0%	.1	.04	.1	.04
2	50%	50%	.105	.05	.105	.036
3	0%	100%	.11	.06	.11	.06

An investor with a high risk preference would select portfolio 3, while an investor with a low risk preference would choose portfolio 1. This technique allows the investor to determine the estimated returns and risk for combinations of securities and various R_{AB} estimates.

Reference: Weston and Brigham, *Managerial Finance,* pp. 366–376.

A Simplified Lease-or-Buy Decision

Before acquiring new equipment a company has to make two basic decisions: one, will acquiring the equipment be a profitable move — that is, will the savings generated by the equipment meet the return rate required by the company — and two, is it better to lease or to purchase the equipment?

With your calculator you can analyze both situations quickly. First, find the present value of the expected annual savings generated by the equipment, using the return rate your company requires on investments. If the present value is equal to or exceeds the purchase price of the equipment, the savings meet or exceed your required return rate. Then, calculate the present value of the lease payments, using the interest rate at which your company usually borrows money. If the present value is less than the purchase price, leasing is the best option. If, however, the present value of the lease payments is more than the purchase price of the equipment, it would be best to buy the equipment outright.

Example: Your business is considering buying or leasing a new computer. According to the lease agreement, the company would pay $36,000 per year for five years, payable at the first of each year. On the other hand, you could buy the machine (with a five year service contract) for $135,000. If the computer is installed, it is expected to save your company $46,000 per year. You have determined that the computer will have no resale value at the end of the five years. Ignoring tax effects, should you acquire the computer, and if so, should you lease it or purchase it?

Your company is a healthy one with good credit and can borrow at 8% annual interest, and you require a 15% annual return on projects and investments of this kind.

Time line for purchase option

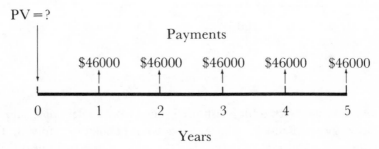

A SIMPLIFIED LEASE-OR-BUY DECISION

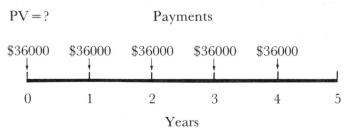

Time line for lease option

PV = ?   Payments

$36000 $36000 $36000 $36000 $36000

0   1   2   3   4   5

Years

i = 8% per year   N = 5 years

Action	Press	Display
1. Clear calculator and select two-decimal display.	CLR 2nd CM 2nd FIX 2	0.00
2. Enter number of years.	5 N	5.00
3. Enter required annual return rate.	15 %i	15.00
4. Enter savings.	46000 PMT	46000.00
5. Calculate present value of savings.	CPT PV	154199.13

The present value of the annual savings exceeds the purchase price of the computer, so the investment will exceed your annual required return rate. Acquiring the computer is a good financial move.

6. Clear calculator.	CLR 2nd CM	0.00
7. Enter number of years.	5 N	5.00
8. Enter interest at which your firm can borrow.	8 %i	8.00
9. Enter annual lease payment.	36000 PMT	36000.00
10. Calculate present value of lease payments.	2nd DUE PV	155236.57

The present value of the lease payments is greater than the purchase price of the computer ($135,000), so it would be best to buy the computer outright.

An Advanced Lease-or-Purchase Model

Assuming that an asset must be acquired, a business has to decide whether to borrow money and purchase the asset outright or to lease it. This model compares the present value of the lease payments to the present value of the credit costs of buying the asset, so that the advantage or disadvantage of leasing can be determined.

The factors that have to be considered are the company's tax rate, the before-tax cost of debt, the after-tax cost of debt, the salvage value of the asset, the interest rate on loans the company can get, and the life and operating expense of the asset.

Formula   Lease advantage =

$$
P + T_X \left[\sum_{i=1}^{n} \frac{L_i}{(1 + d_1)^i} - \sum_{i=1}^{n} \frac{K_i}{(1 + d_1)^i} - \sum_{i=1}^{n} \frac{Dep_i}{(1 + d_1)^i} \right]
$$

$$
- \sum_{i=1}^{n} \frac{L_i}{(1 + d_2)^i} + \sum_{i=1}^{n} \frac{CO_i (1 - T_X)}{(1 + C)^i} - \frac{SAL}{(1 + C)^n}
$$

where:
- P = amount borrowed to purchase asset
- T_X = company's tax rate
- n = life of lease or loan
- L_i = lease payment
- K_i = interest on loan for period i
- Dep_i = depreciation expense for period i
- CO_i = deductible cash operating costs for asset (if purchased) for period i
- d_i = after-tax cost of borrowing
- d_2 = before-tax cost of borrowing
- C = average after-tax cost of capital
- SAL = salvage value of asset

This model illustrates the power of your calculator. A complex situation such as this one can be broken into its component parts and solved quickly and easily. Two programs can be used, one to work out the year-by-year depreciation of the asset and the other to find the net present values of the interest expense and the depreciation expense (and the lease payments, as well, if they vary from year to year). Where payments are a uniform amount, the built-in financial operations of your calculator will handle these with a minimum of keystrokes, and the memories can be used to sum up costs and savings.

4

Program for depreciation of an asset, using the Sum-of-the-Years'-Digits method.

Program Memory		Key Sequence	Program Memory		Key Sequence	Program Memory		Key Sequence
00	61	RCL	11	84	+/−	22	00	
01	21	N	12	71	SUM	23	00	
02	45	÷	13	21	N	24	00	
03	61	RCL	14	41	RST	25	00	
04	01	1	15	00		26	00	
05	55	×	16	00		27	00	
06	61	RCL	17	00		28	00	
07	00	0	18	00		29	00	
08	85	=	19	00		30	00	
09	42	R/S	20	00		31	00	
10	01	1	21	00				

Program for finding the net present value of the monthly interest amounts and/or the yearly depreciation amounts.

Program Memory		Key Sequence	Program Memory		Key Sequence	Program Memory		Key Sequence
00	51	STO	11	61	RCL	22	00	
01	00	0	12	01	1	23	00	
02	01	1	13	42	R/S	24	00	
03	71	SUM	14	41	RST	25	00	
04	01	1	15	00		26	00	
05	61	RCL	16	00		27	00	
06	01	1	17	00		28	00	
07	34	x⇄y	18	00		29	00	
08	61	RCL	19	00		30	00	
09	00	0	20	00		31	00	
10	29	2nd NPV	21	00				

AN ADVANCED LEASE-OR-PURCHASE MODEL

Steps in solving the problem

1. Calculate and list each year's depreciation expense (Dep).
2. Calculate and list interest on loan each year (K).
3. Compute present value of depreciation expenses (Dep) having after-tax interest rate d_1.
4. Calculate present value of interest expenses (K) having after-tax interest rate d_1.
5. Calculate present value of the lease payments (L), using the after-tax interest rate (d_1).
6. Subtract present values of K and Dep from the present value of L.
7. Multiply result by tax factor (T_X).
8. Add purchase price to result. You have now evaluated:

$$P + T_X \left[\sum_{i=1}^{n} \left(\frac{L_i}{(1 + d_1)^i} \right) - \sum_{i=1}^{n} \left(\frac{K_i}{(1 + d_1)^i} \right) - \sum_{i=1}^{n} \left(\frac{Dep_i}{(1 + d_1)^i} \right) \right]$$

9. Compute present value of the lease payments (L), using the before-tax interest rate (d_2), and subtract from previous total.
10. Calculate present value of the operating expenses (CO) using the average cost of capital rate (C).
11. Add to previous total.
12. Calculate present value of the salvage value (SAL) and subtract from previous total.

Steps 9 through *12* evaluate the remainder of the formula:

$$- \sum_{i=1}^{n} \left(\frac{L_i}{(1 + d_2)^i} \right) + \sum_{i=1}^{n} \left(\frac{CO_i (1 - T_X)}{(1 + C)^i} \right) - \frac{SAL}{(1 + C)^n}$$

The result is the net advantage (positive result) or disadvantage (negative result) of leasing the equipment.

Example:

Your company has decided to acquire a certain machine on January 1 of next year. You have the option of borrowing money and buying the machine or leasing it from the manufacturer. The details of each alternative are given below.

Purchase Option

The machine can be purchased for $200,000. It has a ten-year life and is expected to have a salvage (resale) value of $20,000 at the end of the ten years. Also, the tax-deductible, net cash operating costs are expected to be $4,500 per year. Your company can borrow at a 6% annual rate, your average tax rate is 40% and your average after-tax cost of capital is 10%.

Leasing Option

The machine can be leased for annual payments of $30,000, payable at the end of each year. The leasing company will take care of all maintenance at no extra charge.

Which option should you choose?

Calculating Depreciation Expenses (SYD Method)

Action	Press	Display
1. Clear calculator and enter program for depreciation.	[2nd] [CA] [2nd] [LRN] Program [2nd] [LRN] [RST]	00 00 0.
2. Select two-decimal display.	[2nd] [FIX] 2	0.00
3. Enter number of periods.	10 [N]	10.00
4. Enter purchase price.	200000 [PV]	200000.00
5. Deduct salvage value.	[−] 20000 [=] [STO] 0	180000.00
6. Calculate and enter sum of the years' digits.	10 [×] 11 [÷] 2 [=] [STO] 1	55.00
7. Calculate first year's depreciation.	[R/S]	32727.27
8. Repeat *Step 7* for each year. 2nd year	[R/S]	29454.55
3rd year	[R/S]	26181.82
4th year	[R/S]	22909.09
5th year	[R/S]	19636.36
6th year	[R/S]	16363.64
7th year	[R/S]	13090.91
8th year	[R/S]	9818.18
9th year	[R/S]	6545.45
10th year	[R/S]	3272.73

List each year's depreciation for later use.

AN ADVANCED LEASE-OR-PURCHASE MODEL

Calculating Annual Interest on Loan

Action	Press	Display
1. Clear calculator and select two-decimal display.	CLR 2nd CM 2nd FIX 2	0.00
2. Enter number of periods.	10 N	10.00
3. Enter purchase price.	200000 PV	200000.00
4. Enter interest rate.	6 %i	6.00
5. Compute payment.	CPT PMT	27173.59
6. Calculate each year's interest.	1 2nd P/I x:y	12000.00
	2 2nd P/I x:y	11089.58
	3 2nd P/I x:y	10124.54
	4 2nd P/I x:y	9101.60
	5 2nd P/I x:y	8017.28
	6 2nd P/I x:y	6867.90
	7 2nd P/I x:y	5649.56
	8 2nd P/I x:y	4358.12
	9 2nd P/I x:y	2989.19
	10 2nd P/I x:y	1538.13

List each year's interest for later use. Your depreciation expense and loan interest table is now complete.

Year	Depreciation Expense	Interest on Loan
1	$32,727.27	$12,000.00
2	29,454.55	11,089.58
3	26,181.82	10,124.54
4	22,909.09	9,101.60
5	19,636.36	8,017.28
6	16,363.64	6,867.90
7	13,090.91	5,649.56
8	9,818.18	4,358.12
9	6,545.45	2,989.19
10	3,272.73	1,538.13

You are ready to evaluate your lease-purchase options.

Action	Press	Display
1. Clear calculator and enter program for NPV of a series of payments.	2nd CA 2nd LRN	00 00
	Program 2nd LRN RST	0.
2. Select two-decimal display.	2nd FIX 2	0.00
3. Calculate and enter the after-tax cost of borrowing money (d_1).	1 − 40 % = × 6 =	3.60
	%i	3.60
4. Calculate present value of depreciation expenses. $$-\sum_{i=1}^{n}\left(\frac{Dep_i}{(1+d_1)^i}\right).$$	32727.27 R/S	1.00
	29454.55 R/S	2.00
	26181.82 R/S	3.00
	22909.09 R/S	4.00
	19636.36 R/S	5.00
	16363.64 R/S	6.00
	13090.91 R/S	7.00
	9818.18 R/S	8.00
	6545.45 R/S	9.00
	3272.73 R/S	10.00
	RCL PV	156832.36
5. Change sign (see formula) and store in memory 2.	+/− STO 2	− 156832.36
6. Calculate present value of interest on loan $$-\sum_{i=1}^{n}\left(\frac{K_i}{(1+d_1)^i}\right).$$	0 PV STO 1	0.00
	12000 R/S	1.00
	11089.58 R/S	2.00
	10124.54 R/S	3.00
	9101.60 R/S	4.00
	8017.28 R/S	5.00
	6867.90 R/S	6.00
	5649.56 R/S	7.00
	4358.12 R/S	8.00
	2989.19 R/S	9.00
	1538.13 R/S	10.00
	RCL PV	62143.07
7. Change sign (see formula) and sum to memory 2.	+/− SUM 2	− 62143.07
8. Calculate present value of lease payments using after-tax borrowing rate already stored in %i $$\sum_{i=1}^{n}\left(\frac{L_i}{(1+d_1)^i}\right).$$	10 N 30000 PMT	30000.00
	CPT PV	248245.32

Action	Press	Display
9. Sum to memory 2 (see formula).	SUM 2	248245.32
10. Multiply total by tax rate (T_X).	40 % 2nd PROD 2	0.40
11. Add purchase price of machine (P) to total (see formula).	200000 SUM 2	200000.00
12. Compute present value of lease payments using *before-tax* borrowing rate	6 %i	6.00

$$- \sum_{i=1}^{n} \frac{L_i}{(1 + d_2)^i}$$

	Press	Display
	CPT PV	220802.61
13. Change sign (see formula) and sum to memory 2.	+/− SUM 2	− 220802.61
14. Calculate present value of net operating costs, using average cost of capital rate	10 %i	10.00

$$+ \sum_{i=1}^{n} \frac{CO_i \, (1 - T_X)}{(1 + C)^i}$$

	Press	Display
	1 − 40 % = ×	0.60
	4500 = PMT	2700.00
	CPT PV	16590.33
15. Add to memory 2 (see formula).	SUM 2	16590.38
16. Compute present value of salvage (resale) value of machine	0 PMT	0.00
	20000 FV	20000.00
	CPT PV	7710.87

$$- \frac{SAL}{(1 + C)^n}$$

	Press	Display
17. Change sign and sum to memory 2.	+/− SUM 2	− 7710.87
18. **Recall leasing advantage** from memory 2.	RCL 2	− 215.19

Since the final result is negative, this represents a disadvantage for leasing the machine, and the asset should be purchased with borrowed funds. You may want to repeat the procedures above using different interest rates or average cost-of-capital rates. The net disadvantage in this instance is small and the result could be sensitive to slight changes in your estimated rates. Also of interest, if the straight-line depreciation method is used in this particular example, rather than the SYD method, the answer is a lease advantage of $2938.87.

Reference: Weston and Brigham, *Managerial Finance,* pp. 490-496.

Capital Budgeting

This capital budgeting model compares the net cost of a project to the net present value of the total after-tax cash flows or savings generated by the project. If the present value of the savings (using an appropriate discount factor) exceeds the project's cost, the project is profitable.

The basic model is as follows:

$$NCF_n = CF_n (1 - T_1) + D_n \times T_1$$

$$ACF = P - \left[(P - NBV_k) \times T_2\right]$$

$$PV = \left[\sum_{n=1}^{k} NCF_i (1 + i)^{-n}\right] + ACF (1 + i)^{-k}$$

where:

NCF_n	=	net cash flows or savings per period n after taxes and depreciation
ACF	=	after-tax cash flow from selling the asset at the end of decision period k
CF_n	=	cash inflows or savings per period n before depreciation or taxes
D_n	=	depreciation expense per period n
T_1	=	tax rate on annual income
T_2	=	tax rate on gain or loss incurred when the asset is sold at the end of the decision period (k)
i	=	required rate of return on assets after taxes (discount factor)
PV	=	present value of cash flows after taxes
k	=	decision period
P	=	gross proceeds received from selling the asset at period k
NBV	=	net book value of the asset at period n (cost of asset − accumulated depreciation at period n)

This model assumes that, if a loss is incurred, the firm has other income to take advantage of the deduction. Also, keep in mind that the decision period may be shorter than the depreciable life of the asset. Thus, the proceeds may have a value different from the salvage value which is used to calculate depreciation.

The steps for solving this problem are:

1. Compute the net cash outlay for the new asset.
2. Compute the depreciation expense per period for the decision period (k).
3. Compute the net cash flows or savings (NCF) per period n (after taxes and depreciation) and their net present value.
4. Compute the after-tax cash flow (ACF) created by selling the asset at the end of decision period k and its present value.
5. Sum NCF and ACF, and subtract the net cash outlay for the asset to obtain the net present value for the project.

Two programs can be used to reduce repeat keystrokes — one to calculate the depreciation expenses for each period (the Sum-of-the-Years'-Digits method is used here, but any depreciation method could be used) and one to compute the present value of the net cash flows or savings.

Program for computing annual depreciation (SYD method)

Program Memory		Key Sequence	Program Memory		Key Sequence	Program Memory		Key Sequence
00	61	RCL	11	71	SUM	22	00	
01	21	N	12	24	PV	23	00	
02	45	÷	13	61	RCL	24	00	
03	61	RCL	14	24	PV	25	00	
04	01	1	15	42	R/S	26	00	
05	55	×	16	01	1	27	00	
06	61	RCL	17	84	+/−	28	00	
07	00	0	18	71	SUM	29	00	
08	85	=	19	21	N	30	00	
09	42	R/S	20	41	RST	31	00	
10	84	+/−	21	00				

Program for computing the present value of net cash flows (savings)

Program Memory	Key Sequence	Program Memory	Key Sequence	Program Memory	Key Sequence
00 55	×	11 00	0	22 41	RST
01 43	(	12 85	=	23 00	
02 01	1	13 25	FV	24 00	
03 65	−	14 42	R/S	25 00	
04 61	RCL	15 12	CPT	26 00	
05 00	0	16 24	PV	27 00	
06 85	=	17 71	SUM	28 00	
07 75	+	18 02	2	29 00	
08 42	R/S	19 61	RCL	30 00	
09 55	×	20 02	2	31 00	
10 61	RCL	21 42	R/S		

Example: A corporation pays 48% on operating income and a capital gains rate of 25%. Its cost of capital rate is 14% (the "break-even" rate which all investments must meet or exceed). With these facts in mind, a corporate analyst is evaluating a capital budgeting opportunity for the company.

A new machine costs $20,000 today and has a ten-year expected life, again with a salvage value of zero for depreciation (sum-of-years'-digits method). Over its ten-year life, however, the new machine will produce annual cash flows of $2500 per year for the first five years of its life and $2000 per year for the remaining five years. At the end of ten years the market value of the machine is expected to be $500.

Considering the corporation's tax status and their cost of capital rate, should the analyst recommend that the new machine be purchased?

Action	Press	Display
1. Clear calculator and enter program for depreciation.	2nd CA 2nd LRN Program 2nd LRN RST	00 00 0.
2. Select two-decimal display.	2nd FIX 2	0.00
3. Calculate each year's depreciation expense (D_n) and net book value (NBV) for new machine.	10 N	10.00
	20000 PV	20000.00
	− 0 = STO 0	20000.00
	10 × 11 ÷ 2 =	55.00
	STO 1	55.00
1st year's depreciation	R/S	3636.36
1st year's NBV	R/S	16363.64
2nd year's depreciation	R/S	3272.73
2nd year's NBV	R/S	13090.91
3rd year's depreciation	R/S	2909.09
3rd year's NBV	R/S	10181.82
4th year's depreciation	R/S	2545.45
4th year's NBV	R/S	7636.36
5th year's depreciation	R/S	2181.82
5th year's NBV	R/S	5454.55
6th year's depreciation	R/S	1818.18
6th year's NBV	R/S	3636.36
7th year's depreciation	R/S	1454.55
7th year's NBV	R/S	2181.82
8th year's depreciation	R/S	1090.91
8th year's NBV	R/S	1090.91
9th year's depreciation	R/S	727.27
9th year's NBV	R/S	363.64
10th year's depreciation	R/S	363.64
10th year's NBV	R/S	0.00

Action	Press	Display
4. Clear calculator and enter program for computing net present value.	2nd CA 2nd LRN Program 2nd LRN RST	00 00 0.
5. Select two-decimal display.	2nd FIX 2	0.00
6. Enter cost-of-capital rate (discount rate).	14 %i	14.00
7. Enter annual income tax rate (T_1).	48 % STO 0	0.48
8. Enter first period.	1 N	1.00
9. Enter cash savings for that period and begin calculation.	2500 R/S	1300.00
10. Enter depreciation expense for that period and calculate NCF_1.	3636.36 R/S	3045.45
11. **Calculate NPV** at end of first period.	R/S	2671.45
12. Repeat *Steps 7* through *11* for each period.		
	2 N 2500 R/S	1300.00
NCF_2	3272.73 R/S	2870.91
Accumulated NPV	R/S	4880.52
	3 N 2500 R/S	1300.00
NCF_3	2909.09 R/S	2696.36
Accumulated NPV	R/S	6700.49
	4 N 2500 R/S	1300.00
NCF_4	2545.45 R/S	2521.82
Accumulated NPV	R/S	8193.61
	5 N 2500 R/S	1300.00
NCF_5	2181.82 R/S	2347.27
Accumulated NPV	R/S	9412.71
	6 N 2000 R/S	1040.00
NCF_6	1818.18 R/S	1912.73
Accumulated NPV	R/S	10284.12
	7 N 2000 R/S	1040.00
NCF_7	1454.55 R/S	1738.18
Accumulated NPV	R/S	10978.76

Action	Press	Display
	8 [N] 2000 [R/S]	1040.00
NCF$_8$	1090.91 [R/S]	1563.64
Accumulated NPV	[R/S]	11526.91
	9 [N] 2000 [R/S]	1040.00
NCF$_9$	727.27 [R/S]	1389.09
Accumulated NPV	[R/S]	11954.07
	10 [N] 2000 [R/S]	1040.00
NCF$_{10}$	363.64 [R/S]	1214.55
Accumulated NPV	[R/S]	12281.68

The net present value of the yearly savings (NCF) is $12,281.68. Now you need to find the present value of the $500 resale price of the new machine.

13. Enter resale price (P), and	500 [−]	500.00
calculate net after-tax	[(] 500 [−] 0 [)]	500.00
proceeds (ACF).	[×] 25 [%] [=] [FV]	375.00
14. Compute present value, using	14 [%i]	14.00
cost-of-capital rate (discount rate).	10 [N]	10.00
	[CPT] [PV]	101.15
15. **Calculate total present value**	[+] [RCL] 2 [=]	12382.84
of incoming cash flows		
generated by the project.		
16. **Compare this amount to net**	[−] 20000 [=]	− 7617.16
present value of total cost		
of project.		

Since the result is a negative amount, the project does not return the required 14%, and purchasing the new machine would not be an acceptable move for the corporation. If you want to go on to find the actual return rate, you can calculate it easily on your calculator.

Action	Press	Display
1. Clear calculator and select	[2nd] **CA**	0
two-decimal display.	[2nd] **FIX** 2	0.00
2. Enter total cost of new machine.	20000 [STO] 0	20000
3. Enter each net cash flow into	3045.45 [STO] 1	3045.45
corresponding memory.	2870.91 [STO] 2	2870.91
	2696.36 [STO] 3	2696.36
	2521.81 [STO] 4	2521.81
	2347.27 [STO] 5	2347.27
	1912.73 [STO] 6	1912.73
	1738.18 [STO] 7	1738.18
	1563.64 [STO] 8	1563.64
	1389.09 [STO] 9	1389.09
	1214.55 [STO] [·]	1214.55
	375 [SUM] [·]	375.00
4. Calculate return rate.	[2nd] **IRR**	1.73

The return rate on the project is 1.73%, well below the company's
cost-of-capital rate of 14%. The project is clearly unacceptable on economic
grounds.

Reference: Weston and Brigham, *Managerial Finance,* Chapter 10.

Bond Analysis

CHAPTER 5

5

A bond is a financial obligation made by a corporation or a government agency. The purchaser of a bond receives periodic interest payments, usually semiannually, and receives the face value of the bond on the redemption date.

The interest payment each period is the interest rate printed on the bond divided by the number of payments per year multiplied by the face value of the bond. For example, a 7% $1000 bond with interest paid semiannually would pay each six months:

$$\frac{.07}{2} \times \$1000 = \$35$$

This semiannual interest payment is also called the *coupon payment*. In this case the coupon payment is $35, or 3.5%. This payment amount and the rate based on the face value of the bond remain constant. But bonds often sell at prices above or below the face value. A bond selling for an amount greater than the face value (or par) is said to be sold at a *premium* while a bond priced below par sells at a *discount*. The actual selling price can differ from the par value for many reasons. For example, a bond was originally sold when 5% was an acceptable return, but 8% is required currently in the market. This return required by the market is called *yield*.

More specifically, the yield is the return desired by the buyer. Because the face value of the bond and dollar amount of the coupon payment are fixed, the selling price, or present value, of the bond is adjusted to arrive at the current yield. Thus, a bond sells at a premium when its coupon rate exceeds the market yield, while a bond sells at a discount if its coupon rate is below the market yield. The yield desired by an investor is a function of many factors: the issuer's bond rating, state of the economy, and the amount of bonds purchased, to name a few.

Your MBA calculator will compute bond price and yield with great accuracy. The same calculation procedures practiced in the industry are used here in order to have solutions which agree with quoted figures. The more common procedures are explained in the following sections. These procedures are intended for users who require precise calculations, and are thus necessarily quite detailed and should be carefully followed to arrive at desired results. For those applications requiring quick approximations, the programs in the Owner's Manual may be universally applied.

The approaches used in our programs to compute bond price and bond yield are ones commonly used in the field. However, be aware of the fact that the examples shown are specific illustrations and do not take into account all of the factors that may affect the bond market. Historically, bond transactions have incorporated a variety of approximations, and many different types of calculations are still in use today. Because of this, the answers using the following methods may not agree exactly with answers you get from all other sources.

Present Value of Bond on Coupon Payment Date

The present value of a bond on a coupon payment date can be calculated using the following procedure.

1. Determine the number of coupon payments remaining until maturing of the bond. Enter this value and press N .

   A straightforward method of determining the number of coupon payments is:
   a. Enter the settlement date in MM.DDYYYY format and press DBD .
   b. Enter the maturity date in MM.DDYYYY format and press = to obtain the number of days remaining.
   c. Divide the number of days remaining by 182.5 for semiannual payments or 91.25 for quarterly payments.
   d. Press 2nd FIX 0. This is the number of payments.
   e. Press CLR and reenter this number before pressing N . Press 2nd FIX 2 before continuing.

2. Enter the yield per coupon period and press %i . For example, 8% per year would be 4% for semiannual coupon payments.

3. Enter the dollar amount of the coupon payment per $100 of face value of the bond, and press PMT . The payment is computed by dividing the nominal interest rate by the number of coupon payments per year.

4. Enter the bond maturity per $100 of face value and press FV .

5. Press CPT PV to compute the present value of the bond coupon payments. Press STO 0 to store this value in memory 0.

6. Enter a zero in PMT by pressing 0 PMT .

7. Press CPT PV to compute the present value of the bond maturity value. Press SUM 0 to add this to the PV of the coupon payments.

8. Press RCL 0 to display the present value of the coupon payments and maturity value. This is the bond price per $100 of maturity value.

Now work a problem using this procedure.

Example: You are interested in acquiring a bond that has an 8% yield, 7% nominal interest rate, with semiannual payments. The bond matures on January 1, 1988. The purchase date is January 1, 1977. What is the present value, or price, of the bond?

Action	Press	Display
1. Clear calculator.	2nd CA	0
2. Enter settlement date (MM.DDYYYY)	1.011977 DBD	1.011977
3. Enter maturity date and calculate number of days.	1.011988 =	4017.
4. **Calculate number of periods.**	÷ 182.5 =	22.0109589
5. Display number of coupon payments.	2nd FIX 0	22.
6. Enter number of coupon payments and select two-decimal display.	CLR 22 N 2nd FIX 2	22.00
7. Enter yield per coupon period.	8 ÷ 2 = %i	4.00
8. Enter coupon payment per $100 of face value.	7 ÷ 2 = PMT	3.50
9. Enter maturity value of bond per $100 of face value.	100 FV	100.00
10. **Calculate present value of coupon payments.**	CPT PV STO 0	50.58
11. Store a 0 in PMT.	0 PMT	0.00
12. **Calculate present value of redemption value.**	CPT PV	42.20
13. Sum to PV of coupon payments.	SUM 0	42.20
14. Display PV or price of bond rounded to two decimal places.	RCL 0	92.77
15. **Display PV of bond without rounding.**	2nd FIX 9	92.77444234

The present value of the bond is $92.77 per $100 of face value. The present value without rounding has been shown to provide input for the yield example which follows.

Yield of Bond on Coupon Payment Date

The following procedure is used to calculate the yield of a bond on a coupon payment date.

1. Enter the number of coupon payments remaining until maturity of the bond and press N . The number can be determined as described in the present value procedure.
2. Enter coupon payment per $100 of face value of the bond and press PMT .
3. Enter price, or present value of bond per $100 and press PV .
4. Enter the bond maturity value per $100 of face value and press FV .
5. Press CPT %i to compute the yield per coupon period.

Now work the previous example using the bond present value to compute the yield. For convenience, the input values were:

$$N = 22$$
$$PMT = 3.5$$
$$PV = 92.77444234$$
$$FV = 100$$

Action	Press	Display
1. Clear calculator.	2nd CA	0
2. Enter number of coupon payments.	22 N	22.
3. Enter coupon payment per $100.	3.5 PMT	3.5
4. Enter price of bond.	92.77444234 PV	92.77444234
5. Enter redemption value per $100.	100 FV	100.
6. Compute yield per coupon period.	CPT %i	3.999999999
7. Calculate annual yield.	× 2 =	7.999999998

Computed yield has .000000002 accuracy compared with the yield stated in the previous example. Without clearing your calculator perform the following:

8. Enter PV of bond rounded to two places.	92.77 PV	92.77
9. Compute yield per coupon period.	CPT %i	4.000322843
10. Calculate annual yield.	× 2 =	8.000645686

With the bond price rounded to two decimal places, the computed yield has .000645686 accuracy. This illustrates how sensitive the yield calculation is to small changes in the bond price. If you are checking bond yield on quoted bonds which are usually given in dollars and eights, there may be a slight difference because of the rounding of the bond price to the nearest eighth. In the example, if you pay $92.77444234 your yield is 7.999999998%, but if you pay $92.75 the yield is 8.003553152%.

According to one authoritative source the dollar price accuracy of price calculations should be:

> **Municipal Securities** — The price should be computed to seven digits following the decimal. The price is displayed to three decimal places, with the other digits dropped. Rounding *does not* take place.
>
> **Other Securities Including Corporate Bonds** — The price should be computed to seven decimal places *with rounding* to six decimal places.

Thus, in the above example, the price would be $92.774 for a municipal security or $92.774442 for other securities.

The same source states that yield calculations for all securities should be accurate to four places after the decimal, with rounding to three places for displaying the yield.

Assuming the bond in the above example is a municipal bond, the price with a stated yield of 8% is $92.774. If we have a price of $92.774 stated, the yield is 8.000 rounded to three places (unrounded yield is 8.000064291). A stated price of $92.774442 gives a yield of 8.000 rounded to three places (unrounded yield is 8.000000048).

In summary, the calculated yield can be slightly more or less than the stated yield because of rounding of the bond price for market quotation. Furthermore, the calculated price may be slightly more or less than the stated price because the quoted yield may not show all calculated decimal places. Generally, these differences affect the calculations beyond three decimal places.

Reference: Spence, Graudenz and Lynch, *Standard Securities Calculation Methods,* pp. 13, 44.

Computing Bond Price and Yield Between Coupon Payment Dates

Computing the bond price or yield between coupon payment dates is more complex because at the settlement date, the seller is paid his share of the current coupon payment (accrued interest) along with the price of the bond. The accrued interest is calculated using the following formula.

$$\text{Accrued Interest} = \frac{AD}{TD} \times \text{Coupon Payment}$$

where:
AD = Number of days from last coupon payment to settlement date, or accrued days

TD = Total number of days in this coupon period

This simple formula is complicated by the lack of a single method for counting the days in a month and the days in a year.

Day Count Methods

Several different methods are used in industry to count days. Three widely used methods are the "30/360", the "actual/actual", and the "actual/360" methods.

30/360 Method — Each month is assumed to have only 30 days, and the year to have 360 days. A semiannual coupon payment would occur after 180 days.

Actual/Actual Method — The actual number of days in each month and year is calculated.

Actual/360 Method — The actual number of days in each month is counted, but the year is assumed to have 360 days.

When counting the number of days remember that interest is not paid on the settlement date. The DBD routine in the **MBA** automatically calculates the correct number of days for the actual/actual and actual/360 methods.

The Investment Bankers Association of America Subcommittee on Trading and Cashiering Procedures in its report "Recommendations for Computation of Principal and Interest on Transactions in Municipal Securities" suggests the following method of counting days in the 30/360 method:

The number of elapsed days should be computed in accordance with the examples given below.

From the 1st to the 30th of the same month to be figured as 29 days
From the 1st to the 31st of the same month to be figured as 30 days
From the 1st to the 1st of the following month to be figured as 30 days
From the 1st to the 28th of February to be figured as 27 days

Where interest is payable on the 30th or 31st of the month:

From the 30th or 31st to the 1st of the following month to be figured as 1 day
From the 30th or 31st to the 30th of the following month to be figured as 30 days
From the 30th or 31st to the 31st of the following month to be figured as 30 days
From the 30th or 31st to the 1st of the second following month to be figured as 1 month 1 day

To illustrate this method of counting consider a bond with coupon dates of May 1 and November 1. Assume a settlement date of August 9.

The days from the last coupon date (AD) are:
$$(30 \times 3) + 8 = 98$$
The days to the next coupon date (RD) are:
$$(30 - 9) + (30 \times 2) + 1 = 82$$

The number of days in a coupon period also depends on the day count method. For semiannual coupons, the number of days is 180 using the 30/360 method and logically is the actual number of days for the actual/actual and actual/360 methods. The bond calculations use both the number of days from the last coupon date to the settlement date (AD) and the number of days from the settlement date to the next coupon date (RD). If actual days for AD and RD are each divided by the total days in the coupon period (TD), the following may occur if 180 or 182.5 days are used for TD.

$$\frac{AD}{TD} + \frac{RD}{TD} \neq 1$$

To illustrate this with an example, assume the last coupon date is June 1, 1977, the settlement date is September 15, 1977, and the next coupon date is December 1, 1977. Using the DBD routine:

$$TD = 183$$
$$AD = 106$$
$$RD = 77$$

Then:

$$\frac{106}{183} + \frac{77}{183} = 1$$

But if 182.5 days are used for the coupon period:

$$\frac{106}{182.5} + \frac{77}{182.5} = 1.002739726$$

As a result, minor inaccuracies can occur in the price and yield calculation. Logically, then, if actual days are used for AD and RD, the actual number of days in the coupon period should also be used. Therefore, if you are checking yield calculations, you need to know the day count method used in the original calculations and how AD and RD are calculated.

Use the actual number of days in the coupon period if actual days are used for AD and RD. You can use the actual days for AD and RD and an approximation such as 180 or 182.5 days for the coupon period in the following programs, but be aware of the minor inaccuracies introduced.

Bond Price Between Coupon Dates/ More than One Payment Remaining

5

To determine the price from the keyboard manually, the following steps are used:

1. Determine the number of whole coupon payments remaining (N). Use the next coupon date and the redemption date in the DBD routine. Divide this number by 182.5. The whole number nearest to this result is N.

2. Determine the number of days between the settlement date and the next coupon date (RD).

3. Determine the number of days in the coupon period (TD).

4. Compute the present value of the bond at the next coupon date.

5. Add the coupon payment to the present value.

6. Compute the present value of the total in *Step 5* as of the settlement date.

7. Subtract the accrued interest from the total computed in *Step 6* to compute the present value (price) of the bond at the settlement date.

This procedure is summarized by the following formula:

$$
\begin{array}{c}
\text{Present Value} \\
\text{of Bond}
\end{array}
=
\left[
\begin{array}{c}
\text{Present} \\
\text{Value of} \\
\text{Coupon} \\
\text{Payments}
\end{array}
+
\begin{array}{c}
\text{Present} \\
\text{Value of} \\
\text{Redemption} \\
\text{Value}
\end{array}
\right]
-
\begin{array}{c}
\text{Accrued} \\
\text{Interest}
\end{array}
$$

Remember, accrued interest is the seller's share of the current coupon payment. This must be accounted for when determining bond price between coupon dates.

Example: The settlement date is September 15, 1977. The last coupon date was June 1, 1977 and the next coupon date is December 1, 1977. The yield is 8% with a nominal rate of 7%. The bonds mature on December 1, 1993. Compute the bond price using actual days. The following steps comprise the manual keyboard solution.

Action	Press	Display
1. Clear calculator and select two-decimal display.	CLR 2nd CM 2nd FIX 2	0.00
2. Determine number of days to maturity.		
Next coupon date (MM.DDYYYY)	12.011977 DBD	12.01
Maturity date (MM.DDYYYY)	12.011993 =	5844.00
3. Calculate number of coupon periods.	÷ 182.5 =	32.02
4. Number of coupon payments.	2nd FIX 0	32.
5. Determine number of days remaining in coupon period (RD).	9.151977 DBD	9.
	12.011977 =	77.
6. Determine total days in coupon period (TD).	6.011977 DBD	6.
	12.011977 =	183.
7. Enter number of coupon payments, select two-decimal display.	32 N 2nd FIX 2	32.00
8. Enter yield per coupon period.	8 ÷ 2 = %i	4.00
9. Enter coupon payment.	7 ÷ 2 = PMT	3.50
10. Enter redemption value of bond.	100 FV	100.00
11. **Calculate PV of coupon payments** and store in memory 0.	CPT PV STO 0	62.56
12. Store 0 in PMT.	0 PMT	0.00
13. **Calculate PV of redemption value.**	CPT PV	28.51
14. Sum to PV of coupon payments.	SUM 0	28.51
15. **PV of bond and coupon payments.**	RCL 0	91.06
16. PV after next coupon payment.	+ 3.5 =	94.56
17. Enter as future value.	FV	94.56
18. Calculate and enter fractional period remaining in coupon payment period.	77 ÷ 183 = N	0.42
19. Calculate PV on settlement date before accrued interest is subtracted.	CPT PV	93.02
20. **Calculate and subtract accrued interest to obtain PV.**	− (183 − 77)	106.00
	÷ 183 ×	0.58
	3.5 =	90.99
	2nd FIX 9	90.98815901

The present value of the bond on September 15, 1977 is $90.98815901 after the accrued interest is deducted when the actual/actual day count basis is used. As a comparison, work the same example using the 30/360 day count basis.

The procedure follows the same keystrokes except at *Step 5* the remaining days (September 15 to December 1) are calculated as follows:

$$(30 - 15) + (2 \times 30) + 1 = 76$$

The total days in step 6 are 180 days by definition. When you complete *Step 17* perform the following:

Action	Press	Display
18. Calculate and enter fractional period remaining in coupon payment period.	76 $\div$ 180 $=$ N	0.42
19. Calculate PV on settlement date before accrued interest is subtracted.	CPT PV	93.01
20. Calculate and subtract accrued interest to obtain PV.	$-$ (180 $-$ 76)	104.00
	$\div$ 180 $\times$	0.58
	3.5 $=$	90.99
	2nd FIX 9	90.9879433

The present value of the bond on September 15, 1977 is $90.9879433 when the 30/360 day count basis is used.

The program to compute the bond price after accrued interest is deducted when more than one coupon payment remains is shown below. The program uses a modification of the MBA annuity PV calculation and does not follow exactly the same steps as the manual calculation example but gives the correct result.

Program Procedure

1. Compute the number of days remaining in coupon period (RD).
2. Compute the number of days in the coupon period (TD).
3. Compute the number of whole coupon payments remaining (N).
4. Enter N $+ \dfrac{RD}{TD}$ in N and store in memory 2.
5. Store $1 - \dfrac{RD}{TD}$ in memory 0.
6. Enter yield per coupon period as a percent in %i .
7. Store coupon payment in dollars in memory 1.
8. Enter redemption value in FV .
9. Press R/S .

To repeat program reenter the redemption value in FV and press R/S .

Bond Price Between Coupon Dates/
More than One Payment Remaining

Program

Program Memory	Key Sequence	Program Memory	Key Sequence	Program Memory	Key Sequence
00 61	RCL	11 65	−	22 85	=
01 02	2	12 61	RCL	23 42	R/S
02 21	N	13 01	1	24 41	RST
03 12	CPT	14 23	PMT	25 00	
04 24	PV	15 55	×	26 00	
05 75	+	16 61	RCL	27 00	
06 00	0	17 00	0	28 00	
07 23	PMT	18 21	N	29 00	
08 12	CPT	19 75	+	30 00	
09 24	PV	20 12	CPT	31 00	
10 85	=	21 25	FV		

Program Example

Using the same situation as the manual example, the following input values are available without computation.

RD	=	77 days	% i	=	4 percent
TD	=	183 days	PMT	=	3.5 dollars
N	=	32 periods			

Action	Press	Display
1. Clear calculator and enter program.	2nd CA 2nd LRN Program 2nd LRN RST	00 00 0.
2. Select three-decimal display.	2nd FIX 3	0.000
3. Compute and enter N + RD/TD.	32 + 77 ÷ 183 = N STO 2	32.421 32.421
4. Compute and enter 1 − RD/TD.	1 − 77 ÷ 183 = STO 0	0.579 0.579
5. Enter yield per coupon period.	4 %i	4.000
6. Enter coupon payment.	3.5 PMT STO 1	3.500
7. Enter redemption value.	100 FV	100.000
8. Compute PV.	R/S	90.988
9. Unrounded value.	2nd FIX 9	90.988159

Notice that to calculate AD/TD above, RD/TD was subtracted from 1 in the program:

$$AD/TD = 1 - RD/TD$$

If we had used 180 or 182.5 for the total number of days in the coupon period, the value for AD/TD would have been incorrect, thus causing our answer to be slightly inaccurate. We used $100 for the redemption and par value of the bond, but any value can be used. Remember to calculate the correct amount of the coupon payment to enter in memory 1.

Bond Yield Purchased Between Dates/ More Than One Payment Remaining

The yield for bonds with more than one coupon payment remaining is solved by an iteration process. With the MBA, this requires only a few keystrokes. The program and procedure shown using the internal %i calculation determines the yield between interest dates with great accuracy for the method used in practice.

Program
Procedure

1. Determine the number of whole coupon payments remaining (N).
2. Determine the number of days between the settlement date and the next coupon date (RD).
3. Determine the number of days in the coupon period (TD).
4. Enter N + RD/TD in N .
5. Store 1 − RD/TD in memory 0.
6. Enter the coupon payment in dollars in PMT.
7. Enter the bond price in PV and store it in memory 1.
8. Enter the redemption value in FV and store it in memory 2.
9. Press CPT %i to calculate yield between interest dates.
10. Press R/S to adjust variables.
11. Repeat *Steps 9* and *10* until the answer computed in *Step 9* stabilizes (remains the same). This usually requires 3 or 4 cycles of *Steps 9* and *10*.

Program Memory	Key Sequence	Program Memory	Key Sequence	Program Memory	Key Sequence
00 61	RCL	11 21	N	22 00	0
01 00	0	12 55	X	23 66	2nd EXC
02 66	2nd EXC	13 61	RCL	24 21	N
03 21	N	14 23	PMT	25 51	STO
04 51	STO	15 85	=	26 00	0
05 00	0	16 75	+	27 61	RCL
06 12	CPT	17 61	RCL	28 02	2
07 25	FV	18 01	1	29 25	FV
08 84	+/−	19 85	=	30 42	R/S
09 75	+	20 24	PV	31 41	RST
10 61	RCL	21 61	RCL		

Example: To demonstrate the program, we will use the same bond situation used for the price calculations. The pertinent values are:

RD	=	77	coupon payment = 3.5
TD	=	183	price = 90.988159
N	=	32	redemption value = 100

Action	Press	Display
1. Clear calculator and enter program.	2nd CA 2nd LRN **Program**	0
2. Select two-decimal display.	2nd FIX 2	0.00
3. Compute and enter N + RD/TD.	32 + 77 ÷ 183 = N	32.42
4. Compute and enter 1 − RD/TD.	1 − 77 ÷ 183 = STO 0	0.58
5. Enter coupon payment.	3.5 PMT	3.50
6. Enter price.	90.988159 PV STO 1	90.99
7. Enter redemption value.	100 FV STO 2	100.00
8. Remove fix decimal format.	2nd FIX 9	100.
9. Calculate yield between interest dates.	CPT %i	4.000994838
10. Adjust variables.	R/S	100.
11. Repeat *Steps 9-10* until calculated yield stabilizes.	CPT %i	3.999999757
	R/S	100.
	CPT %i	4.
	R/S	100.
	CPT %i	4.
12. Calculate annual yield for bond.	× 2 =	8.000000001

Thus, the yield is computed with accuracy to eight decimal places. However, remember that the calculator computes yield based on the values you enter. So, if you enter the price to the nearest cent, the yield will be slightly different than if it were entered to six decimal places. If you want to check your yield calculation, simply use the calculated yield to compute the bond price using the price program.

Example: Using the bond price calculated using the 30/360 day count basis, the program procedure is the same except for the input values which are:

RD	=	76	coupon payment = 3.5
TD	=	180	price = 90.9879433
N	=	32	redemption value = 100

When the procedure in the previous example is followed using these inputs, the yield computed is 8% with accuracy to nine decimal places.

Purchase of Bond Between Coupon Dates/One Coupon Payment Remaining

5

When a bond is purchased between coupon dates and only one coupon payment remains, the usual practice assumes daily interest periods. The formula for determining the present value (price) is:

$$PV = RV \times \left[\frac{\frac{RV}{100} + C_i}{1 + \left(\frac{RD}{TD} \times Y_i\right)} - \left[\frac{AD}{TD} \times C_i\right] \right]$$

where: PV = Present value of the bond on the settlement date
RV = Redemption value of the bond
C_i = Interest rate per coupon period expressed as a decimal
Y_i = Yield per coupon period expressed as a decimal
AD = Days from last coupon payment to the settlement date
RD = Days from settlement date to the next coupon payment
TD = Total days in the coupon period

Program Procedure

1. Store redemption value in memory 2.
2. Divide redemption value by 100 and enter in FV .
3. Store RD/TD in memory 0.
4. Store yield per coupon period as a decimal in memory 1.
5. Enter coupon interest rate per period as a percent in %i .
6. Press R/S to compute price.

Program Memory	Key Sequence	Program Memory	Key Sequence	Program Memory	Key Sequence
00 61	RCL	11 00	0	22 44	)
01 25	FV	12 55	×	23 55	×
02 75	+	13 61	RCL	24 61	RCL
03 61	RCL	14 01	1	25 22	%i
04 22	%i	15 85	=	26 85	=
05 85	=	16 65	−	27 55	×
06 45	÷	17 43	(	28 61	RCL
07 43	(	18 01	1	29 02	2
08 01	1	19 65	−	30 85	=
09 75	+	20 61	RCL	31 42	R/S
10 61	RCL	21 00	0		

PURCHASE OF BOND BETWEEN COUPON
DATES/ONE COUPON PAYMENT REMAINING

Example: A bond with a maturity date of December 1, 1978 is purchased on October 24, 1978. Coupon payments are made on June 1 and December 1. The bond has a nominal interest rate of 4% and an annual yield of 5%. Using a day basis of actual days, what is the purchase price?

Action	Press	Display
1. Clear calculator and enter program.	[2nd] **CA** [2nd] **LRN** Program	0
2. Select two-decimal display.	[2nd] **FIX** 2	0.00
3. Store redemption value.	100 [STO] 2	100.00
4. Divide RV by 100 and enter.	[÷] 100 [=] [FV]	1.00
5. Calculate RD.	10.241978 [DBD]	10.24
	12.011978 [=]	38.00
6. Calculate TD.	6.011978 [DBD]	6.01
	12.011978 [=]	183.00
7. Store RD/TD.	38 [÷] 183 [=] [STO] 0	0.21
8. Store yield per period as a decimal.	5 [÷] 2 [=] [%] [STO] 1	0.03
9. Enter coupon rate per period.	4 [÷] 2 [=] [%i]	2.00
10. Compute purchase price.	[R/S]	99.89
11. Remove fix decimal format.	[2nd] **FIX** 9	99.88852698

The price is $99.88852698 using industry methods.

Yield of Bond Between Coupon Dates with One Coupon Payment Remaining

The yield is computed using the following formula which is based on the present value formula.

$$Y_i = \frac{\dfrac{RV}{100} + C_i - \dfrac{PV}{100} + \left(\dfrac{AD}{TD} \times C_i\right)}{\dfrac{PV}{100} + \left(\dfrac{AD}{TD} \times C_i\right)} \times \frac{TD}{RD}$$

where the terms are as defined for the present value formula.

Program Procedure

1. Divide redemption value by 100 and enter in $\boxed{FV}$.
2. Store RD/TD in memory 0.
3. Divide PV by 100 and store in memory 3.
4. Enter coupon interest rate per period as a percent in $\boxed{\%i}$.
5. Press $\boxed{R/S}$ to compute yield per period.

Program Memory	Key Sequence	Program Memory	Key Sequence	Program Memory	Key Sequence
00 61	$\boxed{RCL}$	11 43	$\boxed{(}$	22 85	$\boxed{=}$
01 25	$\boxed{FV}$	12 01	1	23 45	$\boxed{\div}$
02 75	$\boxed{+}$	13 65	$\boxed{-}$	24 61	$\boxed{RCL}$
03 61	$\boxed{RCL}$	14 61	$\boxed{RCL}$	25 23	$\boxed{PMT}$
04 22	$\boxed{\%i}$	15 00	0	26 85	$\boxed{=}$
05 85	$\boxed{=}$	16 44	$\boxed{)}$	27 45	$\boxed{\div}$
06 65	$\boxed{-}$	17 55	$\boxed{\times}$	28 61	$\boxed{RCL}$
07 43	$\boxed{(}$	18 61	$\boxed{RCL}$	29 00	0
08 61	$\boxed{RCL}$	19 22	$\boxed{\%i}$	30 85	$\boxed{=}$
09 03	3	20 44	$\boxed{)}$	31 42	$\boxed{R/S}$
10 75	$\boxed{+}$	21 23	$\boxed{PMT}$		

YIELD OF BOND BETWEEN COUPON DATES
WITH ONE COUPON PAYMENT REMAINING

Example: Using the purchase price computed in the previous example, compute the yield. The pertinent values are:

$$RD = 38 \quad RV = 100$$
$$TD = 183 \quad PV = 99.88852698$$
$$C_i = 2\%$$

Action	Press	Display
1. Clear calculator and enter program.	2nd CA 2nd LRN **Program**	0
2. Select two-decimal display.	2nd FIX 2	0.00
3. Divide RV by 100 and enter.	100 ÷ 100 = FV	1.00
4. Store RD/TD.	38 ÷ 183 = STO 0	0.21
5. Divide price by 100 and store.	99.88852698 ÷ 100 =	1.00
	STO 3	1.00
6. Enter coupon rate per period.	2 %i	2.00
7. Compute yield per period.	R/S	0.02
8. Calculate annual yield in percent.	× 100 × 2 =	5.00
9. Remove fix-decimal format.	2nd FIX 9	4.999999907

Callable Bonds

5

Bonds which can be retired by the issuing corporation before their maturity date are *callable bonds*. Usually a premium is paid if the bonds are called. The redemption value of the bond plus the premium equal the call price.

A common practice is to compute the yield-to-call calculation which gives the minimum assured yield to the investor. Therefore, if the callable bond is selling at a discount, use the maturity date for the yield calculation. For a bond selling at a premium, but callable at par, use the next call date for the yield calculation.

The bond programs previously discussed are used for the calculation of price or yield with callable bonds. The following examples reference these programs and procedures. Therefore, many of the details are omitted at this point.

Example: A bond has a call date of November 1, 1988 and a call price of 101. The bond has semiannual coupons with coupon dates of May 1 and November 1. The bond yields 4% and pays a 5% coupon rate. The bond is purchased on August 9, 1978. What is the price if the 30/360 day basis is used?

$$AD = 98$$
$$RD = 82$$
$$TD = 180$$
$$N = 20$$

Use the program for price between coupon dates with more than one coupon payment remaining.

Action	Press	Display
1. Clear calculator and enter	2nd CA 2nd LRN	00 00
program.	Program 2nd LRN RST	0
2. Select two-decimal display.	2nd FIX 2	0.00
3. Compute and enter N + RD/TD.	20 + 82 ÷ 180 = N	20.46
	STO 2	20.46
4. Compute and enter 1 − RD/TD.	1 − 82 ÷ 180 =	0.54
	STO 0	0.54
5. Enter yield per coupon period.	4 ÷ 2 = %i	2.00
6. Enter coupon payment.	5 ÷ 2 = PMT	2.50
	STO 1	2.50
7. Enter call price for FV.	101 FV	101.00
8. Compute price.	R/S	108.99
9. Unrounded price.	2nd FIX 9	108.9875958

CALLABLE BONDS

Using the bond price just calculated, solve for the yield on the callable bond. The pertinent input values are:

RD	=	82	Price = 108.9875958
TD	=	180	Redemption Value = 101
N	=	20	Coupon Rate = 5%

Use the program for yield between coupon dates with more than one coupon payment remaining.

Action	Press	Display
1. Clear calculator and enter program.	2nd CA 2nd LRN **Program**	0
2. Select two-decimal display.	2nd FIX 2	0.00
3. Compute and enter N + RD/TD.	20 + 82 ÷ 180 = N	20.46
4. Compute and enter 1 − RD/TD.	1 − 82 ÷ 180 =	0.54
	STO 0	0.54
5. Enter coupon payment.	5 ÷ 2 = PMT	2.50
6. Enter price.	108.9875958 PV STO 1	108.99
7. Enter redemption value.	101 FV STO 2	101.00
8. Remove fix-decimal format.	2nd FIX 9	101.
9. Calculate yield.	CPT %i	2.0003488
10. Adjust values.	R/S	101.
11. Repeat *Steps 9-10* until yield	CPT %i	1.999999937
stabilizes.	R/S	101.
	CPT %i	1.999999998
	R/S	101.
	CPT %i	1.999999998
12. Calculate annual yield.	× 2 =	3.999999996

The programs for bonds purchased on coupon dates and for bonds with one coupon payment remaining are used as shown in the examples for those programs. In each program the call price is substituted for the redemption value.

Investor's Rate of Return on a Convertible Bond

5

When an investor purchases a convertible bond, he generally expects the price of the stock to increase so he can convert the bond in the future. Upon conversion the investor will have received interest payments (CP) for n years and receives stock with a value CN. The following analysis ignores taxes, assumes reinvestment at the rate (h) and assumes that the investor sells the stock upon conversion.

If the bond originally sells at par value, the investor's rate of return (h) is found using the following relationship.

$$BP = CP \left(\frac{1 - (1 + h)^{-n}}{h} \right) + \frac{CN}{(1 + h)^{n}}$$

$$CN = \frac{BP\,(P)\ (1 + r)^{n}}{C}$$

where:

BP	=	Purchase price, or par value, of the bond.
CP	=	Coupon payment, or interest received, per year.
h	=	Internal rate of return, or rate of return investor will receive.
n	=	Numbers of years until bond is converted into stock.
CN	=	Conversion value of the bond.
P	=	Present price per share of the stock.
C	=	Conversion price per share of the stock.
r	=	Projected increase in value of stock per year.

The procedure for solving this formula for the rate of return (h) involves the following steps.

1. Enter CN in $\boxed{FV}$, BP (P) / C in $\boxed{PV}$, $\dot{r}$ in $\boxed{\%i}$, and solve for n by pressing $\boxed{CPT}$ $\boxed{N}$. This step requires the conversion value of the bond (CN) at which conversion would occur, and solves for the number of periods (N). It also requires the expected growth rate of the stock (r). The current price of the stock (P) and the conversion price of the shares (C) are given (fixed by bond terms).

2. After determining the year for conversion in *Step 1*, solve for CN* after rounding n to the nearest whole number (n*). Here we are assuming conversion occurs on an interest date.

$$CN^* = \frac{BP\,(P)}{C}\ (1 + r)^{n^*}$$

Enter BP (P) / C in $\boxed{PV}$, n* in $\boxed{N}$, and r in $\boxed{\%i}$. Solve for CN* by pressing $\boxed{CPT}$ $\boxed{FV}$. If the values for BP (P) / C and r were entered in *Step 1,* they do not have to be reentered at this point.

INVESTOR'S RATE OF RETURN
ON A CONVERTIBLE BOND

3. Now compute the rate of return (h) using the appropriate bond yield method discussed previously. Use the between interest dates routine if the bond is convertible between dates. In this example bonds are converted on a payment date. In this case enter CN* in [FV], BP in [PV], CP in [PMT], and n* in [N]. Solve for h by pressing [CPT] [%i].

Example:

An investor purchases a convertible bond at par for $1000 that pays 5% interest due in 20 years. The stock is currently selling for $20 a share with a conversion price of $25 per share. The investor wants to know his rate of return (h) if he converts the bond when the conversion value equals $1300. The stock has an expected growth rate of 5%. Conversion occurs on an interest payment date.

BP	=	$1000
CN	=	$1300
CP	=	$50
P	=	$20
C	=	$25
r	=	5%
n	=	?
h	=	?

Action	Press	Display
1. Clear calculator and select two-decimal display.	[CLR] [2nd] **CM** [2nd] **FIX** 2	0.00
2. Enter CN.	1300 [FV]	1300.00
3. Compute and enter BP (P) / C.	1000 [×] 20 [÷] 25 [=]	800.00
	[PV]	800.00
4. Enter r.	5 [%i]	5.00
5. Compute n.	[CPT] [N]	9.95
6. Enter n*.	10 [N]	10.00
7. Compute CN*.	[CPT] [FV]	1303.12
8. Enter CP.	50 [PMT]	50.00
9. Enter BP.	1000 [PV]	1000.00
10. Compute h.	[CPT] [%i]	7.18

The bond if converted at the end of the tenth year yields 7.18%, assuming a 5% increase in the stock price each year.

Reference: Weston and Brigham, *Managerial Finance,* pp. 508-515.

Bond Refunding

5

If a company has sold callable bonds at a time when interest rates are relatively high and interest rates subsequently drop, the company may wish to sell a new issue of lower-yielding bonds and use the proceeds to retire the high-yield bonds. This is called a *refunding operation.*

A recommended procedure for evaluating the decision to refund a bond issue is to compare the present value refunding costs to the present value of the savings in future interest costs. The refunding costs *after taxes* are composed of the following items.

Call Premium — the bonus paid to the bond holder when his bond is called. This expense is deducted in the year it is incurred.

Flotation Costs — the costs incurred in selling a new issue. These costs are usually amortized over the life of the bond, or a period of time such as twenty years. In a refunding decision, there are two groups of flotation costs: 1) the unamortized flotation costs of the old bond issue, and 2) the flotation costs of the new issue.

Extra Interest — If the new bonds are issued before the old bonds are retired, this extra interest must be considered.

The annual interest savings are composed of the present value after tax of the difference between the old bond interest and the new bond interest.

The calculations are summarized as follows:

    A.   Compute present value of refunding costs.
        1. After tax cost of call premium.
        2. Present value of flotation costs on new issue.
        3. Present value of unamortized flotation costs on old issue.
        4. Interest costs on new issue incurred before the old issue is retired.
        5. The net of 1, 2, 3, and 4 is the total after-tax investment.

    B.   Compute present value of interest savings.
        1. After-tax annual amount of old bond interest minus after-tax annual amount of new bond interest.
        2. The present value of this annual savings over the life of the bonds is the total savings.

    C.   Compare A and B.

Note: The tax shield relationship is:
    Non-cash deductions
        Expense × Tax Rate
    Cash deductions
        Expense × (1 − Tax Rate)

BOND REFUNDING

Example:

A corporation has a $450,000, 20-year bond issue outstanding. The debt is five years old, with a coupon interest rate of 10% paid annually. The flotation costs are $18,000 and are being amortized on a straight-line basis over the life of the bonds. The call price is 105, or at a premium of 5% of the par value. The bonds were issued at par.

The corporation now has the opportunity to refinance the debt with 15-year bonds at a 7% coupon rate paid annually. The flotation costs would be $22,000. No further decline in interest rates is expected. The new bonds would be issued one month before the old issue is retired. The corporation has an average tax rate of 40%.

Based on these facts, should the old bond issue be refunded?

Action	Press	Display
1. Clear calculator and select two-decimal display.	CLR 2nd CM 2nd FIX 2	0.00
2. Compute before tax cost of call premium.	5 % ✕ 450000 =	22500.00
3. Compute after tax cost of call premium.	✕ (1 − 40 % =	13500.00
4. Compute annual deduction for flotation costs of new issue before tax.	22000 ÷ 15 =	1466.67
5. Compute and enter the after tax deduction.	✕ 40 % = PMT	586.67
6. Compute and enter the after tax interest rate of the new debt.	7 ✕ (1 − 40 %	0.40
	) = %i	4.20
7. Enter life of new bonds.	15 N	15.00
8. **Compute PV of tax savings.**	CPT PV	6432.51
9. Compute net after-tax effect of new flotation costs.	+/− + 22000 =	15567.49
10. Compute annual deduction before tax from old flotation costs.	18000 ÷ 20 =	900.00
11. Compute after tax deduction and enter as annual savings.	✕ 40 % = PMT	360.00
12. Enter number of years.	15 N	15.00
13. Enter rate (same as new issue).	4.2 %i	4.20
14. **Compute PV of future tax savings on all the old issue flotation costs.**	CPT PV	3947.22

Action	Press	Display
15. Compute current tax savings from old issue flotation costs.	15 ÷ 20 × 18000	18000
	× 40 % =	5400.00
16. Compute net tax benefit from retiring the old issue.	− 3947.22 =	1452.78
17. Compute additional interest because the bonds overlap one month.	450000 × 7 % ÷ 12	12
	× (1 − 40 %	0.40
	) =	1575.00
18. Compute after tax present value cost of refunding old bond issue.		
a. Enter call premium	13500	13500
b. Add new bond flotation cost	+ 15567.49	15567.49
c. Subtract old bond flotation cost	− 1452.78	1452.78
d. Add additional interest and total	+ 1575 =	29189.71
19. Compute annual after tax interest savings.		
a. Old bond interest	450000 × 10 % ×	45000.00
	(1 − 40 %) =	27000.00
b. New bond interest	450000 × 7 % ×	31500.00
	(1 − 40 %) =	18900.00
c. Annual savings	+/− + 27000 =	8100.00
20. Enter annual savings.	PMT	8100.00
21. Compute and enter after tax interest rate.	(1 − 40 %)	0.60
	× 7 = %i	4.20
22. Enter life of new bonds.	15 N	15.00
23. Compute PV of interest savings.	CPT PV	88812.45
24. Compute net advantage from refunding.	− 29189.71 =	59622.74

The net advantage to the firm for refunding the bond issue is $59,622.77 because the net after-tax cost of refunding is $29,189.68, while the interest savings are $88,812.45.

Reference: Weston and Brigham, *Managerial Finance*, pp. 459-463.

Real Estate

Real estate is considered to be a most dynamic field with changes occurring almost daily. These changes are reflected in the creative financing area, that is, in the area of mortgage packing, income tax applications, determining rates of return and, in the ultimate decision process, whether to invest in a real estate package or not. Interested individuals run the gamut from the one-time, unsophisticated investor who might want to know how much to invest in a single family house to that individual-builder-developer who is interested in tax cover, depreciation allowances and reduced taxable income.

In the past the mathematical and statistical applications required to make a decision were often tedious, time consuming and prone to error. Not so anymore.

Welcome to the world of calculator analysis for real estate. Your calculator brings you, the individual investor in whatever category of sophistication, the means of calculating many of the ratios, rates of return and other analytical techniques that will assist you in arriving at the best real estate decision. The range of the calculator's applications is limited only by your curiosity, imagination and real estate knowledge.

To give you an idea of possible applications, this section shows a variety of problems ranging from simple home ownership to the complex sale-leaseback situation. Keep in mind that these problems are set up to show you the potential of your calculator. They are meant to stimulate you to explore its vast potential.

Home Financing
Monthly Payment for Home Mortgage

You are buying a $37,550 house, putting $5000 down and financing the rest at 8.75% annual interest for 30 years (excluding taxes and insurance). How much will your monthly payments be on the loan?

If taxes and insurance will average 30% of your loan payment each month, how much will your house payment be?

$$PV = \begin{array}{r} \$37550 \\ - 5000 \\ \hline \$32550 \end{array}$$

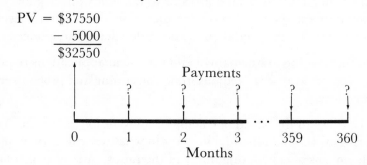

$i = 8.75\%/12$ per month $\qquad\qquad$ N $= 360$ months

Action	Press	Display
1. Clear calculator and select two-decimal display.	CLR 2nd CM 2nd FIX 2	0. 0.00
2. Calculate loan amount.	37550 − 5000 = PV	32550.00
3. Calculate monthly interest rate.	8.75 ÷ 12 = %i	0.73
4. Calculate number of payments.	30 × 12 = N	360.00
5. **Compute monthly payment.**	CPT PMT	256.07
6. **Compute total monthly house payment.**	+ 30 % =	332.89

Loan Amount a Buyer Can Afford

6

A loan company will usually finance a house if the potential monthly payment does not exceed 25% of a buyer's gross income. Assume you have a gross monthly income of $1550. What price house can you afford to finance at an 8.75% annual interest rate for 30 years with 5% down? Monthly taxes and insurance will be 30% of the loan payment.

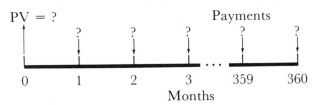

PV = ?   Payments

0   1   2   3   359   360
                     Months

i = 8.75% per month   N = 360 months

Action	Press	Display
1. Clear calculator and select two-decimal display.	CLR 2nd CM 2nd FIX 2	0. 0.00
2. Calculate maximum allowable monthly payment (total).	1550 X 25 % =	387.50
3. Calculate maximum allowable loan payment.	÷ (1 + 30 %) = PMT	298.08
4. Calculate number of monthly payments.	30 X 12 = N	360.00
5. Calculate monthly interest rate.	8.75 ÷ 12 = %i	0.73
6. **Compute maximum allowable loan amount.**	CPT PV	37889.51
7. **Calculate affordable house price.**	÷ (1 − 5 %) =	39883.69
8. **Calculate down payment.**	− RCL PV =	1994.18

Property Appreciation

The house you bought for $37,075 five years ago is now appraised at $52,000. What was the annual appreciation rate? What will the house be worth in three years?

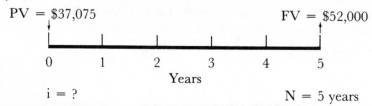

Action		
1. Clear calculator and select two-decimal display.	CLR 2nd CM 2nd FIX 2	0. 0.00
2. Enter former value.	37075 PV	37075.00
3. Enter current value.	52000 FV	52000.00
4. Enter number of years.	5 N	5.00
5. **Calculate annual appreciation rate in percent.**	CPT %i	7.00
6. Enter new present value.	52000 PV	52000.00
7. Enter new period.	3 N	3.00
8. **Calculate future value.**	CPT FV	63702.53

The house is appreciating at an average annual rate of 7%. In three years your house should be worth about $63,700 if the 7% appreciation rate continues.

Original Cost and Appreciation

6

Your friend has a five year old house that has been appraised at $48,000. He has an 8.5%, 30-year loan and an unpaid balance of $26,834. Five years ago, 8.5%, 30-year loans required 20% down payment. You want to know two things: one, what was the original price of the house and, two, if he sells the house for $48,000, what would his average yearly appreciation rate be?

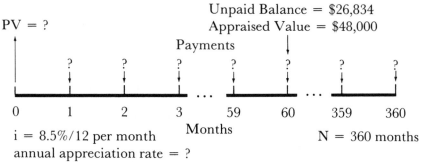

PV = ?

Unpaid Balance = $26,834
Appraised Value = $48,000

Payments

0   1   2   3 ... 59   60   ... 359   360

Months

i = 8.5%/12 per month
annual appreciation rate = ?

N = 360 months

Action	Press	Display
1. Clear calculator and select two-decimal display.	CLR 2nd CM 2nd FIX 2	0. 0.00
2. Calculate monthly interest rate.	8.5 ÷ 12 = %i	0.71
3. Calculate number of remaining payments.	30 − 5 = × 12 = N	300.00
4. Enter unpaid balance.	26834 PV	26834.00
5. **Calculate monthly loan payment.**	CPT PMT	216.07
6. Calculate original number of periods.	30 × 12 = N	360.00
7. Compute original loan amount.	CPT PV	28101.29
8. Calculate original price of home.	÷ (1 − 20 % = PV	35126.62
9. Compute annual appreciation rate.	5 N 0 PMT 48000 FV CPT %i	5.00 0.00 48000.00 6.44

Principal and Interest

Assume that you have made 85 payments on your home. Your original loan was for $32,000 with an 8.5% interest rate, and your payments (less taxes and insurance) are $250 per month. You would like to know how much of your next loan payment will be interest and how much will be added to your equity (the amount of your loan that is paid off). Also how much principal has been paid off on the loan?

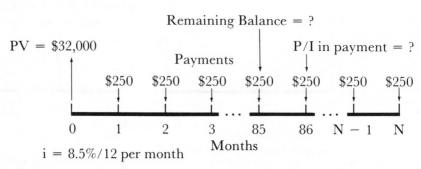

Action	Press	Display
1. Clear calculator and select two-decimal display.	CLR 2nd CM 2nd FIX 2	0. 0.00
2. Enter original loan amount.	32000 PV	32000.00
3. Enter monthly payment.	250 PMT	250.00
4. Calculate monthly interest rate.	8.5 ÷ 12 = %i	0.71
5. **Enter number of payments made and compute loan balance at intermediate period.**	85 2nd BAL	29292.08
6. **Calculate principal paid off.**	+/– + RCL PV =	2707.92
7. **Enter number of next period and calculate amount that applies to principal.**	86 2nd P/I	42.51
8. Calculate interest amount.	x:y	207.49

You have decided to buy a $35,000 house and would also like to make some improvements. You can finance the house for 20 years at 8.4% annual interest rate with 10% down. You need $3,400 for improvements which you could borrow from another source. The improvement loan would be at 9.6% annual interest for two years. What would your monthly loan payment be for the two loans (during the first two years)? What would your monthly loan payment be if the improvement loan was included in the original house loan (added to the purchase price of the house)?

Step 1

Calculate the total monthly payment when the home and improvement loans are financed separately.

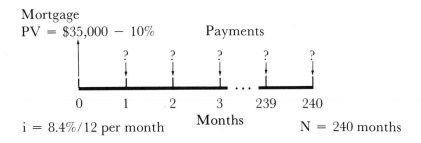

Mortgage
PV = $35,000 − 10%   Payments

0   1   2   3   239   240
               Months

i = 8.4%/12 per month   N = 240 months

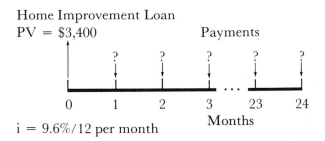

Home Improvement Loan
PV = $3,400   Payments

0   1   2   3   23   24
               Months

i = 9.6%/12 per month

HOME IMPROVEMENT

Action	Press	Display
1. Clear calculator and select two-decimal display.	CLR 2nd CM 2nd FIX 2	0. 0.00
2. Calculate home loan after down payment.	35000 − 10 % = PV	31500.00
3. Calculate interest rate for home loan.	8.4 ÷ 12 = %i	0.70
4. Calculate months of home loan.	20 × 12 = N	240.00
5. Calculate payment for home loan.	CPT PMT STO 1	271.37
6. Enter home improvement amount.	3400 PV	3400.00
7. Calculate interest rate on home improvement loan.	9.6 ÷ 12 = %i	0.80
8. Calculate months in home improvement loan.	2 × 12 = N	24.00
9. Compute monthly payment for home improvement loan.	CPT PMT SUM 1	156.27
10. Display total payment for both loans financed separately.	RCL 1	427.64

Step 2 Calculate the total monthly payment for financing both for 20 years.

$$PV = (\$35,000 + \$3400) - 10\%$$

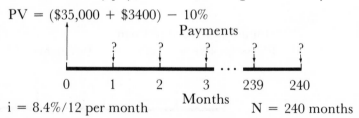

i = 8.4%/12 per month   Months   N = 240 months

Action	Press	Display
1. Calculate total amount for house and improvement loan.	35000 + 3400 =	38400.00
2. Subtract down payment.	− 10 % = PV	34560.00
3. Calculate interest rate.	8.4 ÷ 12 = %i	0.70
4. Calculate total number of payments.	20 × 12 = N	240.00
5. Compute total monthly payment.	CPT PMT	297.74

The combined loan payments would be $427.64 the first two years. If the improvement loan could be included in the purchase price, the monthly payments would be $297.74 for 20 years.

Mortgage with Balloon Payment

There are many financial situations that involve not only a series of regular payments, but also a payment at the end (that may be larger or smaller than the regular payment). These payments are called balloon payments (or balloons), and can be used to pay off a loan before its normal duration is complete — or in a variety of other circumstances.

Example: You are considering buying a $15,000 lake house, but you need the payments to be as small as possible. You know that you'll receive $3000 from an insurance policy in 14 years and would like that money to be a balloon payment on the lake house mortgage (and also serve as the last payment). If the 14 year mortgage (including the balloon payment) is set at 9.25% annual interest, what would your monthly payment be?

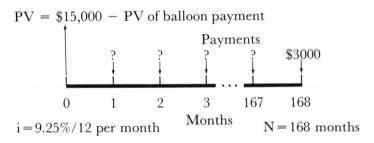

PV = $15,000 − PV of balloon payment

Payments

$3000

0   1   2   3   167   168

Months

i = 9.25%/12 per month   N = 168 months

Action	Press	Display
1. Clear calculator and select two-decimal display.	CLR 2nd CM	0.
	2nd FIX 2	0.00
2. Enter balloon payment.	3000 FV	3000.00
3. Calculate monthly interest rate.	9.25 ÷ 12 = %i	0.77
4. Calculate number of payments.	14 × 12 = N	168.00
5. Calculate present value of balloon payment.	CPT PV	825.78
6. Calculate present value of loan.	+/− + 15000 = PV	14174.22
7. Enter number of payments (balloon payment is last payment).	167 N	167.00
8. Calculate monthly payment.	CPT PMT	151.20

Investments in Real Estate
Time to Pay Off a Loan

Assume that when you bought some property at $5,000, you borrowed at 10% annual interest. You plan to use the $90 per month income from the property to repay the loan. How long will it take?

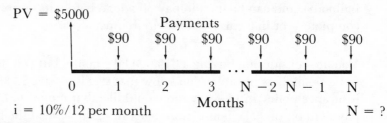

$PV = \$5000$

$i = 10\%/12$ per month

$N = ?$

Action	Press	Display
1. Clear calculator and select two-decimal display.	CLR 2nd CM 2nd FIX 2	0. 0.00
2. Enter present value.	5000 PV	5000.00
3. Enter payment.	90 PMT	90.00
4. Calculate interest rate.	10 ÷ 12 = %i	0.83
5. Compute months to pay off loan.	CPT N	74.91
6. Convert months to years.	÷ 12 =	6.24

Buying Loan Payments

Joe Brown loaned Fred Smith $10,000 at 8.5% annual interest for ten years. Fred's payments to Joe are $123.99 per month. Two years later (right after the 24th payment), Joe has an immediate need for cash so he asks you to buy the remaining loan payments from him. You earn a 9% annual rate compounded monthly from your other investments, so you are only willing to buy the mortgage if you can realize a 9% rate of return. What would you offer to pay Joe Brown for the balance of the loan?

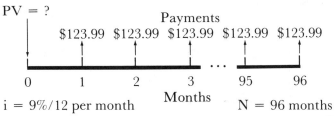

Action	Press	Display
1. Clear calculator and select	CLR 2nd CM	0.
two-decimal display.	2nd FIX 2	0.00
2. Enter payment.	123.99 PMT	123.99
3. Calculate number of periods	10 − 2 =	8.00
left in loan.	× 12 = N	96.00
4. Calculate interest rate.	9 ÷ 12 = %i	0.75
5. Compute present value of	CPT PV	8463.36
future payments.		

Any offer under $8464 would represent a profitable investment returning at least 9% annually.

Purchase Price of Rental Property

One quick method that can be used to determine whether or not to buy a piece of rental property is to assume that you will buy only if the rent income from the property covers taxes, maintenance, insurance, and the loan payment for the value of the property. Say a house rents for $210 a month. You estimate that taxes, insurance, and maintenance will run $75 each month. If you can get a 25 year loan for the full cost of the house at 9¾% yearly interest compounded monthly, how much can you afford to pay for the house?

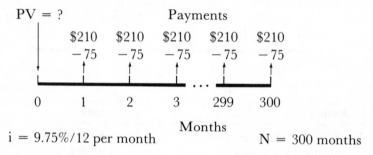

$i = 9.75\%/12$ per month $N = 300$ months

Action	Press	Display
1. Clear calculator and select two-decimal display.	CLR 2nd CM 2nd FIX 2	0. 0.00
2. Calculate amount of rent applicable to loan payment.	210 − 75 = PMT	135.00
3. Calculate monthly interest rate.	9.75 ÷ 12 = %i	0.81
4. Calculate number of payments.	25 × 12 = N	300.00
5. **Compute the amount of the loan necessary to fulfill your specifications.**	CPT PV	15149.18

A $15,150 house would be within your purchase limit.

Investing in a Rental Property

6

Example: You're considering buying a house that is presently rented for $375 per month (payable at the first of each month) as an investment. You have $10,000 available cash for the investment. You realize that buying a house involves some risk, so you are planning the move only if you can make a sizable profit on the deal (15% annual rate).

After checking with a real estate agent, you find that you can buy the house by placing $10,000 down and assuming a $25,000 mortgage. You figure that your expenses, including mortgage payments, will be about $250 per month. You expect to keep the property for 10 years, sell the property, pay off the mortgage, and net $20,000. Should you invest in the house?

You are dealing here with two types of cash flows: one, the income produced by the property (the monthly rental payments and the $20,000 profit from selling the house in ten years), and, two, the expenses of buying the house (the monthly mortgage payment, taxes, insurance, maintenance and down payment). The first step in solving the problem will be to find the present value of the income. Then, find the present value of expenses and compare the two amounts. If the present value of the income equals or exceeds the present value of the expenses, you should buy the house.

Income

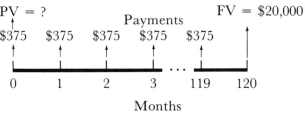

$i = 15\%/12$ per month $N = 120$ months

Expenses

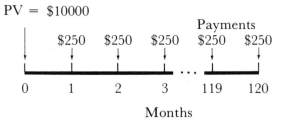

$i = 15\%/12$ per month $N = 120$ months

INVESTING IN A RENTAL PROPERTY

Action	Press	Display
1. Clear calculator and select two-decimal display.	CLR 2nd CM	0.
	2nd FIX 2	0.00
2. Enter number of periods.	10 × 12 = N	120.00
3. Enter desired interest rate (use this as a discount factor in finding the present values).	15 ÷ 12 = %i	1.25
4. **Enter monthly rental income and calculate present value** (an annuity due situation, since lease payments are usually made at the beginning of each period).	375 PMT	375.00
	2nd DUE PV	23534.11
	STO 0	23534.11
5. Eliminate payment and enter $20,000 sale profit.	0 PMT 20000 FV	20000.00
6. **Calculate present value and add to monthly rental payment present value.**	CPT PV SUM 0	4504.29
7. **Enter monthly expenses** (mortgage payment, taxes, insurance, and maintenance) **and calculate present value** (an ordinary annuity situation).	250 PMT CPT PV	15495.71
8. **Add down payment to find total present value of expenses.**	+ 10000 =	25495.71
9. **Compare to present value of income.**	+/− + RCL 0	28038.40
	=	2542.69

Purchasing the house will give you more than the 15% annual return you want — by $2542.69.

Calculating Required Balloon Payment

6

It is sometimes advantageous to pay off a loan with a balloon payment before the scheduled termination of the mortgage.

The following procedure easily calculates the size of balloon payment needed for early payoff of a mortgage.

Example: Consider a mortgage balance of $250,000 that is to terminate in 25 years. Paying 10½% annual interest rate (compounded monthly), what balloon payment must be made in 15 years to pay off the loan?

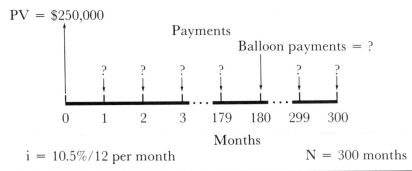

Action	Press	Display
1. Clear calculator and select two-decimal display.	CLR 2nd CM	0.
	2nd FIX 2	0.00
2. Calculate original mortgage term.	25 ✕ 12 = N	300.00
3. Calculate monthly interest rate.	10.5 ÷ 12 = %i	0.88
4. Enter mortgage amount.	250000 PV	250000.00
5. Calculate monthly payment.	CPT PMT	2360.45
6. Calculate number of payments you will have made at end of 15th year.	15 ✕ 12 =	180.00
7. Calculate balloon payment.	2nd BAL	174932.70

Price of a Mortgage with a Balloon Payment

You are looking for an investment that will pay 15% annual interest compounded monthly on your money. A friend offers to sell you a new $12,000 ten-year mortgage. The monthly payments are $141.92 with a final balloon payment of $3000. What would you pay for the mortgage to earn 15% annual interest compounded monthly?

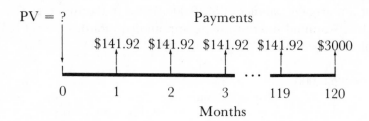

PV = ?   Payments

$141.92 $141.92 $141.92 $141.92 $3000

0   1   2   3   119   120

Months

i = 15%/12 per month   N = 120 months

Action	Press	Display
1. Clear calculator and select two-decimal display.	CLR 2nd CM	0.
	2nd FIX 2	0.00
2. Enter balloon payment.	3000 FV	3000.00
3. Calculate number of periods.	10 ✕ 12 = N	120.00
4. Calculate monthly interest rate.	15 ÷ 12 = %i	1.25
5. **Compute present value of balloon payment.**	CPT PV STO 1	675.64
6. Enter payment.	141.92 PMT	141.92
7. Calculate number of payments (balloon is last payment).	10 ✕ 12 − 1 = N	119.00
8. **Compute present value of loan.**	CPT PV	8764.64
9. **Calculate total price.**	+ RCL 1 =	9440.29

The present value of the payments and the balloon payment, assuming a 15% annual return, is about $9440. If your friend will sell you the mortgage for this amount, you will achieve your desired return.

Present Value of Income-Producing Property

6

This is an old standby method used by appraisal people when they forecast a constant income stream (ordinary annuity) and a reversion value (the value of the property at the end of the time period). It is natural to presuppose a "stabilized" level stream for discounting to the present value. The procedure is:

1. Find present value of lease payments.
2. Calculate present value of reversion (future) value.
3. Sum the present values above to find the total present value of the property.

Example: A piece of property has 20 years remaining on a $22,000 per year lease, with payments made at the end of each year. The reversion value of the property is forecast to be $100,000. The applicable discount rate is 9% (rate of interest). What should you expect to pay for the land today to meet the specified reversion value and discount rate?

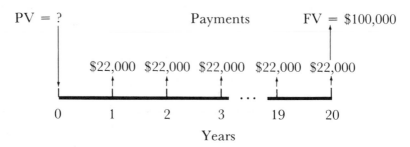

i = 9% per year   N = 20 years

Action	Press	Display
1. Clear calculator and select two-decimal display.	CLR 2nd CM 2nd FIX 2	0. 0.00
2. Enter number of years remaining on lease.	20 N	20.00
3. Enter annual payment.	22000 PMT	22000.00
4. Enter annual interest rate.	9 %i	9.00
5. Compute present value of income stream.	CPT PV STO 1	200828.00
6. Remove annual lease payment.	0 PMT	0.00
7. Enter reversion value.	100000 FV	100000.00
8. Compute present value of reversion value.	CPT PV SUM 1	17843.09
9. Display present value of property.	RCL 1	218671.09

Reversion Value for Specified Yield

Appraisers periodically need to calculate the reversion (future) value of a certain piece of property based on some expected or desired yield. The traditional method is to:

1. Solve for periodic rent per dollar of purchase price $= \dfrac{\text{monthly rent}}{\text{purchase price}}$
2. Calculate monthly reversion yield $= (1 + i)^n$, where i is monthly interest rate
3. Calculate accumulation per period $= \dfrac{(1 + i)^n - 1}{i}$
4. Calculate required reversion $=$ purchase price $\times \left[\text{monthly reversion yield} - \text{rent per dollar} \times (1 + i) \times \text{accumulation per period}\right]$

Example:
A lease that expires in 22 years requires a $15,500 monthly rental, payable in advance. As holder of this lease, you are negotiating with a prospective client who is considering offering $1,500,000 for the property holding. He asks what should the reversion value be at the end of the 22-year lease period to realize a yield of 12%. He says that his real estate people quoted him a reversion value of $850,000. Do you agree or disagree?

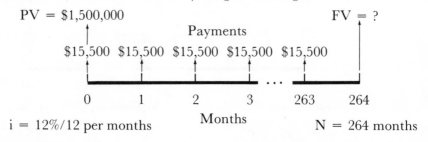

PV = $1,500,000   FV = ?

Payments

$15,500 $15,500 $15,500 $15,500 $15,500

0   1   2   3   263   264

i = 12%/12 per months   Months   N = 264 months

Action	Press	Display
1. Clear display and memories and select two-decimal display.	CLR 2nd CM	0.
	2nd FIX 2	0.00
2. Enter payment.	15500 PMT	15500.00
3. Calculate monthly interest rate.	12 ÷ 12 = %i	1.00
4. Calculate number of payments.	22 × 12 = N	264.00
5. Calculate future value of rent payments.	2nd DUE FV	
	STO 1	20086387.01
6. Enter lease sale price.	1500000 PV	1500000.00
7. Calculate future value of lease sale price.	0 PMT CPT FV	20745979.25
8. Calculate difference.	− RCL 1 =	659592.24

The investor's advisors suggested a reversion value of $850,000, but your calculations indicate that the value of the property can drop to $660,000 at the end of 22 years and the investor will still receive his 12% return.

Indicated Overall Rate Using Mortgage Constant

6

An alternative procedure used by real estate practitioners to derive an overall capitalization rate is described below. This rate is then used to determine an income-producing property's value.

1. Determine annual mortgage constant as shown below.
2. Solve for the indicated overall rate which is the following sum: (mortgage × mortgage constant) + (equity × desired equity yield).
3. Calculate the present value by $\dfrac{\text{Net Operating Income}}{\text{Overall Rate}}$.

Example: What is the present value of a $500,000 office complex? A survey of the records indicates that the predicted level net income stream of $35,000 annually is valid. It is possible to obtain a 75% mortgage at 10.25% for a term of 25 years, payable monthly. An equity yield rate of 13% is required.

Action	Press	Display
1. Clear calculator and select four-decimal display.	CLR 2nd CM 2nd FIX 4	0.0000
2. Calculate number of periods.	25 × 12 = N	300.0000
3. Calculate monthly interest rate.	10.25 ÷ 12 = %i	0.8542
4. Enter 1 as present value.	1 PV	1.0000
5. Compute monthly mortgage constant.	CPT PMT	0.0093
6. Calculate annual mortgage constant.	× 12 =	0.1112
7. Calculate indicated overall rate.	× .75 =	0.0834
	+ .25 × .13 =	0.1159
8. Calculate present value of property.	1/x × 35000 =	302050.9382

These calculations indicate that the property is worth no more than $302,051 assuming the 13% equity yield rate must be met.

Reference: Kinnard, *Income Property Valuation.*

Capitalization Rates and Rates of Return

These mathematical techniques are used by real estate analysts and appraisers to determine important and meaningful capitalization rates and rates of return.

1. Calculate the overall capitalization rate $= \dfrac{\text{Net Operating Income}}{\text{Total Property Investment}}$

2. Calculate the cash throw-off before taxes
   $= \text{Net Operating Income} - \text{Annual Debt Service}$

3. Calculate equity dividend rate $= \dfrac{\text{Cash throw-off}}{\text{Equity Investment}}$
   where equity investment $=$ property value $-$ mortgage

4. Compute capital recovery amount per year $= \dfrac{\text{purchase price} - \text{selling price}}{\text{number of years}}$

Example: You are an investor who has paid $300,000 for a small garden-type office building. This income-producing property yields a level yearly net operating income of $30,000. This income should continue another 10 years. You have obtained a 30-year, 9½% level monthly mortgage for $240,000. The property is to be sold in 10 years for an anticipated 80% of its original purchase price:

Calculate: Overall capitalization rate
Cash throw-off (cash before tax)
Equity dividend rate (before taxes)
Capital recovery amount for 10-year period

Action	Press	Display
1. Clear calculator and select four-decimal display.	CLR 2nd CM / 2nd FIX 4	0. / 0.0000
2. **Calculate overall capitalization rate.**	30000 ÷ 300000 =	0.1000
3. Calculate number of periods.	30 × 12 = N	360.0000
4. Calculate monthly interest rate.	9.5 ÷ 12 = %i	0.7917
5. Enter mortgage amount as present value.	240000 PV	240000.0000
6. Compute monthly payment.	CPT PMT	2018.0501
7. Calculate annual debt service.	× 12 =	24216.6011
8. **Calculate annual cash throw-off.**	+/− + 30000 =	5783.3989
9. **Calculate equity dividend rate.**	÷ (300000 −	
	240000) =	0.0964
10. **Calculate capital to be recovered.**	300000 − 80 % =	60000.0000
11. **Calculate capital recovery rate per year on a straight line basis.**	÷ 10 =	6000.0000

Leased Fee and Leasehold Valuations

6

The leased fee valuation is the present values of the rent paid to the owner and the reversion (future) value of the property. Leasehold valuation is the present value of the annual rents paid by tenants to the leased fee holder.

1. Find the present value of the annual rent incomes.
2. Calculate the present value of the reversion value.
3. Determine leased fee value as the sum of the two present values calculated above.
4. Calculate present value of leasehold.

Formerly, you would have had to multiply the annuity factor $\dfrac{1 + \dfrac{1}{(1 + i)^n}}{i}$ by the annual rental to find the present value of the leasehold. Note how easily this is handled by the calculator.

Example: Mrs. Willow leases a vacant lot to Mr. Oak for $10,000 per year for 50 years. Mr. Oak erects a building on the lot at a cost of $200,000 with a 50 year economic life. He then leases space in the building to several tenants, and his net income from the building is $20,000 annually. The land reversion value is $250,000. Using 5% annual rate for Mrs. Willow and 7% for Mr. Oak, determine the value of the leased fee and leasehold. (Assume that all lease payments are made at the beginning of the period.)

Action	Press	Display
1. Clear calculator and select two-decimal display.	CLR 2nd CM 2nd FIX 2	0. 0.00
2. Enter number of periods.	50 N	50.00
3. Enter Mrs. Willow's rate of return.	5 %i	5.00
4. Enter Mrs. Willow's rent income.	10000 PMT	10000.00
5. **Compute present value of rents.**	2nd DUE PV STO 1	191687.22
6. Enter reversion value of property.	250000 FV	250000.00
7. Enter 0 as payment.	0 PMT	0.00
8. **Compute present value of** reversion value.	CPT PV SUM 1	21800.93
9. **Display leased fee value.**	RCL 1	213488.15
10. Enter Mr. Oak's rate of return.	7 %i	7.00
11. Enter Mr. Oak's annual income from building rentals.	20000 PMT	20000.00
12. **Compute present value of** Mr. Oak's income.	2nd DUE PV	295335.97
13. **Subtract cost of building** to find leasehold value.	− 200000 =	95335.97

The leasehold value exceeds the value of the building by $95,335.97. This excess rental makes the business venture worthwhile.

Sale – Leaseback

A sale-leaseback situation involves a sale of real estate (either land, building or both) with a lease given back to the seller by the buyer. It is a technique used by large industrial and commercial firms as a means of reducing their involvement in capital investment and management of real estate.

General Notes on Sale-Leaseback Decisions

- Advantages and disadvantages to lessor and lessee are the same as a leased property would provide.

- Tax treatment of the transaction is a very important consideration. A competent tax attorney should be consulted before the transaction is attempted.

- Seller-Lessee enjoys significant tax advantages since the entire rent becomes tax deductible as a cost of business.

- Sale-Leaseback provides, in essence, 100% financing of the property, e.g., $100,000 cost to construct, owner sells for no less than $100,000, so, 100% financing. An excellent financing tool.

- Purchaser-Lessor realizes an adequate rate of return on his property in the form of an annuity stream income.

- Seller-Lessee is released from major capital investment in property. He now leases. In addition, seller-lessee is out of the business of property management.

- Purchaser-Lessor can realize added value in the form of property appreciation over time.

- Sale-Leaseback payments are traditionally calculated on a beginning of the period payment (in advance) as opposed to mortgage payments made at end of period.

Example:

Fairbanks Publications, Inc. (FPI) has the opportunity for the cash acquisition of a new subsidiary. FPI can either borrow the necessary capital or establish a sale-leaseback arrangement using one of FPI's existing properties.

A private investor has agreed to work with FPI to arrive at an equitable agreement for either. He will loan the necessary $1,175,000 for 30 years at an annual 8% rate or purchase from FPI for leaseback a 20-year-old piece of property.

The property originally cost $1,500,000, of which $500,000 was allocated for the site. The ensuing $1,000,000 structure was built to have an economic life of 50 years. It is currently being depreciated using the straight-line method. Because $60\%\left(\dfrac{30 \text{ years}}{50 \text{ years}}\right)$ of the depreciable value remains, the building basis is 60% of 0.6 × $1,000,000, or $600,000.

The property is offered for sale and leaseback by FPI for $1,200,000, anticipating a 30-year lease from the investor in return. The net rental is to be calculated as the sale price amortized over the 30-year life at a 9% return rate.

The positive and negative aspects (including taxes) need to be analyzed for each party for both the mortgage and sale-leaseback situations.

FPI Sets Up a Sale-Leaseback

The property is to be sold for $1,200,000 and leased back to FPI with rentals to repay the sale price plus a 9% annual return. Part of the rent is tax deductible. The sale price of $1,200,000 provides the necessary $1,175,000 because 25% capital gain tax must be paid on the profit from the sale, that is, the sale price less the purchase price of site less the current structure basis. This is 25% × (1,200,000 − 500,000 − 600,000) = $25,000.

Action	Press	Display
1. Clear calculator and select	CLR 2nd CM	0.
two-decimal display.	2nd FIX 2	0.00
2. **Calculate annual rent payment.**		
Enter number of periods	30 N	30.00
Enter annual interest rate	9 %i	9.00
Enter sale price	1200000 PV	1200000.00
Calculate payment	2nd DUE PMT	107159.29
3. **Calculate total 30-year rentals.**	× 30 = STO 0	3214778.58
4. Calculate tax deduction at 48%	− 48 %	1543093.72
corporate tax rate.		
5. **Calculate actual rental cost to FPI.**	=	1671684.86
6. **Add capital gains tax to actual**	+ 25000 =	1696684.86
rental cost to obtain total cost to FPI.		

FPI Establishes a Mortgage

FPI can borrow the $1,175,000 from the investor at 8% for 30 years.

Action	Press	Display
1. Clear calculator.	CLR	0
2. Enter annual interest rate.	8 %i	8.00
3. Enter mortgage value.	1175000 PV	1175000.00
4. Calculate annual mortgage payment.	CPT PMT	104372.23
5. Calculate total mortgage cost.	X 30 = STO 1	3131167.03
6. Calculate interest cover by subtracting mortgage.	− 1175000 =	1956167.03
7. Calculate total tax deduction by adding remaining depreciable value.	+ 600000 =	2556167.03
8. Calculate the tax savings for a corporate tax rate of 48%.	X 48 % =	1226960.17
9. Calculate cost of mortgage after taxes.	+/− + RCL 1 =	1904206.85

The 30-year cost of the mortgage after taxes would be $1,904,206.85 to be paid to the investor by FPI for the $1,175,000 cash loan now.

In summary, it appears that the sale-leaseback option is better for FPI by $207,521.99.

Mortgage cost after taxes	$1,904,206.85
Lease cost after taxes	1,696,684.86
Difference	$ 207,521.99

Investor's Leasing Position

Assume that the investor, in buying the property, can allocate $800,000 to the building for depreciation purposes. This amount can be deducted from the rental income before calculating the required taxes.

Action	Press	Display
1. Calculate taxable rental income.	RCL 0 − 800000 =	2414778.58
2. Calculate taxes due on rental income at 48% tax rate.	X 48 % =	1159093.72
3. Calculate net income from rental by subtracting rental income after taxes from 30 years of rentals.	+/− + RCL 0 =	2055684.86

The rental income after taxes is $2,055,684.86.

Investor Issues a Loan

If the investor loans the $1,175,000 for 30 years at 8% he must pay a 48% income tax on the interest.

Action	Press	Display
1. Calculate interest (taxable) part of payment.	RCL 1 − 1200000 =	1931167.03
2. Calculate 48% income tax.	× 48 % =	926960.17
3. **Calculate income (after taxes) paid to investor.**	+/− + RCL 1 =	2204206.85

In summary, the mortgage seems the better investment for the investor.

Net to investor in mortgage	$2,204,206.85
Net to investor in sale-leaseback	2,055,684.86
Difference	$ 148,521.99

Conclusions

The sale-leaseback is financially more attractive to FPI by $207,521.99. The mortgage is better for the investor by $148,521.99. Because of this difference, the final transaction must be arbitrated taking into account the following facts concerning the sale-leaseback.

FPI gives up ownership of the property, but readily gets the necessary cash for the new subsidiary. Any buildings built by FPI on the leased property would be depreciated by FPI.

The investor receives his yield of 9% per year and the principal payments. He gets ownership of the property at the end of the lease. This property is worth at least $500,000 (site value) and possibly more if there is any remaining value in the remaining structures. He can possibly recover sale-leaseback versus mortgage difference through a short-term lease.

Investment Feasibility Program

The investment feasibility model is used to determine the quality of a real estate investment based on the cost of money, the income produced from the property, and the risks involved. It can also be used to determine the required income based on a desired return on equity; or the risks involved can be determined based on a required return on equity and the income produced.

To evaluate an investment in any income producing property where the majority of the purchase price must be financed, there are four factors which primarily determine the quality of the investment.

Net Income — This the income after allowance for all expenses. For example, if an apartment house is being evaluated, net income is the gross potential income less vacancy costs and less operating costs. If the property is being considered as a tax shelter, the tax savings and depreciation allowance can be added to net income.

Debt Coverage Ratio — This is a measure of the investment risk. It is the ratio of net income to debt service. A high risk investment would be where net income would just cover interest payments.

Mortgage or Loan Constant — This is a measure of the cost of money. It is the ratio of debt service to the loan amount. Since debt service can vary by the going interest rate and the amortization schedule, the mortgage constant will vary as a function of the type of financing planned. However, it will normally be about one percentage point above the interest rate on home mortgages (except for balloon notes).

Return on Equity — This is a measure of the profit on the investment. It is the ratio of cash flow to down payment. It should be at least as good as the rate on similar risk opportunities for investment.

The variables used in the feasibility model are:

$$\text{Net Income} = \text{Gross Rent} - (\text{Gross Rent} \times \text{Vacancy Rate}) - \text{Operating Expense}$$

$$\text{Debt Coverage Ratio} = \frac{\text{Net Income}}{\text{Debt Service or (Interest} + \text{Principal Payment)}}$$

$$\text{Mortgage Constant} = \frac{\text{Debt Service}}{\text{Loan Amount}}$$

$$\text{Return on Equity} = \frac{\text{Net Income} - \text{Debt Service}}{\text{Down Payment}}$$

$$\text{Property Price} = \text{Available loan amount} + \text{down payment compatible with desired return on equity}$$

To actually solve for these values in terms of each other, use the following programs:

Program to Calculate Net Income

Program Memory	Key Sequence	Program Memory	Key Sequence	Program Memory	Key Sequence
00 61	RCL	11 61	RCL	22 00	
01 02	2	12 02	2	23 00	
02 55	X	13 45	÷	24 00	
03 61	RCL	14 61	RCL	25 00	
04 05	5	15 04	4	26 00	
05 45	÷	16 65	−	27 00	
06 43	(	17 61	RCL	28 00	
07 61	RCL	18 04	4	29 00	
08 03	3	19 32	1/x	30 00	
09 32	1/x	20 85	=	31 00	
10 75	+	21 42	R/S		

Program to Calculate Debt Coverage Ratio

Program Memory	Key Sequence	Program Memory	Key Sequence	Program Memory	Key Sequence
00 61	RCL	11 03	3	22 01	1
01 01	1	12 44	)	23 85	=
02 45	÷	13 45	÷	24 42	R/S
03 61	RCL	14 43	(	25 00	
04 03	3	15 61	RCL	26 00	
05 55	X	16 04	4	27 00	
06 43	(	17 55	X	28 00	
07 61	RCL	18 61	RCL	29 00	
08 04	4	19 05	5	30 00	
09 65	−	20 65	−	31 00	
10 61	RCL	21 61	RCL		

INVESTMENT FEASIBILITY PROGRAM

Program to Calculate Mortgage Constant

Program Memory		Key Sequence	Program Memory		Key Sequence	Program Memory		Key Sequence
00	61	RCL	11	04	4	22	61	RCL
01	01	1	12	55	×	23	01	1
02	55	×	13	61	RCL	24	85	=
03	61	RCL	14	05	5	25	42	R/S
04	04	4	15	65	−	26	00	
05	45	÷	16	61	RCL	27	00	
06	43	(	17	02	2	28	00	
07	61	RCL	18	55	×	29	00	
08	02	2	19	61	RCL	30	00	
09	55	×	20	01	1	31	00	
10	61	RCL	21	75	+			

Program to Calculate Return on Equity

Program Memory		Key Sequence	Program Memory		Key Sequence	Program Memory		Key Sequence
00	61	RCL	11	44	)	22	65	−
01	01	1	12	45	÷	23	61	RCL
02	55	×	13	43	(	24	01	1
03	61	RCL	14	61	RCL	25	85	=
04	03	3	15	02	2	26	42	R/S
05	55	×	16	55	×	27	00	
06	43	(	17	61	RCL	28	00	
07	61	RCL	18	03	3	29	00	
08	02	2	19	55	×	30	00	
09	65	−	20	61	RCL	31	00	
10	01	1	21	05	5			

Program to Calculate Property Price

Program Memory		Key Sequence	Program Memory		Key Sequence	Program Memory		Key Sequence
00	61	RCL	11	02	2	22	03	3
01	01	1	12	65	−	23	55	×
02	55	×	13	61	RCL	24	61	RCL
03	43	(	14	03	3	25	04	4
04	61	RCL	15	44	)	26	85	=
05	04	4	16	45	÷	27	42	R/S
06	75	+	17	43	(	28	00	
07	61	RCL	18	61	RCL	29	00	
08	03	3	19	02	2	30	00	
09	55	×	20	55	×	31	00	
10	61	RCL	21	61	RCL			

Example: An investor is considering buying an apartment house if he can realize a 10% return on his investment. The apartment produces a gross rent of $30,000 per year. Vacancies and bad debts account for 10% of the rent. The operating expense is $3,000 per year. The mortgage company requires a mortgage constant of at least 11% on its loans, and it feels the investor can qualify for a loan if the debt coverage ratio is 1.2 or greater. What is the maximum price the investor should pay for the apartment house?

Action	Press	Display
1. Clear calculator and enter program to solve for your unknown.	[2nd] [CA] [2nd] [LRN] Program [2nd] [LRN] [RST]	00 00 0.
2. Select two-decimal display.	[2nd] [FIX] 2	0.00
3. Store the four known values in memories, leaving memory that would contain the unknown empty. Intermediate calculations can take place wherever necessary.		
For example, net income is gross income − vacancies − operating expense.		
Net income in 1	30000 [−] 3000 [−] 3000 [=] [STO] 1	27000.00 24000.00
Debt Coverage Ratio in 2	1.2 [STO] 2	1.20
Mortgage Constant in 3	11 [%] [STO] 3	0.11
Return on Equity in 4	10 [%] [STO] 4	0.10
Property Price in 5	(not needed here)	
4. Calculate unknown.	[R/S]	221818.18

To fulfill all requirements, no more than $221,818.18 should be paid for the apartment house.

Decision-Making with Statistics

CHAPTER 7

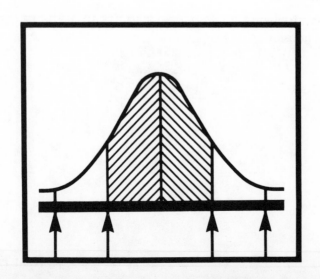

As mentioned in the introduction to this book, our primary concentration is on how to use your calculator in a variety of business situtations, and we hope you'll find these techniques valuable (and even enjoyable) in your decision-making. As we work through the statistical functions of the calculator, however, we'll give you a bit of theory in addition to the "how to" routines.

Basic Statistics Keys

The statistical features built into your calculator handle the complex mathematics needed to analyze groups of statistical data so that you can focus your attention on using the results. The detailed statistical theory behind these features is beyond the scope of this book, but as you'll see, it is not necessary to have a detailed background in statistics in order to use the analytical capabilities your calculator provides. The special statistical keys are defined below.

Key Definitions

- $\boxed{x\!:\!y}$ and $\boxed{\Sigma+}$: Are used for data entry in mean, standard deviation, and variance calculations and in linear regression and trend line analysis.

- $\boxed{2nd}$ $\boxed{\Sigma-}$: Removes an incorrect data entry.

- $\boxed{2nd}$ $\boxed{MEAN}$ Calculates the mean value or "central" tendency of your data.

- $\boxed{2nd}$ $\boxed{S.D.}$: Computes the standard deviation. This gives an indication of how the data points vary from the mean, with n − 1 weighting.

- $\boxed{2nd}$ $\boxed{VAR}$: Calculates the variance of your data with N weighting.

Linear Regression Keys

Linear regression is simply having the calculator plot the best line it can through your data points (a line that comes closest to all the data points). The slope of the line as well as where it crosses the y-axis (intercept) can also be determined. You can find out how well the line "fits" the data and, if the fit is satisfactory, predict new data points along the line.

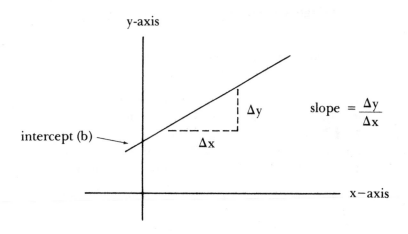

Key Definitions

This is accomplished with the following keys.

- 2nd SLOPE : Calculates the slope of the line through your data points.
- 2nd INTCP : Computes the y-intercept of the line.
- 2nd x' : Finds the "x" value for any "y" you select.
- 2nd y' : Finds the "y" value for any "x" you select.
- 2nd CORR : Finds the correlation coefficient for two sets of data, indicating how closely they are related.

Data Entry

Your data points can be entered as points on an x-y graph with each point being represented by its own unique coordinate (x_i, y_i), where i represents the point number, (x_1, y_1) is the first point, (x_2, y_2) is the second, etc.

As the data points are entered they are stored in memory, so you should always begin statistical calculations with 2nd CM .

For a **single set of data,** enter the values as shown below.

y_1 Σ+ , y_2 Σ+ , y_3 Σ+ , etc.

For an **array of data with two variables,** the entry procedure is as follows:

x_1 x:y y_1 Σ+ , x_2 x:y y_2 Σ+ , etc.

The data point number i is displayed after each point is entered. To remove an unwanted data point, reenter both the undesired x and y values again, but press 2nd Σ- instead of Σ+ . If only the y values are being entered, simply enter the unwanted y and press 2nd Σ- . The data point number i is automatically decreased by 1 and displayed after this procedure.

As each data point is keyed in it is assimilated into memory locations 1-7 as follows:

Memory Location	Contents
1	Used
2	$\Sigma\ x$
3	$\Sigma\ x^2$
4	$\Sigma\ xy$
5	$\Sigma\ y$
6	$\Sigma\ y^2$
7	N

The symbol Σ means "the sum of all the following items from i = 1 to N."

Data that have already been grouped as above can be entered directly into these locations and analysis can begin immediately.

Mean, Standard Deviation and Variance   7

In many situations, you have had a large volume of data that needs to be analyzed. These data could be test scores, sales figures, weights of an incoming shipment, etc. The most commonly used statistical calculations used to reduce those data to a manageable size for analysis are the **mean, standard deviation,** and **variance.** The *mean* gives you the average or central value of your data, while the *standard deviation* and *variance* tell you about the variability of your data points or how reliable the mean value really is.

The following equations are used by the calculator.

$$\text{Mean of x -array of values} = \bar{x} = \frac{\Sigma\, x}{N} \qquad \text{Mean of y -array of values} = \bar{y} = \frac{\Sigma\, y}{N}$$

where N is the total number of data points entered.

$$\text{Standard Deviation of x -array} = \sigma_x = \sqrt{\frac{\Sigma\,(x_i - \bar{x})^2}{n - 1}}$$

$$\text{Standard Deviation of y -array} = \sigma_y = \sqrt{\frac{\Sigma\,(y_i - \bar{y})^2}{n - 1}}$$

where n is the number of samples used out of the total population N.

For purposes here n = N. More on this later.

$$\text{Variance of x-array} = \sigma_x{}^2 = \frac{\Sigma(x_i - \bar{x})^2}{N}$$

$$\text{Variance of y-array} = \sigma_y{}^2 = \frac{\Sigma(y_i - \bar{y})^2}{N}$$

The symbol Σ means "the sum of all following items from i = 1 to N."

Instead of having to remember all of these formulas, the statistics keys on the calculator evaluate them internally for you. To find the standard deviation of the y-array of data once the data have been entered, just press `2nd` `S.D.` . If the x-array is variable also, press `CPT` `2nd` `S.D.` to compute the standard deviation of that dimension.

For your convenience, the option has been provided to select N or n − 1 weighting for standard deviation and variance calculations. N weighting results in a maximum likelihood estimator that is generally used to describe populations (N), while n − 1 is un unbiased estimator customarily used for a sample of data (n) from some larger population. The difference between N and n − 1 weighting becomes very small when more than thirty data points are used. Thirty data points are considered to be the breakover point between "small" and "large" samples. This makes a difference in the way some situations are treated. More on this later.

Note that the variance key uses N weighting while the standard deviation key uses n − 1 weighting. Note also that variance (σ^2) is the square of standard deviation (σ). So, to find the variance with n − 1 weighting, press 2nd S.D. x^2 . To find the standard deviation with N weighting, press 2nd VAR 2nd $\sqrt{x}$.

Follow the table below to calculate the specific statistics you require.

Function	Weighting	Key Sequences y-array	x-array
Mean		2nd MEAN	CPT 2nd MEAN
Standard Deviation	N	2nd VAR 2nd $\sqrt{x}$	CPT 2nd VAR 2nd $\sqrt{x}$
Variance	N	2nd VAR	CPT 2nd VAR
Standard Deviation	n − 1	2nd S.D.	CPT 2nd S.D.
Variance	n − 1	2nd S.D. x^2	CPT 2nd S.D. x^2

For single variance data (y-array only) you do not need to use the $x{:}y$ key for entering data points or the CPT key for calculating x-array statistics.

To get into applications, begin with an analysis of a small body of data, one that can be handled completely without having to take a sample.

Example: The company's personnel department has recently given an office skills test to the five members of your clerical staff. The test scores are in now, and you'd like to analyze the data to see how well your staff did. The scores were 4, 5, 6, 7, and 8, out of a possible score of 10.

With your calculator you can easily calculate the mean (labeled $\bar{y}$), and the standard deviation (labeled σ_y):

Action	Press	Display
1. Clear calculator and select two-decimal display.	CLR 2nd CM 2nd FIX 2	0.00
2. Enter data. (Calculator keeps a count of your data entries.)	4 Σ+	1.00
	5 Σ+	2.00
	6 Σ+	3.00
	7 Σ+	4.00
	8 Σ+	5.00
3. Calculate mean.	2nd MEAN	6.00
4. Calculate standard deviation.	2nd VAR 2nd $\sqrt{x}$	1.41

The median score is 6, and the standard deviation is 1.41. This means that the majority of your test scores fall within the range of 6 ± 1.41.

Remember, the key sequence 2nd VAR 2nd $\sqrt{x}$ is used to find the standard deviation using N weighting, because calculations involve the entire population.

Consider a Huge Population

What happens when you'd like to know the population mean (μ), but the population is made up of thousands (or even millions) of items. Even with your calculator helping, entering all that data may be nearly impossible. In addition, sometimes the measurements made destroy the item. For example, imagine that you're testing a shipment (population) of 5000 batteries to determine their lifetime. You have to deplete a battery to know how long it lasted in the lifetime test. If you did this to the entire population, you'd know exactly what the mean lifetime for the population was. You'd also have no batteries left to use!

In situations like this, one logical alternative is to select a smaller number of items from the population and test this sample. This calls for the science of statistics. Based on analyzing the smaller sample (which is cheaper, easier, and more possible than testing the population), you can use methods of statistical inference to make statements about the population mean (μ). Your first step would be to calculate the sample mean ($\bar{x}$) and the sample standard deviation (s_x). Then apply some statistical techniques to get back to information about the population as diagrammed below.

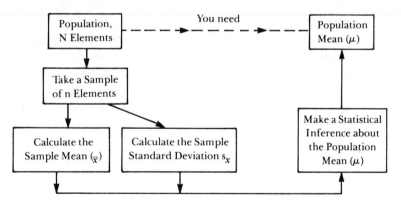

As a general rule, it is assumed in most common situations that the sample elements ($\bar{x}$) are *distributed normally* whenever the population has over 100 elements and the sample size is greater than 30. That is, if you graphed many sample means, your graph would assume a classic, symmetric shape called the **Normal Curve.**

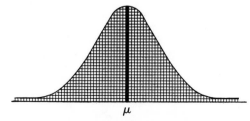

THE NORMAL CURVE

Much has been written about the normal (or "Bell" or "Gaussian") curve, but it's the area under the curve that is used to get more information about the population mean from the sample mean. The standard deviation of the sample means, $s_{\bar{x}}$, is the primary ingredient in the calculations.

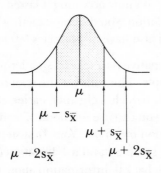

Because of the fact that the sample means follow this "normal" behavior (for large populations and samples), some mathematical predictions can be made using the normal curve that apply to just about any situation where large populations and samples are concerned. Remember that statisticians calculated these results by examining areas under the normal curve.

First of all, examine the normal curve above and note that its area is partitioned into four sections, each of which is separated by $s_{\bar{x}}$. Look at the shaded area. It includes all the sample means whose values are between $\mu \pm s_{\bar{x}}$. The ratio of this area to the total is always the same: 68.26%. This means that whenever you pick a sample from a population, your chances are 68.26 out of 100 that you have picked a sample mean that is within $\pm s_{\bar{x}}$ of the population mean. Another way of saying this is that you can be 68.26% sure that the population mean lies somewhere in the range of your sample mean plus or minus $s_{\bar{x}}$.

Now it turns out that $s_{\bar{x}}$, the standard deviation of the sample means, is fairly easy to calculate from your sample data. For samples with larger than 30 elements (n > 30), $s_{\bar{x}}$ can be considered equal to

$$s_{\bar{x}} = \frac{s_x}{\sqrt{n}}$$

where s_x is just the sample standard deviation with an (n-1) weighting which estimates σ. The sample standard deviation is readily available—this is the number you see displayed in your calculator after you enter your sample data (with the $\boxed{\Sigma+}$ key) and then press $\boxed{\text{2nd}}$ $\boxed{\text{S.D.}}$

7

Determining the Predicted Range For μ

With the help of the normal curve you can analyze a population, based on a sample; use the following procedure.

First, enter the sample data into your calculator with the $\boxed{\Sigma+}$ key. Then use the $\boxed{\text{2nd}}$ $\boxed{\text{MEAN}}$ and $\boxed{\text{2nd}}$ $\boxed{\text{S.D.}}$ key sequences to find the sample mean ($_x$) and the sample standard deviation (s_x). Using your sample data you can say with 68.26% certainty that the population mean (μ) lies between:

$$\bar{x} + \frac{s_x}{\sqrt{n}} \quad \text{and} \quad \bar{x} - \frac{s_x}{\sqrt{n}}$$

That is, you can use your sample data to set up a predicted range for the population mean. This range is as close as you can get to using sample data to draw conclusions about the population. You can only state, to a specific degree of certainty, that the population mean lies somewhere in that range.

ANALYZING WITH LARGE SAMPLES: z SCORES

Notice that the predicted range for the population mean above gave us the limits for the value of μ to one specific degree of certainty—68.26%. In most applications it is advisable to select the degree of certainty that you desire (or need) when making any decision about a population based on sample data.

To make this easy to do, tables have been constructed based on the areas under different portions of the normal curve. These tables are called tables of **z values** or **z scores,** and they enable you to calculate a predicted range for μ to a degree of certainty you select. (A **z value** table is included for your use in the *Appendix.*)

To use the table, decide how sure you want to be that your calculated range will include the population mean. Check in the z table to find the appropriate z score.

UPPER/LOWER LIMITS

Note that two columns are included in the z table. The column used to find your z score depends on your particular decision situation. If your decision involves just an upper or lower value for μ, just one limit, use column I; otherwise use column II.

To explain why the z values are different for these two situations, consider the normal curve that we have been discussing.

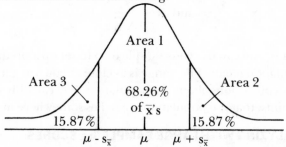

Your chance of picking an x in area 1 (range $\mu \pm s_{\bar{x}}$) is 68.26% as discussed earlier. Looking at this another way, your chance of picking an x outside of area 1 is $\dfrac{\text{area 2 + area 3}}{\text{total area}}$ or $\dfrac{15.87\% + 15.87\%}{100\%}$ or about $\dfrac{32}{100}$. But suppose you are only interested in your chance of picking an x greater than $\mu + s_{\bar{x}}$ (checking only an upper limit). Your chance is $\dfrac{\text{area 2}}{\text{total area}}$ or $\dfrac{15.87\%}{100\%}$ or about $\dfrac{16}{100}$. Since different proportions of the total area are used, different z scores must be used for these two situations — so two columns are provided in the table.

Procedure for Using z Tables to Calculate the Range for μ

Once you've located the z score, you can calculate the predicted range for μ using the general formula below.

$$\text{Predicted range for } \mu = \bar{x} \pm \frac{s_X}{\sqrt{n}}\, z$$

where x is your sample mean, and s_X is the sample standard deviation.

Note:

For large samples the sample standard deviation (s_X) turns out to be very nearly equal to the population standard deviation (usually labeled σ). The formula for the range is always correct when written with σ in place of s_X and you'll see it written that way quite often in textbooks. z is the z score for the degree of certainty you select.

Remember, that this particular technique works only for large samples taken from larger populations. Again the boundary line for large samples is usually taken to be 30 elements, a large population is considered to be 100 elements or more.

Let's look at a situation that requires analyzing a large sample from a population.

Example:

Your company is manufacturing an electronic toy into which you put a battery. A battery manufacturer has just delivered a shipment of 5000 to you, and he claims the mean lifetime for this shipment (population) is 180 hours. You want to check his claim to be sure that the mean lifetime of the batteries is no *less* (as near as you can tell) than 180 hours. It will be fine (great, in fact) if the mean lifetime were *more* than 180 hours, but you're concerned only with checking the "low side" of their performance. (This is called a "one-sided" or "one-tailed" process.)

To test the population of 5000 (N), you have a technician select a sample (n) of 100 batteries and measure their average lifetime under standard load conditions. Since this test ruins the batteries, you decide you can't afford a much larger sample than 100 items. Your technician finds out that the sample mean lifetime ($\bar{x}$) is 175 hours, with a sample standard deviation (s_x) of 18 hours.

Actually, you already have quite a bit of information. First of all, since 100 batteries qualifies as a "large" sample (n > 30), the sample standard deviation (s_x) is considered to be equal to the population standard deviation (σ). So you really have an immediate decision to make: is the standard deviation of the shipment acceptable to you? In this case, $\sigma = 18$ hours. Let's say that you can accept this variability in the shipment. Now you need to make a judgment about the population mean (μ). Your sample mean ($\bar{x}$) is 175 hours. How can you use this information to draw a conclusion about the population mean lifetime?

You need to make a decision about whether or not to accept the shipment, based on the sample data, and suppose you want to be 95% certain that you don't reject good batteries. Your primary concern is that the battery life be not much less than 180 hours. If the average life is longer than this, fine!

There's a formula from statistics that allows you to calculate, from your sample data, a range in which the population mean will lie. With this range you know, based on your sample data and degree of certainty you select, an upper and a lower limit for the actual population mean.

This formula is:

$$\text{Range for population mean} = \bar{x} \pm \left[\frac{(N-n)}{(N-1)} \right]^{\frac{1}{2}} \frac{\sigma}{\sqrt{n}} z$$

(This formula may look complex, but it's easy to evaluate on your calculator.)
Where:
$\bar{x}$ is the sample mean lifetime — 175 hours
N is the population size = 5000
n is the sample size = 100
σ is the standard deviation of the population, which in this case can be approximated by s_x (= 18 hours)
z is the z value found from *Table A*. For the degree of certainty you select (here 95% found from column I), the z value is 1.65. You will reject the shipment based on only one boundary in this case.

In this formula the expression $\left[\frac{(N-n)}{(N-1)} \right]^{\frac{1}{2}}$ allows for the fact that when you test the batteries in the sample you remove them from the population and can't return them after the test. This removal of sample items, strictly speaking, affects the "randomness" of your selection. This factor effectively restores the randomness.

In doing this calculation, first evaluate the quantity $\left[\frac{(N-n)}{(N-1)} \right]^{\frac{1}{2}} \frac{\sigma}{\sqrt{n}} z$ and store it. Then complete the calculation.

Action	Press	Display
1. Clear calculator and select two-decimal display.	CLR 2nd CM 2nd FIX 2	0.00
2. Calculate and store.	((5000 − 100)	4900.00
$\left[\frac{(N-n)}{(N-1)} \right]^{\frac{1}{2}} \frac{\sigma}{\sqrt{n}} z$	÷ (5000 − 1)	4999.00
	) 2nd √x̄ X	0.99
	18 ÷ 100 2nd √x̄	10.00
	X 1.65 =	2.94
3. Now add x̄ to **find the**	STO 1	2.94
upper limit.	+ 175 =	177.94
4. **Calculate lower limit.**	175 − RCL 1 =	172.06

Here you are predicting that the population mean actually has a value somewhere between 172.06 and 177.94 — and what you really want to focus your attention on here is that you now know from your sample (with 95% certainty) that the population mean is not greater than 177.94. So, based on your sample data, you can be 95% certain that the battery mean lifetime is less than 180 hours, and based on this analysis you'd reject the shipment (or talk with your vendor about correcting the problem).

ANALYZING WITH SMALL SAMPLES: t SCORES

As the number of samples goes below 30, the normal curve can no longer be accurately used to describe the distribution of the sample means. Statisticians have found a different family of curves that does work — if the population is nearly normally distributed — called **t curves.**

The shape of any t curve depends on what is called the number of degrees of freedom (df) for your particular sample. The number of degrees of freedom in most cases is considered to be equal to the number of elements in your sample minus one (df = n − 1). The shapes of various t curves are shown in the figure below. Note, for a very large number of degrees of freedom (essentially df = 31 or greater), the t curve becomes the normal curve (and z scores can be used).

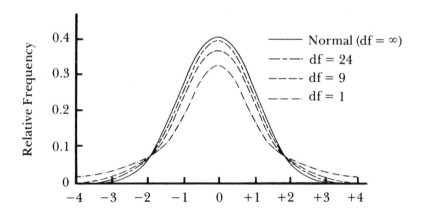

Areas under the t curves have also been tabulated for you in the t score tables (*Tables C* and *D* in the *Appendix* are t score tables for your use). With t scores you can analyze small sample data in much the same way large sample data are analyzed with z scores. Here's the step-by-step procedure to follow:

With the aid of your calculator, calculate the sample mean ($\bar{x}$) and sample standard deviation (s_x).

With this information, you'll be calculating a predicted range for the population mean. Decide how certain you want (or need) to be that the population mean will be in your predicted range. For this level of certainty look up the appropriate t score in *Table C* or *D* in the *Appendix*. (Use *Table C* if your decision involves only a maximum or minimum value for μ; otherwise use *Table D*.) The value for df you use (the degrees of freedom) is the number of elements in your sample minus one (n − 1).

Once you have located the t score, the predicted range for the population mean can be calculated using the following formula:

$$\text{Predicted range for the population mean} = \bar{x} \pm \frac{s_x}{\sqrt{n}}\, t$$

Now let's see how you would use the data from a small sample for determining both upper and lower limits.

Example:

Your paint manufacturing company is checking on the amount of red dye being mixed into five-gallon containers of "rose" colored paint. The process specification calls for 15.5 ounces of red tint in each can. You select a random sample of eight cans, and through analysis find the tint content to be:

15.2 oz.	15.8 oz.
15.0 oz.	16.1 oz.
15.7 oz.	15.6 oz.
15.9 oz.	15.9 oz.

If the analysis is expensive, you are limited to this small sample quantity.) Your decision in this case: should you stop the manufacturing and adjust the process ?

You want to get as much information as you can about the population mean for the amount of red tint, based on data from the small sample you have to work with. To do this you can use a statistical technique especially designed to handle the small-sample situation. This technique allows you to calculate a predicted range of values that the population mean (μ) will fall into, with a degree of certainty you select.

7

This predicted range of values can form the basis for your decision. If your calculated range of values includes the specification value of 15.5 oz., you don't have enough indication of trouble to stop the line. If the range of values you calculate from your sample data does not include your specification value, however, you can be sure (to the degree of certainty you selected) that you have a problem and an adjustment should be made. Also, note in this case that you are concerned about both limits on the amount of tint. Too much will give you a color that's too red, while too little tint will yield too weak a color.

Since your sample size in this case is less than 30, it falls into the "small" sample category, and some statistical methods especially suited to this situation should be used.

First, decide on a degree of certainty you need for the decision — let's say 90% in this case. Then, calculate the predicted range for the mean tint (population value), using the formula below:

$$\text{Predicted Range for Population Mean} = \bar{x} \pm \frac{s_x}{\sqrt{n}} t$$

where:

$\bar{x}$ is the mean value for your sample

s_x is the sample standard deviation which estimates

n is the size of the sample

t is a value found from *Table D* in the *Appendix*. For the degree of certainty you select (90%) and the number of degrees of freedom ($n - 1 = 7$), the t value is 1.895.

To find the sample mean ($\bar{x}$) and sample standard deviation (s_x), you can use special keys on your calculator.

Action	Press	Display
1. Clear calculator and set select two-decimal display.	CLR 2nd CM 2nd FIX 2	0.00
2. Enter data points.	15.2 Σ+	1.00
	15.0 Σ+	2.00
	15.7 Σ+	3.00
	15.9 Σ+	4.00
	15.8 Σ+	5.00
	16.1 Σ+	6.00
	15.6 Σ+	7.00
	15.9 Σ+	8.00
3. Calculate the sample mean, $\bar{x}$.	2nd MEAN	15.65
4. Calculate the sample standard deviation (s_x).	2nd S.D.	0.37

At this point you already have quite a bit of information. The sample mean looks pretty close to 15.5 and the standard deviation is low, indicating that there's a relatively low "spread" in your measured sample red tint values. But remember, your sample is a small one, and you need to make an important decision about a much larger population based on it. This is where the statistical method can be helpful. Now go on to calculate the predicted range of the population mean (μ).

$$\text{Predicted Range for } \mu = \bar{x} \pm \frac{s_x}{\sqrt{n}} t$$

Now you know that $\bar{x} = 15.65 \quad n = 8$

$$s_x = 0.37 \quad t = 1.895$$

Begin by calculating $\dfrac{s_x}{\sqrt{n}} t$

Action	Press	Display
1. Clear calculator and select two-decimal display.	CLR 2nd CM 2nd FIX 2	0.00
2. Calculate and store $\dfrac{s_x}{\sqrt{n}} t$	0.37 ÷ 8 2nd √x̄	2.83
	× 1.895 = STO 1	0.25
3. Now add this to $\bar{x}$ to **find upper range limit:** $= \bar{x} + \dfrac{s_x}{\sqrt{n}} t$	+ 15.65 =	15.90
4. Calculate lower limit: $= \bar{x} - \dfrac{s_x}{\sqrt{n}} t$	15.65 − RCL 1 =	15.40

Your sample states that with 90% certainty the population mean lies between these two values. From your small sample of eight cans you can state that with 90% certainty the population mean value for the red tint is between 15.4 and 15.9 oz. Since your specified value of 15.5 lies in between these limits, the process appears to be satisfactory.

Summary on Statistical Inference

One process of statistical inference that can be of great use to you in decision-making involves taking data from a sample and from those calculating a predicted range for the population mean. This range will tell you, to the degree of certainty you select, where the population mean lies.

The steps involved in the process of statistical inference are summarized in the following diagram.

Steps in Analyzing Sample Data, to Calculate the Predicted Range for the Population Mean:

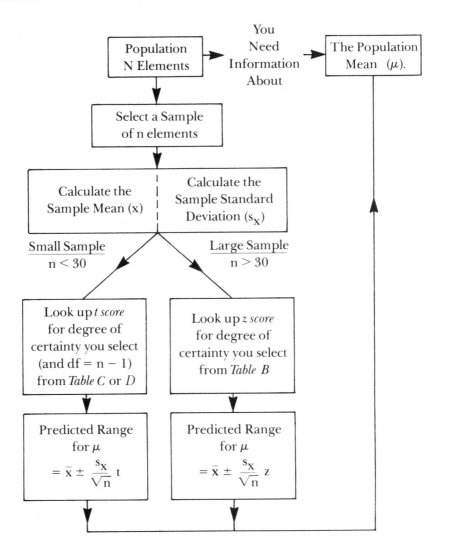

Linear Regression

"Linear Regression" may sound like a highly technical or threatening title, but it is a very valuable process that your calculator makes easy to use. And it's one that deals with one of the oldest problems in the world for the businessman — predicting the future. With the linear regression keys on your calculator you can use data about past performance or relationships to make forecasts of future performance (assuming that whatever relationship exists in your data keeps on working).

In the linear regression situation, you usually have data expressed as pairs of variables that you could plot on a graph. Label each pair of variables with the letters x and y, like this (x,y). x may be dollars in advertising while y is unit sales, or x may be a test score and y a performance record in the field, etc. You want to make a prediction: for any given x value that you select, what will happen to y (or vice versa)? Your calculator can do this for you by mathematically drawing the "best straight line" through your data points. You may then use the straight line to make predictions. Here are the simple steps you follow to do this.

- First, press CLR 2nd CM — do this when starting any statistical calculation.
- Enter an "x" value and press x:y
- Enter the corresponding "y" value, and press Σ+
- Continue until all data points are entered.

Your calculator is now ready to draw the best straight line through your points, and give you the following information from it:

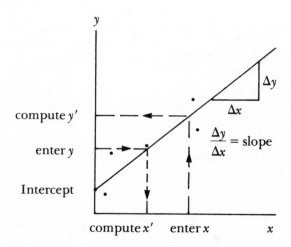

Knowledge about (and some control over) what will happen in the future is an important aspect of managing any type of business enterprise today. The more you can predict about how prices will vary, how well a sales force will perform, how advertising will affect sales, etc., the easier it will be to make sound decisions in a variety of business situations. Knowing how well one variable will relate to another can allow you to make better things happen in your everyday life, as well as in your business.

Now apply linear regression to a typical business situation.

Example: Your company has recently started advertising in a series of magazines on a weekly basis. Your marketing manager figures that the advertising campaign of one week will affect the sales volume of the following week, and he has a record of the amount spent on advertising each week (x) and the corresponding sales volume (y). There seems to be a fairly good relationship between the two. What would be the expected sales volume if $4750 is spent on advertising next week? What advertising expense is required to produce $300,000 in sales?

Amount Spent on Advertising (x)	Weekly Sales Volume (y)
$1000	$101,000
$1250	$116,000
$1500	$165,000
$2000	$209,000
$2500	$264,000
$4750	???
???	$300,000

Action	Press	Display
1. Clear calculator and select two-decimal display.	CLR 2nd CM 2nd FIX 2	0.00
2. Enter data.	1000 x:y 101000 Σ+	1.00
	1250 x:y 116000 Σ+	2.00
	1500 x:y 165000 Σ+	3.00
	2000 x:y 209000 Σ+	4.00
	2500 x:y 264000 Σ+	5.00
3. Calculate the y value for x = $4750.	4750 2nd y′	514672.41
4. Calculate x value for y = $300,000.	300000 2nd x′	2813.61

Based on the best straight line approximation, the projected weekly sales volume for $4750 spent on advertising is $514,672.41. For $300,000 in sales, you should spend $2813.61 on advertising.

When you press the [2nd] [𝒚'] key, you'll note a slight pause before the result is displayed. That's because your calculator has the chore of handling the linear regression calculation (not you). Here's the formula for what it's doing:

$$y' = \left[\frac{\frac{\Sigma x_i \, \Sigma y_i}{N} - \Sigma x_i y_i}{\frac{(\Sigma x_i)^2}{N} - \Sigma x_i^2} \right] \times (\text{your ``x'' value})$$

$$+ \left\{ \frac{\Sigma y_i}{N} - \left[\frac{\frac{\Sigma x_i \, \Sigma y_i}{N} - \Sigma x_i y_i}{\frac{(\Sigma x_i)^2}{N} - \Sigma x_i^2} \right] \left(\frac{\Sigma x_i}{N} \right) \right\}$$

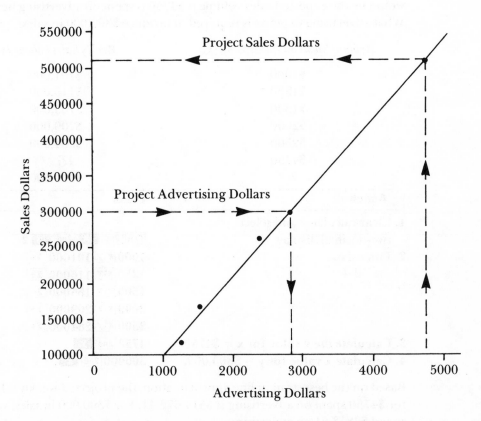

(Think of the "fun" you'd have doing this calculation yourself!)

Trend Line Analysis

Trend line analysis is a variation of linear regression that's very handy in making predictions based on trends or growth. The only thing that makes trend line analysis different from linear regression is that the x values are automatically increased by 1 for each data point. Your calculator does this for you. All you need to do is enter the first x value with the $\boxed{x:y}$ key, and then enter consecutive y values with the $\boxed{\Sigma+}$ key. Your machine automatically increments the x variable by one for each y value you enter. To remove an unwanted data point, reenter both the faulty x and y values, press $\boxed{2nd}$ $\boxed{\Sigma-}$, and reenter the correct point.

Your calculator now computes the best line it can through the data. Once the line is determined, you can use your calculator to find the following:

Key Definitions

- Predict a new y value for any x you select   Enter new x, press $\boxed{2nd}$ $\boxed{y'}$
- Predict a new x value for any y you select   Enter new y, press $\boxed{2nd}$ $\boxed{x'}$
- Calculate the slope of the line   Press $\boxed{2nd}$ $\boxed{SLOPE}$
- Calculate the intercept of the line   Press $\boxed{2nd}$ $\boxed{INTCP}$
- See how well the data points are related   Press $\boxed{2nd}$ $\boxed{CORR}$

You'll find many instances when your data are collected in the form of a series of yearly figures. Your job is to predict what will happen in years to come. This type of prediction is a common application of trend line analysis.

Slope, Intercept and Correlation

Once your data are entered, your calculator can also tell you some other things about the relationship of your x and y values. Earlier we looked at a graph showing how your calculator was "drawing a line" through the data points you entered. To find out more about that line, after you've entered all your x and y values:

**Key
Definitions**

- Press 2nd SLOPE to calculate the slope of the line through your points, and
- Press 2nd INTCP to calculate the y-intercept of the line.

The **correlation coefficient** is an important factor in determining the *relationship* between your data. After all your x and y values are entered, you can calculate the correlation coefficient by pressing 2nd CORR.

The correlation coefficient tells you something about how your data points are related. A correlation coefficient near +1 indicates a good positive relationship between your data points. A good positive correlation means that as your x value increases, so does your y value, as shown in *Figure a,* below. You might expect, for example, that the number of sales people on your staff and your total sales volume should be positively correlated. The more sales people you have, the higher your sales should be.

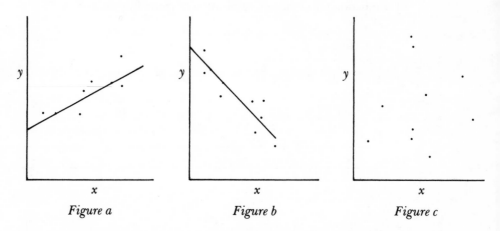

| *Figure a* | *Figure b* | *Figure c* |

A correlation coefficient close to −1 indicates a strong negative relationship in your data: as your x value increases, your y value decreases, as shown in *Figure b.* For example, as your sales staff increases, you'd expect that your backlog of unanswered sales inquiries should decrease.

A correlation factor near zero means that there is little or no relationship between the two sets of data *(Figure c).* The size of your sales staff would probably not correlate to the number of rainy days in your area by month during 1976, for example.

Example: A stock that you've been keeping your eye on has reported the following earnings per share during the past few years:

> $1.52 in 1972
> 1.35 in 1973
> 1.53 in 1974
> 2.17 in 1975
> 3.60 in 1976

You'd like to predict the earnings per share for the next 3 years. You'd also like to know in what year you could expect the earnings per share to reach $6.50.

First, you'll enter your data, using the $\boxed{x \colon y}$ and $\boxed{\Sigma +}$ keys. In this case the "x" values are a series of years in sequence, and the "y" values are the stock dividends recorded for each year. (Data for a series of successive years are common for trend line analysis situations.)

Remember, if you enter any set of data incorrectly in a linear regression calculation, you can remove those data points by the following method:

- Reenter the undesired x value,
- Press $\boxed{x \colon y}$
- Reenter the undesired y value, and
- Press $\boxed{2nd}$ $\boxed{\Sigma -}$
- Reenter the desired x and y values.

Also, after your data are entered, you can get some further information from the calculator:

- $\boxed{2nd}$ $\boxed{\text{MEAN}}$, $\boxed{2nd}$ $\boxed{\text{S.D.}}$ –These key sequences calculate the mean and standard deviation (using n − 1 weighting) of your y data points.
- $\boxed{\text{CPT}}$ $\boxed{2nd}$ $\boxed{\text{MEAN}}$, $\boxed{\text{CPT}}$ $\boxed{2nd}$ $\boxed{\text{S.D.}}$ –These key sequences calculate the mean and standard deviation (using n − 1 weighting) of your x data points.

Here's an important feature: for trend line analysis your calculator will automatically add 1 to the x variable for you.

This means that you can enter the first x value (the first year, 1972) and press x:y, then enter the y value ($1.52 earnings per share) and press Σ+. The first data point is entered.

Then you can enter the second data point by just entering the y value (in our case $1.35) and pressing Σ+. The calculator automatically increments the x variable for you by one for each entry. This comes in handy when you're analyzing data from successive years or wherever your x variable increments by 1.

To make predictions on earnings for future years, just enter the year and press 2nd y'

To predict in what year a certain level of earnings per share will be reached, enter the earnings and press 2nd x'.

Action	Press	Display
1. Clear calculator and select two-decimal display.	CLR 2nd CM 2nd FIX 2	0.00
2. Enter data into statistical routine.	1972 x:y 1.52 Σ+	1.00
	1.35 Σ+	2.00
	1.53 Σ+	3.00
	2.17 Σ+	4.00
	3.6 Σ+	5.00
3. Predict earnings for 1977, 1978, 1979	1977 2nd y'	3.53
	1978 2nd y'	4.03
	1979 2nd y'	4.52
4. Predict when earnings should reach $6.50.	6.5 2nd x'	1982.97

Now, see how well the two sets of data are correlated by pressing 2nd CORR and finding 0.85, a fairly good correlation.

You can get an idea as to how valid the correlation coefficient is by checking *Table A* in the *Appendix*. First, find the line with the same number of samples you have here (5). Now, scan across to the right and find the first value that's larger than your r value (.85). (You should find the value .878.) You can now glance up to the Level of Certainty values at the top of the table to draw a conclusion: you can be about 90-95% sure that this correlation coefficient is valid.

So, using the linear regression and correlation keys can give you quite a bit of information about (and analysis of) your data. To use the calculator to do this, you just:

Enter each x value and press $x\text{:}y$.
Enter each y value and press $\Sigma+$.

The calculator mathematically draws the "best fitting line" for your data points, and you can use the information about this line to predict:

Given any new x value, what is the corresponding y value? (Enter the new value of x, press 2nd y'.)
Given any new y value, what is the corresponding x value? (Enter new y, press 2nd x'.)

You can also get an idea of how well the data correlates.

Press 2nd CORR. The closer the display reads to plus or minus 1, the better the correlation.
To calculate the slope and intercept of the line, press 2nd SLOPE and 2nd INTCP.

A plot of the previous example looks like this.

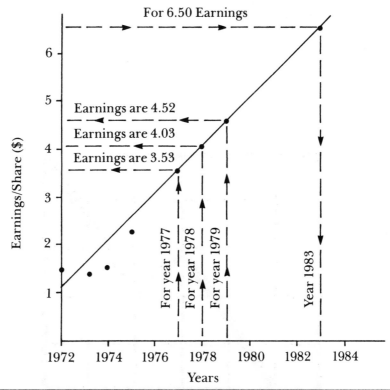

Marketing and Forecasting

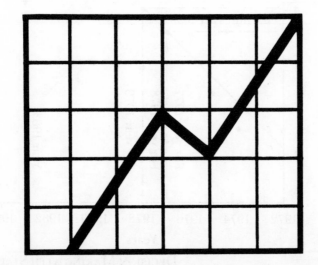

CHAPTER 8

Marketing and Sales

Times are changing. More and more mathematics are required to efficiently manage and maintain any business from the one-man operations to the large conglomerates. Consequently, the handheld calculator is becoming increasingly indispensable at all levels, especially for marketing and forecasting. So much time can be saved through simple uses as well as complex applications of a calculator.

Sales Tax

In many areas today, sales taxes are charged on most retail sales. These add-on taxes are usually expressed as a percentage, and you can easily calculate the amount of the tax and the total price you'll pay.

Example:
(determining sales tax)

You are buying a new sorting machine from a local business supply store and have bargained to a price of $4632, plus 4% sales tax. How much will the tax and the total cost be?

Action	Press	Display
1. Clear calculator and select two-decimal display.	CLR 2nd FIX 2	0.00
2. Enter purchase price.	4632	4632
3. Calculate amount of sales tax.	+ 4 %	185.28
4. Calculate total cost.	=	4817.28

The sales tax is $185.28 and the total cost is $4817.28.

Example:
(determining price before sales tax)

You and a salesman have just agreed that the final price you'll pay for a refrigerator is $550.00 which includes the 5% sales tax. How much are you paying for the refrigerator, and how much is paid in taxes?

Action	Press	Display
1. Clear calculator and select two-decimal display.	CLR 2nd FIX 2	0.00
2. Enter final price.	550	550
3. Calculate selling price.	÷ (1 + 5 % =	523.81
4. Calculate amount of tax.	X 5 % =	26.19

The price of the refrigerator is $523.81 and the tax is $26.19.

Markups and Selling Prices

8

To establish their selling prices, retail businesses add a markup percentage to the wholesale costs of their merchandise. Below are three examples of the relationships between cost, markup percentage, and selling price.

Example:
(calculating selling price)

A grocery store manager has purchased a load of bananas for $0.21 per pound. At what price should he sell the bananas if his standard markup is 20% of cost?

Action	Press	Display
1. Clear calculator and select two-decimal display.	CLR 2nd FIX 2	0.00
2. Enter cost per pound.	.21	0.21
3. **Add markup percentage to determine selling price.**	+ 20 % =	0.25

The selling price should be $0.25 per pound.

Example:
(calculating cost before markup)

The list price of a certain microwave oven is $342.56, and the store's markup is 22% of cost. How much did the microwave oven cost the store?

Action	Press	Display
1. Clear calculator and select two-decimal display.	CLR 2nd FIX 2	0.00
2. Enter list price.	342.56	342.56
3. **Calculate cost.**	÷ (1 + 22 % =	280.79

The cost of the oven to the store was $280.79.

Example:
(calculating percentage of markup)

A store is selling stereo speakers for $42.50 each. The wholesale cost of the speakers was $31.23 each. What is the percentage of markup?

Action	Press	Display
1. Clear calculator and select two-decimal display.	CLR 2nd FIX 2	0.00
2. Enter wholesale cost.	31.23	31.23
3. **Calculate percent of markup.**	2nd Δ% 42.50 =	36.09

The markup from cost is about 36%.

Discounts and Selling Prices

Discounts are a common occurrence in business. Often items are offered for sale at "25% off" the regular price or with a "10% discount" for orders placed before a certain date. These discount percentages are usually based on the regular or list selling price of an item.

Example:
(calculating a discounted price)

A store near your home recently advertised a lawnmower, which usually sells for $239.45, at a 15% discount. What is the sale price?

Action	Press	Display
1. Clear calculator and select two-decimal display.	CLR 2nd FIX 2	0.00
2. Enter regular price.	239.45	239.45
3. Calculate sale price.	− 15 % =	203.53

The sale price of the lawnmower is $203.53.

Example:
(calculating price before discount)

A stereo system is on sale for $323.55. The salesman explains that the sale price is a 35% saving from the regular price. What is the regular price?

Action	Press	Display
1. Clear calculator and select two-decimal display.	CLR 2nd FIX 2	0.00
2. Enter the sale price.	323.55	323.55
3. Calculate regular price.	÷ (1 − 35 %	0.35
	=	497.77

The price was $497.77 before discount.

Gross Profit Margin

8

Gross Profit Margin (GPM) is used by businesses to measure the profitability of products or services and is a kind of benchmark below which the corporation does not want its before-tax profits to fall. GPM is often expressed as a percentage based on the difference between the selling price and the cost of producing the product or service.

The relationships between GPM, sales price, and cost are expressed in the formulas:

$$GPM = \frac{SP - Cost}{SP}$$

$$SP = \frac{Cost}{(1 - GPM)}$$

$$Cost = SP(1 - GPM)$$

where   GPM = gross profit margin
        SP   = selling price of the item
        Cost = production costs of making the item

Example:
(calculating GPM)

You are making macrame bags, and your total material, labor, and incidental costs per bag are $13.75. A local store pays you $17.47 for each bag you make. What is your gross profit margin?

Action	Press	Display
1. Clear calculator and select two-decimal display.	CLR 2nd FIX 2	0.00
2. Enter selling price.	17.47 STO 1	17.47
3. Deduct costs.	− 13.75 =	3.72
4. Calculate GPM.	÷ RCL 1 =	0.21

Your GPM would be 21%.

Example:
(calculating selling price)

You need to determine the retail price for an item that cost your store $22.50. If you require a 35% gross profit margin, what should the retail price be?

Action	Press	Display
1. Clear calculator and select two-decimal display.	CLR 2nd FIX 2	0.00
2. Enter cost.	22.50	22.50
3. Calculate selling price.	÷ (1 − 35 %	0.35
	=	34.62

The retail price should be at least $34.62.

GROSS PROFIT MARGIN

Example:
(calculating cost)

A new compact car on a showroom floor has a base sticker price of $3995. You read in a consumer magazine that compacts are generally priced to provide the dealer about a 17% margin. If this report is correct, how much did the car cost the dealer?

Action	Press	Display
1. Clear calculator and select two-decimal display.	CLR 2nd FIX 2	0.00
2. Enter selling price.	3995	3995
3. Calculate cost.	× (1 − 17 %	0.17
	=	3315.85

The cost was approximately $3315.85.

Example:
(designing to cost)

You are manufacturing a better mousetrap retailed by a local store for $24.50. The store requires a GPM of 30% on all merchandise. What is the maximum cost you can charge the store for your product?

Action	Press	Display
1. Clear calculator and select two-decimal display.	CLR 2nd FIX 2	0.00
2. Enter retail price.	24.50	24.50
3. Calculate cost.	× (1 − 30 %	0.30
	=	17.15

The highest price the store will be willing to pay is $17.15 per unit.

An Itemized Invoice

8

The orders received by a company usually consist of requests for different quantities of several different items, each priced separately. To invoice the buyer, the quantity of each item must be multiplied by its unit price to find the line total, the line totals added to determine the total billing amount, and the quantities of each item added together to find the total number of items ordered. The process is not difficult, but it can be time-consuming and therefore costly.

Your calculator and a simple program can greatly reduce the calculation time needed to prepare itemized invoices.

Program Memory	Key Sequence	Program Memory	Key Sequence	Program Memory	Key Sequence
00 71	SUM	11 00		22 00	
01 01	1	12 00		23 00	
02 55	X	13 00		24 00	
03 42	R/S	14 00		25 00	
04 85	=	15 00		26 00	
05 71	SUM	16 00		27 00	
06 02	2	17 00		28 00	
07 42	R/S	18 00		29 00	
08 41	RST	19 00		30 00	
09 00		20 00		31 00	
10 00		21 00			

Example:

Your firm must prepare an itemized invoice billing Company A for a recent purchase order. The order consisted of the following items:

Line Item	Quantity	Unit Price
1	100	$0.25
2	200	0.15
3	50	0.35
4	150	0.40
5	300	0.10

AN ITEMIZED INVOICE

Find the totals needed for the itemized invoice.

Action	Press	Display
1. Clear calculator and enter program.	2nd CA 2nd LRN	00 00
	Program 2nd LRN RST	0.
2. Select two-decimal display.	2nd FIX 2	0.00
3. Enter quantity of line item 1.	100 R/S	100.00
4. Enter unit price of line item 1 and		
calculate total line item price.	.25 R/S	25.00
5. Repeat steps 3 and 4 for each		
line item.		
Line item 2	200 R/S .15 R/S	30.00
Line item 3	50 R/S .35 R/S	17.50
Line item 4	150 R/S .4 R/S	60.00
Line item 5	300 R/S .1 R/S	30.00
6. Once each line item has been entered		
and line item price calculated, **recall**		
total number of items ordered.	RCL 1	800.00
7. Recall the total billing amount.	RCL 2	162.50

You may also want to determine the average unit price of the order for your records. The information you need has already been generated for you, and you can find the average easily.

8. Calculate the average unit price.	RCL 2 ÷	162.50
	RCL 1 =	0.20

Your completed invoice has the following information:

Line Item	Quantity	Unit Price	Line Item Price
1	100	$0.25	$ 25.00
2	200	0.15	30.00
3	50	0.35	17.50
4	150	0.40	60.00
5	300	0.10	30.00

Total Order: 800 units   162.50 billing amount
Average Unit Price: 0.20

Note: If you go on to prepare other invoices with the program already entered in the calculator, be sure to clear the memories by pressing 2nd CM before starting a new invoice, to prevent incorrect results. 2nd CM will clear the memory registers of their accumulated totals without disturbing the program.

Forecasting

Forecasting plays an important role today in financial planning. Projecting trends in sales, forecasting financial requirements, and planning production needs and output are only a few of the areas in business that call for sound forecasting techniques. This section contains forecasting programs that can be used here and separately as building blocks for other applications not discussed. While these programs are not exhaustive, they provide basic routines useful in forecasting.

The forecasting program and seasonal index programs used here assume a multiplicative model.

$$\text{Forecast value} = T \times S \times C \times I$$

where:
- T = general trend relationship expressed as a unit value
- S = seasonal variations that occur within a year
- C = long-run variations that occur over long run periods
- I = random variations other than T, S, or C

The values for S and C are expressed as index values. Thus, if you had a situation with the values of $T = 515$, $S = 1.05$, $C = 0.99$, the forecast would be:

$$\text{Forecast value} = 515 \times 1.05 \times 0.99$$
$$= 535.34$$

The programs here show methods to estimate the seasonal variation or index value. The trend relationship determined is equal to $T \times C \times I$. This is computed by dividing the original value by S.

$$\text{Original forecast value} = T \times S \times C \times I$$

$$\text{Value to estimate trend} = \frac{T \times S \times C \times I}{S} = T \times C \times I$$

The values T, C, and I are used to determine the trend line. Once the trend values are determined, they are used to project a future value, which is then multiplied by the seasonal index to arrive at the forecast value.

For more information refer to forecasting texts such as Chisholm & Whitaker, *Forecasting Methods*, and Croxton, Cowden and Bolch, *Practical Business Statistics*.

Determining Validity of Relationships

In this section the linear regression capability of your calculator, in particular the correlation feature ([2nd] [CORR]) is used to help make a decision on whether or not two variables are related. It may often appear that one factor in your business life is related to another, but just how closely they really "track" is often unclear. With your calculator you can get a more accurate picture of just how much relation there is between two variables.

Example:

Your sales manager is spending a considerable sum on a test for prospective sales employees. You'd like to see if this test is actually telling you anything about how well the employee will function in the field. Does a higher test score mean superior sales performance? How strong a correlation is there between these two factors in your business?

You have samples of the test scores for 10 employees, along with records on sales performance expressed as the percentage of the time that each employee exceeded his or her weekly sales goals last year. The data are tabulated below:

Employee	Employee Test Score (s)	Employee Sales Performance (y)
Ken	5	10
Ross	13	30
Joe	8	30
Ralph	10	40
Mary	15	60
Gary	20	50
Judy	4	20
Alecia	16	60
Roger	18	50
Jackie	6	20

Action	Press	Display
1. Clear calculator and select two-decimal display.	CLR 2nd **CM** 2nd **FIX** 2	0.00
2. Enter test scores and sales performance into regression routine.	5 [x:y] 10 [Σ+]	1.00
	13 [x:y] 30 [Σ+]	2.00
	8 [x:y] 30 [Σ+]	3.00
	10 [x:y] 40 [Σ+]	4.00
	15 [x:y] 60 [Σ+]	5.00
	20 [x:y] 50 [Σ+]	6.00
	4 [x:y] 20 [Σ+]	7.00
	16 [x:y] 60 [Σ+]	8.00
	18 [x:y] 50 [Σ+]	9.00
	6 [x:y] 20 [Σ+]	10.00
3. Calculate correlation coefficient.	2nd **CORR**	0.87

The correlation factor of 0.87 tells you that there is a pretty good relationship between the test scores and the indicator for employee performance that you're using.

To get a general feel for how valid this correlation factor is, glance at *Table A* in the *Appendix.* Find the line for the number of samples you have (in this case 10) and examine the degree-of-certainty values listed to the right. Your correlation coefficient (0.87) falls between .765 and .872 listed on the table. So, you can be between 99% and 99.9% sure it's a valid situation—that there is a definite relationship between these variables.

DETERMINING VALIDITY OF RELATIONSHIPS

Now that the validity of the information has been established, you can go on to predict employee performance for any test score.

Action	Press	Display
1. **Predict performance based on a test score of 7.**	7 [2nd] [y']	24.92
2. **Predict performance based on a test score of 25.**	25 [2nd] [y']	73.23
3. **Predict performance based on a test score of 30.**	30 [2nd] [y']	86.65
4. **Calculate the slope of the line.**	[2nd] [SLOPE]	2.68
5. **Calculate the intercept of the line.**	[2nd] [INTCP]	6.14

Note above that the slope and intercept of the line the calculator derived to fit to the points have been calculated. This allows you to return to the data at some future time and plot this line. The equation for a straight line is

$$y = mx + b$$

where: m = slope
b = intercept

Using the slope and intercept in the example, the equation of the line becomes y = 2.68x + 6.14.

So, if at some future date you wish to make a prediction, you only need note the slope and intercept values. If an employee then scores a 24.2 on his test, you can substitute that result for x in the equation for the line to predict his or her performance:

2.68 × 24.2 + 6.14 = 70.996   A good prospect for field sales!

Three-Point Moving Average

8

The associated program computes a three-point moving average using the following formula.

$$\text{Moving Average} \ = \ \frac{\text{Point } i + \text{Point } (i + 1) + \text{Point } (i + 2)}{3}$$

Beginning with points 1, 2 and 3, then 2, 3 and 4, etc., the resulting moving–average value for each triad of points can be plotted.

The following program simplifies the calculation of each point.

Program Memory	Key Sequence	Program Memory	Key Sequence	Program Memory	Key Sequence
00 51	STO	11 00	0	22 00	
01 00	0	12 45	÷	23 00	
02 66	2nd EXC	13 03	3	24 00	
03 02	2	14 85	=	25 00	
04 71	SUM	15 42	R/S	26 00	
05 00	0	16 41	RST	27 00	
06 66	2nd EXC	17 00		28 00	
07 01	1	18 00		29 00	
08 71	SUM	19 00		30 00	
09 00	0	20 00		31 00	
10 61	RCL	21 00			

Example: Clothing sales from a local chain department store are as follows.

Month	Sales (in $000)	3-Month Moving Average
January	105	
February	110	110.00
March	115	115.00
April	120	117.67
May	118	117.67
June	115	114.33
July	110	111.00
August	108	109.61
September	111	111.33
October	115	116.00
November	122	115.33
December	109	

The three-point moving averages calculated on the next page are also shown here. Note that the average on any three points actually applies to the center point of the three.

Three-Point Moving Average

Action	Press	Display
1. Clear calculator and enter program.	[2nd] [CA] [2nd] [LRN]	00 00
	Program [2nd] [LRN] [RST]	0.
2. Select two-decimal display.	[2nd] [FIX] 2	0.00
3. Enter first data point.	105 [STO] 1	105.00
4. Enter second data point.	110 [STO] 2	110.00
5. Enter next data point and calculate		
moving average.	115 [R/S]	110.00
Repeat *Step 5* for each data point.	120 [R/S]	115.00
	118 [R/S]	117.67
	115 [R/S]	117.67
	110 [R/S]	114.33
	108 [R/S]	111.00
	111 [R/S]	109.67
	115 [R/S]	111.33
	122 [R/S]	116.00
	109 [R/S]	115.33

Reference: Croxton, Cowden, and Bolch, *Practical Business Statistics,* pp. 338-342.

Four-Point Centered Moving Average

8

As with the three-point moving average, the four-point centered moving average can be used to "smooth" data, minimizing periodic variations. Each application of this type of averaging produces the following:

$$\text{moving average} \ = $$

$$\frac{\text{Point i} + 2\,[\text{Point (i}+1) + \text{Point (i}+2) + \text{Point (i}+3)] + \text{Point (i}+4)}{8}$$

What actually happens is that two four-point averages are taken and summed together.

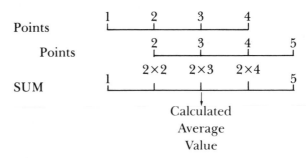

Calculated
Average
Value

Program Memory	Key Sequence	Program Memory	Key Sequence	Program Memory	Key Sequence
00 24	PV	11 71	SUM	22 61	RCL
01 66	2nd EXC	12 00	0	23 00	0
02 04	4	13 66	2nd EXC	24 85	=
03 51	STO	14 01	1	25 45	÷
04 00	0	15 71	SUM	26 08	8
05 66	2nd EXC	16 24	PV	27 85	=
06 03	3	17 61	RCL	28 42	R/S
07 71	SUM	18 24	PV	29 41	RST
08 00	0	19 75	+	30 00	
09 66	2nd EXC	20 02	2	31 00	
10 02	2	21 55	×		

FOUR-POINT CENTERED MOVING AVERAGE

Example: A diaper company had the following quarterly sales (in $000) over 4 years.

		Quarter		
Years	1	2	3	4
1974	370	389	440	510
1975	395	410	485	545
1976	428	445	520	575
1977	460	480	550	610

Calculate a four-point moving average for these sales.

Action	Press	Display
1. Clear calculator and enter program.	2nd CA 2nd LRN	00 00
	Program 2nd LRN RST	0.
2. Select two-decimal display.	2nd FIX 2	0.00
3. Enter first data point.	370 STO 1	370.00
4. Enter second data point.	389 STO 2	389.00
5. Enter third data point.	440 STO 3	440.00
6. Enter fourth data point.	510 STO 4	510.00
7. Enter next data point and calculate	395 R/S	430.38
average for current four points.	410 R/S	436.13
	485 R/S	444.38
	545 R/S	454.38
	428 R/S	462.88
	445 R/S	471.38
	520 R/S	480.13
	575 R/S	488.25
	460 R/S	496.00
	480 R/S	504.38
	550 R/S	512.50
	610 R/S	520.63

Below is a summary of these quarterly sales.

		Quarter		
Year	1	2	3	4
1974			430.38	436.13
1975	444.38	454.38	462.88	471.38
1976	480.13	488.25	496.00	504.38
1977	512.50	520.63		

Reference: Croxton, Cowden, and Bolch, *Practical Business Statistics*, pp. 338-342.

Seasonal Index Using Ratio to Centered Moving Average

8

Seasonal index values can be determined by the ratio of periodic sales to a four-point centered moving average to annual sales.

1. Compute a four-point moving average for the periodic data using the "Four-Point Centered Moving Average" program.
2. Divide each periodic value by its associated average calculated above yielding a periodic ratio.
3. Compute the average of these periodic ratios for each quarter to determine the seasonal index.

Example: Compute the seasonal index values for the following quarterly sales data (in $000).

			Quarter	
Year	1	2	3	4
1974	450	486	553	583
1975	453	488	562	593
1976	476	517	588	614
1977	482	524	607	623

The four-point moving average program run on this data produces the following.

			Quarter	
Year	1	2	3	4
1974			518.38	519.00
1975	520.38	522.75	526.88	533.38
1976	540.25	546.13	549.50	551.13
1977	554.38	557.88		

SEASONAL INDEX USING RATIO TO CENTERED MOVING AVERAGE

Action	Press	Display
1. Clear calculator and select two-decimal display.	CLR 2nd CM 2nd FIX 2	0.00
2. Divide each quarter's data by the weighted average for that quarter.	553 ÷ 518.38 = SUM 3	1.07
	583 ÷ 519 = SUM 4	1.12
	453 ÷ 520.38 = SUM 1	0.87
	488 ÷ 522.75 = SUM 2	0.93
	562 ÷ 526.88 = SUM 3	1.07
	593 ÷ 533.38 = SUM 4	1.11
	476 ÷ 540.25 = SUM 1	0.88
	517 ÷ 546.13 = SUM 2	0.95
	588 ÷ 549.5 = SUM 3	1.07
	614 ÷ 551.13 = SUM 4	1.11
	482 ÷ 554.38 = SUM 1	0.87
	524 ÷ 557.88 = SUM 2	0.94
3. Calculate the seasonal index values.		
Quarter 1	RCL 1 ÷ 3 2nd CONST =	0.87
Quarter 2	RCL 2 =	0.94
Quarter 3	RCL 3 =	1.07
Quarter 4	RCL 4 =	1.12

Remember to divide the accumulation of indexes by the number of observations for each quarter as was done in *Step 3*.

Note: For simplicity the results above have been rounded to two decimal places. For greater accuracy, however, you may want to display and use more significant digits for your seasonal indexes. Also, the sum of the indexes should always equal the number of seasonal periods with which you are working (in this case, four).

References: Croxton, Cowden, and Bolch, *Practical Business Statistics*, pp. 350-359.

Parsons, *Statistical Analysis*, pp. 669-675.

Seasonal Index Using Ratio to Yearly Sales Method

8

Seasonal index values can be determined by the ratio of periodic sales to yearly sales.

1. Find the average sales per period (usually a quarter).
2. Divide average sales per period by the average sales per year.
3. Average the ratios from the first period of each year to get the seasonal index for that period. Repeat for each period.

Example: Compute the seasonal index for each quarter of the sales data (in $000) shown below.

		Quarter		
Year	1	2	3	4
1974	450	486	553	583
1975	453	488	562	593
1976	476	517	588	614
1977	482	524	607	623

Action	Press	Display
1. Clear calculator and select two-decimal display.	CLR 2nd CM 2nd FIX 2	0.00
2. Calculate average sales for each year.	450 Σ+	1.00
	486 Σ+	2.00
	553 Σ+	3.00
	583 Σ+	4.00
Average for 1974	2nd MEAN	518.00
	2nd CM 453 Σ+	1.00
	488 Σ+	2.00
	562 Σ+	3.00
	593 Σ+	4.00
Average for 1975	2nd MEAN	524.00
	2nd CM 476 Σ+	1.00
	517 Σ+	2.00
	588 Σ+	3.00
	614 Σ+	4.00
Average for 1976	2nd MEAN	548.75
	2nd CM 482 Σ+	1.00
	524 Σ+	2.00
	607 Σ+	3.00
	623 Σ+	4.00
Average for 1977	2nd MEAN	559.00

SEASONAL INDEX USING RATIO TO YEARLY SALES METHOD

Now enter the following program to compute the index based on each year's sales and accumulate the first quarter ratios in memory 1, second quarter in memory 2, etc.

Program to determine seasonal indexes from ratios

Program Memory	Key Sequence	Program Memory	Key Sequence	Program Memory	Key Sequence
00 45	÷	11 85	=	22 00	
01 38	2nd CONST	12 71	SUM	23 00	
02 42	R/S	13 03	3	24 00	
03 85	=	14 42	R/S	25 00	
04 71	SUM	15 85	=	26 00	
05 01	1	16 71	SUM	27 00	
06 42	R/S	17 04	4	28 00	
07 85	=	18 42	R/S	29 00	
08 71	SUM	19 41	RST	30 00	
09 02	2	20 00		31 00	
10 42	R/S	21 00			

Action	Press	Display
1. Clear calculator and enter program.	2nd CA 2nd LRN	00 00
	Program 2nd LRN RST	0.
2. Select two-decimal display.	2nd FIX 2	0.00
3. Enter average yearly sales starting with first year.	518 R/S	518.00
4. Enter each year's sales for periods 1, 2, 3 and 4.	450 R/S	0.87
	486 R/S	0.94
	553 R/S	1.07
	583 R/S	1.13
Repeat *Steps 3-4* for each year.	524 R/S	524.00
	453 R/S	0.86
	488 R/S	0.93
	562 R/S	1.07
	593 R/S	1.13
	548.75 R/S	548.75
	476 R/S	0.87
	517 R/S	0.94
	588 R/S	1.07
	614 R/S	1.12
	559 R/S	559.00
	482 R/S	0.86
	524 R/S	0.94
	607 R/S	1.09
	623 R/S	1.11
5. Calculate seasonal indexes for		
First quarter	RCL 1 ÷ 4 2nd CONST =	0.87
Second quarter	RCL 2 =	0.94
Third quarter	RCL 3 =	1.07
Fourth quarter	RCL 4 =	1.12

Remember to divide the accumulation of indexes by the total number of observations for that quarter as was done in *Step 5*.

Trend Projections (Forecasting) Using Seasonal Indexes

Once the seasonal indexes have been determined for a set of information, projection of future events (sales, growth, etc.) can easily be made using the regression capabilities built into your calculator. The existing data are first deseasonalized to make projections more accurate, then reseasonalized to obtain the forecast values.

1. Store the initial data point number (usually 1) in memory 0.
2. Deseasonalize the information from each period of each year by dividing each by the seasonal index of that period.
3. Enter the deseasonalized data into the regression routine. You can find the slope, intercept and correlation coefficient if you want to analyze the data.
4. Now future information can be projected.
5. Seasonalize the data for the actual forecast.

Program to deseasonalize data and enter it into regression routine.

Program Memory	Key Sequence	Program Memory	Key Sequence	Program Memory	Key Sequence
00 45	÷	11 01	1	22 00	
01 42	R/S	12 71	SUM	23 00	
02 85	=	13 00	0	24 00	
03 51	STO	14 61	RCL	25 00	
04 01	1	15 00	0	26 00	
05 61	RCL	16 65	−	27 00	
06 00	0	17 01	1	28 00	
07 34	x:y	18 85	=	29 00	
08 61	RCL	19 42	R/S	30 00	
09 01	1	20 41	RST	31 00	
10 35	Σ+	21 00			

Example: Forecast 1978 quarterly sales based on the following historical data (in $000).

		Quarter		
Year	1	2	3	4
1974	450	486	553	583
1975	453	488	562	593
1976	476	517	588	614
1977	482	524	607	623

The seasonal indexes for the above data are

Quarter	Index	Quarter	Index
1	0.87	3	1.07
2	0.94	4	1.12

Action	Press	Display
1. Clear calculator and enter program.	2nd CA 2nd LRN	00 00
	Program 2nd LRN RST	0.
2. Select two-decimal display.	2nd FIX 2	0.00
3. Store number of first data point (usually 1).	1 STO 0	1.00
4. Enter data point.	450 R/S	450.00
5. Enter seasonal index for data point just entered.	.87 R/S	1.00
Repeat *Steps 4-5* for each data point. Display counts the entries.	486 R/S	486.00
	.94 R/S	2.00
	553 R/S	553.00
	1.07 R/S	3.00
	583 R/S	583.00
	1.12 R/S	4.00
	453 R/S	453.00
	.87 R/S	5.00
	488 R/S	488.00
	.94 R/S	6.00
	562 R/S	562.00
	1.07 R/S	7.00
	593 R/S	593.00
	1.12 R/S	8.00
	476 R/S	476.00
	.87 R/S	9.00
	517 R/S	517.00
	.94 R/S	10.00
	588 R/S	588.00
	1.07 R/S	11.00
	614 R/S	614.00
	1.12 R/S	12.00
	482 R/S	482.00
	.87 R/S	13.00
	524 R/S	524.00
	.94 R/S	14.00
	607 R/S	607.00
	1.07 R/S	15.00
	623 R/S	623.00
	1.12 R/S	16.00

TREND PROJECTIONS (FORECASTING) USING SEASONAL INDEXES

6. Calculate slope, intercept and correlation coefficient of data.

2nd SLOPE	3.56
2nd INTCP	506.96
2nd CORR	0.95

7. Calculate future data points by entering future period number. Sixteen periods of data have been entered, so the first period of 1978 is 17, the second period is 18, etc.

| 17 2nd y' | 567.55 |

8. Reseasonalize new point.

| X .87 = | 493.76 |

Repeat *Steps 7-8* to forecast the remainder of 1978.

18 2nd y'	571.11
X .94 =	536.84
19 2nd y'	574.67
X 1.07 =	614.90
20 2nd y'	578.24
X 1.12 =	647.63

The projected sales for 1978 are:

Quarter	Sales
1	493.76
2	536.84
3	614.90
4	647.63

The above technique can be used with any type of statistically derived trend line, but the assumptions underlying the data used should be closely evaluated. Be sure the relationships being made are valid and that the data satisfy the statistical assumptions. Another problem in forecasting is autocorrelation or serial correlation. For a description of these problems refer to a textbook on statistical forecasting.

Linear Transformations

The calculator computes a linear regression on a series of data points that results in a line that can be represented by the equation $y = mx + b$, where m is the slope of the line and b is where the line crosses the y-axis.

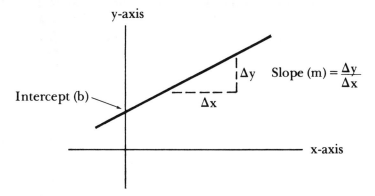

Once you know the slope and intercept of a particular line, you can calculate a y value for any x or an x value for any y.

The calculator can also fit a curved line to the data points. For instance, population growths are characterized by the curve $y = be^{mx}$. Below are listed six equations for some common curves that are offered by many time-sharing computers for trend-line forecasting:

1. $y = bx^m$ (Power Curve)   **4.** $y = b + m/x$

2. $y = be^{mx}$ (Exponential Curve)   **5.** $y = \dfrac{1}{b + mx}$

3. $y = b + m \ln x$ (Logarithmic Curve)   **6.** $y = \dfrac{x}{b + mx}$

To compute these curves, the data must be transformed into linear equivalents. This is done by adjusting the x or y values or both prior to entry into the regression routine with the $\boxed{x:y}$ and $\boxed{\Sigma +}$ keys.

The following table shows the equation for particular curves, the mathematical equivalent for each, and how to adjust each data entry and result to obtain the correct values.

Linear Transformations

Equation	Linear Transformation	Data Entry $x:y$ $\Sigma+$	Computations intercept (b)	slope (m)	new y for new x
1. $y = bx^m$	$\ln y = \ln b + m \ln x$	x [lnx] : y [lnx]	[2nd] [INTCP] [2nd] [e^x]	[2nd] [SLOPE]	x [lnx] [2nd] [y'] [2nd] [e^x]
2. $y = be^{mx}$	$\ln y = \ln b + mx$	x : y [lnx]	[2nd] [INTCP] [2nd] [e^x]	[2nd] [SLOPE]	x [2nd] [y'] [2nd] [e^x]
3. $y = b + m \ln x$	$y = b + m \ln x$	x [lnx] : y	[2nd] [INTCP]	[2nd] [SLOPE]	x [lnx] [2nd] [y']
4. $y = b + m/x$	$y = b + m\left(\dfrac{1}{x}\right)$	x [1/x] : y	[2nd] [INTCP]	[2nd] [SLOPE]	x [1/x] [2nd] [y']
5. $y = \dfrac{1}{b + mx}$	$\dfrac{1}{y} = b + mx$	x : y [1/x]	[2nd] [INTCP]	[2nd] [SLOPE]	x [2nd] [y'] [1/x]
6. $y = \dfrac{x}{b + mx}$	$\dfrac{1}{y} = b\left(\dfrac{1}{x}\right) + m$	x [1/x] : y [1/x]	[2nd] [SLOPE]	[2nd] [INTCP]	x [1/x] [2nd] [y'] [1/x]

Note: Because of the nature of this last regression (6), the values of m and b are reversed by the built-in regression routine. When solving on the calculator, therefore, find the intercept (b) by pressing [2nd] [SLOPE] and the slope (m) by pressing [2nd] [INTCP].

As each data point is keyed in, it must be correctly adjusted as shown in the table. Just as important is the need to properly readjust the results. Forgetting this step can create false results and a misinterpretation of the data. Short programs can be written to facilitate the data entry process. Calculation of the correlation coefficient requires no readjustments. This coefficient can be used to determine which curve best fits the data—the higher the magnitude of the coefficient, the more closely that curve fits.

Example: O. G. Whiz Desserts Unlimited has just opened a new store. Management want to determine if a relationship exists between the sales data and advertising expenses in order to predict advertising expenses for coming months. The deseasonalized sales figures and advertising costs for the last six months are shown below.

Deseasonalized sales ($000)	8.0	17.0	23.2	26.0	27.0	29.0
Advertising Costs ($000)	0.4	1.0	1.7	2.6	3.3	4.5

Test the data for a linear fit ($y = mx + b$), then for the curves $y = bx^m$, $y = be^{mx}$ and $y = b + m \ln x$ for a best fit. Project the sales that should result from $5100 advertising.

8

First, see how the calculator's built-in linear regression handles the data.

Action	Press	Display
1. Clear calculator and select four-decimal display.	CLR 2nd **CM** 2nd **FIX** 4	0.0000
2. Enter x and y data pairs.	.4 $\boxed{x:y}$	0.0000
	8 $\boxed{\Sigma+}$	1.0000
	1 $\boxed{x:y}$	1.4000
	17 $\boxed{\Sigma+}$	2.0000
	1.7 $\boxed{x:y}$	2.0000
	23.2 $\boxed{\Sigma+}$	3.0000
	2.6 $\boxed{x:y}$	2.7000
	26 $\boxed{\Sigma+}$	4.0000
	3.3 $\boxed{x:y}$	3.6000
	27 $\boxed{\Sigma+}$	5.0000
	4.5 $\boxed{x:y}$	4.3000
	29 $\boxed{\Sigma+}$	6.0000
3. Calculate correlation coefficient.	2nd **CORR**	0.8969

Test the curve $y = bx^m$

A short program here can help enter the data by not only lessening the number of keystrokes required, but by decreasing the chance for key-in errors.

Program for $y = bx^m$ data entry

Program Memory	Key Sequence
00 13	$\boxed{\ln x}$
01 34	$\boxed{x:y}$
02 42	R/S
03 13	$\boxed{\ln x}$
04 35	$\boxed{\Sigma+}$
05 42	R/S
06 41	RST

LINEAR TRANSFORMATIONS

Action	Press	Display
1. Clear calculator and enter program.	2nd CA 2nd LRN	00 00
	Program 2nd LRN RST	0.
2. Select four-decimal display.	2nd FIX 4	0.0000
3. Enter x and y data pairs.	.4 R/S	0.0000
	8 R/S	1.0000
	1 R/S	0.0837
	17 R/S	2.0000
	1.7 R/S	1.0000
	23.2 R/S	3.0000
	2.6 R/S	1.5306
	26 R/S	4.0000
	3.3 R/S	1.9555
	27 R/S	5.0000
	4.5 R/S	2.1939
	29 R/S	6.0000
4. Calculate correlation coefficient.	2nd CORR	0.9643

Test the curve $y = be^{mx}$

Program for $y = be^{mx}$ data entry

Program Memory	Key Sequence
00 34	x:y
01 42	R/S
02 13	lnx
03 35	Σ+
04 42	R/S
05 41	RST

Action	Press	Display
1. Clear calculator and enter program.	2nd CA 2nd LRN	00 00
	Program 2nd LRN RST	0.
2. Select four-decimal display.	2nd FIX 4	0.0000
3. Enter x and y data pairs.	.4 R/S	0.0000
	8 R/S	1.0000
	1 R/S	1.4000
	17 R/S	2.0000
	1.7 R/S	2.0000
	23.2 R/S	3.0000
	2.6 R/S	2.7000
	26 R/S	4.0000

Action	Press	Display
	3.3 R/S	3.6000
	27 R/S	5.0000
	4.5 R/S	4.3000
	29 R/S	6.0000
4. Calculate correlation coefficient.	2nd CORR	0.8261

Test the curve y = b + m lnx

Program for y = b + m lnx data entry

Program Memory	Key Sequence
00 13	lnx
01 34	x:y
02 42	R/S
03 35	Σ+
04 42	R/S
05 41	RST

Action	Press	Display
1. Clear calculator and enter program.	2nd CA 2nd LRN	00 00
	Program 2nd LRN RST	0.
2. Select four-decimal display.	2nd FIX 4	0.0000
3. Enter x and y data points.	.4 R/S	0.0000
	8 R/S	1.0000
	1 R/S	0.0837
	17 R/S	2.0000
	1.7 R/S	1.0000
	23.2 R/S	3.0000
	2.6 R/S	1.5306
	26 R/S	4.0000
	3.3 R/S	1.9555
	27 R/S	5.0000
	4.5 R/S	2.1939
	29 R/S	6.0000
4. Calculate correlation coefficient.	2nd CORR	0.9915
5. Calculate intercept.	2nd INTCP	16.8967
6. Calculate slope.	2nd SLOPE	8.8191
7. Project sales for $5100 advertising.	5.1 lnx 2nd y'	31.2652

The correlation coefficients for each type of curve tried are listed below.

Curve Type	Correlation Coefficient
$y = mx + b$	0.8969
$y = bx^m$	0.9643
$y = be^{mx}$	0.8261
$y = b + m \ln x$	0.9915

It is easy to see that the curve $y = b + m \ln x$ best fits the data because of its high correlation coefficient. The selection of a particular curve to fit data should be made very carefully. Frequently a plot of the data can give an indication of what type of curve to use. The characteristic curves for the curve equations given in the table at the first of this section are shown below.

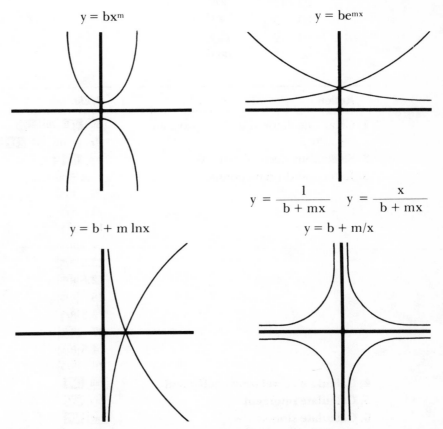

$y = bx^m$

$y = be^{mx}$

$$y = \frac{1}{b + mx} \qquad y = \frac{x}{b + mx}$$

$y = b + m \ln x$

$y = b + m/x$

After plotting your data, choose a curve that most closely resembles it and follow the instructions in the table to calculate additional information.

A plot of the dessert company's data looks like this.

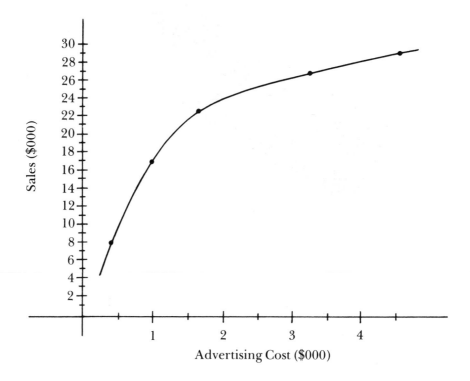

As you can see, these data look most like the plot above for y = b + m lnx which is the same thing the correlation coefficients showed. The example data have the equation y = 16.8967 + 8.8191 lnx.

A closer look at the data plot shows that advertising costs much above $2000 produce relatively little in the way of sales dollars. Notice that $2000 worth of advertising produces over $24000 worth (deseasonalized) of sales. This amounts to $12 sales for each advertising dollar spent. An additional $2000 worth of advertising produces only $4000 more sales or $2 sales for each advertising dollar. So, even though $5100 advertising cost would yield over $31,000 in sales, this advertising investment should be closely analyzed. Is the limited increase in sales worth the necessary advertising dollar outlay?

Quantitative Methods

CHAPTER 9

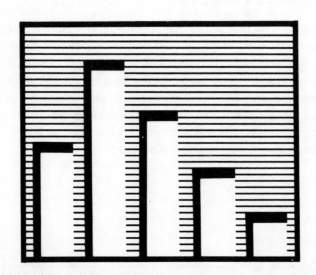

Success or failure of almost any endeavor is heavily dependent on the accuracy of decisions that must be made along the way. The more information available at the time of decision, the better the decision, the more successful the endeavor. Statistics can provide a wealth of information beneficial to the decision-making process. The concepts are simple. The statistical features on your calculator make applications straightforward. The remainder of this book is devoted to suggestions and examples of how statistics and quantitative techniques can be applied to various situations.

The quality of information obtained from statistics depends primarily on two factors: how much historical data you have and how well correlated are the variables being analyzed.

"Cause and Effect"

Note an important point here: Be careful about drawing conclusions about cause and effect. Two variables that are related to a third can show a relation to each other without a "cause and effect" relation between them.

For example, you may have data on children that relate manual dexterity (the time to finish a simple jigsaw puzzle for example) directly to mathematical ability (performance on a math test). The relation may show quite a good correlation coefficient. It may turn out, however, that age is the dominant factor "driving" the variables. Further analysis may show that the older children naturally display both better manual coordination and mathematical skill and that, if your sample is restructured to include only children of the same age, an entirely different relationship may result. So be careful about how you apply your results in making decisions. Consider the makeup of your sample and exactly what you are measuring and testing.

In general, the less data you have to work with, the more "chancy" your prediction will be. *Table A* in the *Appendix* is designated to measure how valid your correlation coefficient is under different data conditions. Simply find the number of samples you have, then proceed laterally to the correlation coefficient of your data. Now read up to find the degree of certainty, which really tells you how valid are the predictions made from this data. If the correlation coefficient for the number of samples you have is too small for the table, you can be no more than 80% sure of the validity of the data.

Many of the techniques applied here have been discussed in *Chapter 7*, "Decision-Making with Statistics." It is best to become acquainted with these techniques for a full understanding of the Quantitative Methods.

Predicted Range for Large Samples Upper Limit Only

For large samples the standard deviation of the sample is very nearly equal to the population's standard deviation. Again, the definition boundary for sample sizes (large or small) is usually taken to be 30 elements while 100 elements is the breakover point from small to large population size.

Example: You are called in to aid the manufacturer of Elflasho flashlights. They have just received their first shipment of flashlight bulbs from a new manufacturer and want to be particularly sure of a good shipment before accepting it. Testing the parts is quite simple in this case — they either light or they don't — so a sizeable sample can be easily tested. The new bulb manufacturer, Brite Spot Systems, Inc., insists that the shipment (population) will contain no more than 12% defective bulbs.

The Elflasho line foreman has 250 of the bulbs tested, and of these, 43 fail (17.2%). He asks your advice — should he accept or reject the shipment based on this data? He'd like to be 90% sure the lot has more than 12% defective bulbs before he rejects the shipment and looks for a new vendor.

Here you are dealing with a claim about a proportion of defective parts, and so you should use a statistical technique especially suited to handling the problem. First, use the formula below to calculate the predicted range of the population mean, as in previous examples. However, instead of the population mean being a numerical value (such as weight, or % volume), it's the proportion of defective parts in the population.

Formula Predicted Range of the Population Mean Proportion $= P \pm \left[\dfrac{P(1-P)}{n} \right]^{\frac{1}{2}} z$

where: P = Proportion of defective parts found in the sample, in
this case, $\dfrac{43}{250}$ or 0.172
n = Sample size (250)
z = z value found from *Table B* in the *Appendix*

You are concerned with the upper limit here (you should reject the shipment if it is over 12% defective, and accept otherwise). Since you wish to be 90% sure of the reject decision, the z value from *Table B* is found from column 1 to be 1.28.

Once you have calculated a range for the population mean, you can compare it to the manufacturer's claim and make your decision.

You already know the proportion of defective parts in the sample is 17.2%. Now evaluate the following expressions to calculate the predicted range of the mean.

$$P + \left[\frac{P(1-P)}{n}\right]^{\frac{1}{2}} z \quad \text{and} \quad P - \left[\frac{P(1-P)}{n}\right]^{\frac{1}{2}} z$$

Action	Press	Display
1. Clear calculator and select three-decimal display.	CLR 2nd CM 2nd FIX 3	0.000
2. Enter P as a decimal value.	.172 STO 1	0.172
3. Calculate second term of expression.	× (1 − RCL 1	0.172
	) ÷ 250 = 2nd √x̄	0.024
	× 1.28 = STO 2	0.031
4. Calculate upper limit.	+ RCL 1 =	0.203
5. Calculate lower limit.	RCL 1 − RCL 2 =	0.141

The sample indicates that the lowest expected percentage of defective parts is 14.1%. You can be 90% sure that the manufacturer is not living up to his claim and Elflasho's needs. Based on this analysis, you advise their foreman to reject the shipment.

As it turns out, the foreman at Elflasho is not immediately ready to ship back the bulbs. (It seems the president of Brite Spot Systems is also the son-in-law of Mr. Elflasho.) He needs to be very sure. You can recheck the decision at a higher degree of certainty quite easily. You both agree that if he's 95% sure the shipment is bad, it will go back and hang the consequences. First, locate the z score in *Table B* for a 95% degree of certainty and repeat the calculation.

At 95% certainty, you would still reject the shipment!

Predicted Range of Population Mean (Upper and Lower Limits)

Here is a situation that calls for a decision about a population based on a sample with concern for both limits.

Example: A large shipment (population) of aerosol cans of insecticide has just arrived at your receiving dock. The manufacturer claims that the cans contain, on the average, 510 grams of insecticide each. Maybe you usually just take this fact at face value, but this time you would like to be sure that he is meeting this claim.

You are concerned about this problem for two reasons: these particular cans don't work properly if they're overfull and you're getting gypped if they're less than full. The ideal case is when each can contains exactly 510 grams and you're concerned about the manufacturer meeting his obligation — both on the high and low end. This is called a "two-sided" or "two-tailed" decision-making process.

You have a technician measure the weight of 40 cans (the sample) and tabulate the data for you. With a quick calculation on your calculator, you found:

> The mean sample weight is 508.75 g (usually labeled $\bar{x}$)
> The sample standard deviation (labeled s_x) is 19.97g.

Is the manufacturer meeting his claim? Should you accept the shipment or reject it? Can the sample data give you a little more to go on?

Assume you want to be 95% sure that the manufacturer has not met his claim before you reject the shipment. Your target here is to get as much information as you can about the population based on the data you have from the sample.

Here your sample size is over 30 items which statisticians generally agree to as an informal boundary between "large" and "small" samples. For your "large" sample of 40 items you may assume that the sample standard deviation (s_x) is a pretty good estimate of the population standard deviation (usually labeled with the lower case Greek letter sigma, σ).

This fact often allows you to immediately reach some important conclusions. Most manufacturing processes deviate from the specified or target value in a "normal" way. This means that the population values can often be considered to follow the normal curve. If this is the case, then about 95% of the cans will be within ± 2 standard deviations of the mean. The sample standard deviation of 19.97 implies a range of ± 2 (19.97) ($\pm$ about 40 grams) for about 95% of the cans. If, in your case, a ± 40 grams variation in the weight of the cans is by itself unacceptable, you may need to reject the cans based on this standard deviation value alone.

If the standard deviation value is acceptable, you now need to proceed to a little more complete analysis. There is a tool for statistics that lets you:

a) Select a degree of certainty for your decision to accept or reject, say 95%.

b) With a straightforward calculation you can now establish a range within which the population mean (labeled μ) lies, to the degree of certainty you selected. The formula for this range is:

$$\text{Range for } \mu \text{ at degree of certainty you select} = \bar{x} \pm \frac{\sigma}{\sqrt{n}} z$$

In this formula $\bar{x}$ is your sample mean, n is the number of samples, and z is the z value for the degree of certainty you select. The z value is found in *Table B* in the *Appendix*. Column II is where z values for checking both upper and lower levels are tabulated. If you check in that table, Column II reads a z value of 1.96 at 95% degree of certainty.

Now, evaluate $\bar{x} \pm \frac{\sigma}{\sqrt{n}} z$ for

$$z \quad = 1.96$$
$$\sigma = s_x = 19.97 \text{ (for large samples, } n > 30, \text{ only)}$$
$$n \quad = 40$$
$$\bar{x} \quad = 508.75$$

PREDICTED RANGE OF POPULATION MEAN
UPPER AND LOWER LIMITS

Action	Press	Display
1. Clear calculator and select two-decimal display.	CLR 2nd CM 2nd FIX 2	0.00
2. Evaluate for ($\bar{x}$ +) limit of population mean.	508.75 STO 0 + (	508.75
	19.97 × 1.96 ÷	39.14
	40 2nd √x) STO 1 =	514.94
3. Evaluate for ($\bar{x}$ −) limit of population mean.	RCL 0 − RCL 1 =	502.56

The manufacturer's claim of 510g falls inside the limits of 502.56 to 514.94 so the shipment should be accepted. The weight is between $\bar{x} - \dfrac{\sigma}{\sqrt{n}} z$ and $\bar{x} + \dfrac{\sigma}{\sqrt{n}} z$. The sample is indicating that the population mean is somewhere between these two numbers, with 95% certainty.

When selecting the degree of certainty for a problem, it is important to realize how the statistical process works. The amount of information you have in your sample does not change. If you select a very high degree of certainty, then what you are certain about is less definite.

Here's an example. A mechanic looks at your car and tells you that he is pretty sure that it will cost about $80 to $100 to fix it. If you tell him that he has to be 99.9% sure of his estimate, he will probably estimate a wider range, say $50 to $200. If the situation you are investigating demands more certainty about a smaller range, then you may need to take a larger sample.

Testing Upper Limit by a Small Sample

When the number of samples goes below 30, the normal curve can no longer be accurately used to describe the distribution of the sample means. A different family of curves does work for these situations. They are called **t curves**. See page **7-14** for more information.

The shape of any t curve depends on what is called the *number of degrees of freedom (df)* for your particular sample. The number of degrees of freedom in most cases is considered to be equal to the number of elements in your sample minus one (df = n − 1).

Example: A government is concerned about its monetary status and closely monitors the currency exchange rates with its closest neighbor. The government must be 95% sure at all times that the exchange rate doesn't consistently exceed 8 to 1 for internal stability reasons. The rate is constantly changing, so the government simply checks the exchange rate at the close of each day's trading. The latest week's closes were 7.85, 8.33, 7.97, 8.31 and 7.76. Is the government nearing an unstable economic condition?

An analysis of the population mean (μ) must be made using relatively small samples. The statistical analysis method shown here is for small samples (n < 30).

1. Enter the sample data into statistical routine.
2. Find the mean ($\bar{x}$) and standard deviation (s_x) of the sample.
3. Calculate the predicted range for the population mean (μ) by

$$\mu = \bar{x} \pm \frac{s_x}{\sqrt{n}} t$$

where:
$\bar{x}$ = Sample mean
s_x = Sample standard deviation
n = Number of items in sample
t = Test value from the Appendix

In this case the t value is found in *Table C* in the *Appendix*, because only one limit is involved. In this table, locate the t value for the degree of certainty you require (here 95%) and the number of degrees of freedom = n − 1 = 4. These intersect at the t value 2.132.

Action	Press	Display
1. Clear calculator and select two-decimal display.	CLR 2nd CM 2nd FIX 2	0.00
2. Enter sample data.	7.85 Σ+	1.00
	8.33 Σ+	2.00
	7.97 Σ+	3.00
	8.31 Σ+	4.00
	7.76 Σ+	5.00
3. Calculate sample standard deviation.	2nd S.D. STO 0	0.26
4. Calculate sample mean.	2nd MEAN STO 1	8.04
5. Evaluate ($\bar{x}+$) limit of population mean.	+ (RCL 0 X	0.26
	2.132 ÷ 5 2nd √x̄	2.24
	) STO 2 =	8.29
6. Evaluate ($\bar{x}-$) limit of population mean.	RCL 1 − RCL 2 =	7.79

Based on the analysis of this week's trading, the economy doesn't seem to be in any great trouble. For this situation the entire predicted range of the population mean would have to be greater than 8 before trading would be considered consistently above 8 with 95% certainty.

Confidence Interval Method for Analyzing Change

9

There are a variety of situations where decisions concerning change are involved. You need to decide whether or not some new process, method, policy, etc. has created some genuine change over an old one. Situations such as this may arise when trying new educational techniques, production methods, engineering systems, etc.

A change may appear overwhelming and it's an "open and shut" case that something is clearly different. In other cases, however, it may appear that some improvement has been made, but it's not an overwhelming change. Here's where decision-making becomes more difficult. A decision to endorse or institute a new procedure or process based on data from small samples, can be a pretty tricky business.

Several methods from statistics are available to aid in the study of change. These methods involve some fairly sophisticated techniques. Your advanced business calculator, with AOS and parentheses, will be a powerful ally here. (In fact, without your calculator handling the arithmetic involved, using these techniques would be quite difficult.)

The specific statistical method used here is called a **confidence interval method.** This procedure often works together with the *F-test.* These two procedures enable you to decide, with a degree of certainty that you select, whether or not a genuine difference exists between one set of data and another (assuming that the populations are at least approximately normal). In cases where your decision involves a considerable sum of money, these tests can be an important part of your decision-making process. In cases where lives may be involved, such as in pharmaceutical research or immunology, these procedures can be crucial!

The next two examples use *confidence interval* and *F-test* methods in analyzing two "case histories" where a decision must be made based on whether or not a change or difference exists between the results of two processes.

Uncorrected *Confidence Interval* Method

Example: A new pipe supplier on the scene (Apex) claims that a new *neverust* coating process on his company's product will provide "up to three times longer life" over standard, noncoated pipe. Your decision to change to the new pipe will involve a significant cost increase and your pipeline requires several hundred miles of pipe, so you need to be pretty sure (say 95%) about any decision made.

The data which supports Apex's claim of up to three times longer life came from the results of six experiments. In each experiment a length of standard pipe and a length of coated pipe were buried side by side (in six different locations), and the weight loss due to corrosion was measured (in ounces per foot per year). The results of their tests are tabulated below:

APEX NEVERUST PIPE CO.
TEST DATA
(yearly weight loss in ounces/foot/year)

Uncoated Steel Pipe	Apex Neverust Coated Pipe
3.68	2.68
1.28	0.45
1.84	0.92
3.68	1.69
1.83	0.05
6.00	0.16

The agent claims that from this data you can "clearly see" that Apex's new coating process results in pipe that lasts "up to three times longer". He has nothing more to say on the matter, so you tell him you'd like to think about it.

The goal is to determine just how much you know about the pipe's performance, based only on the sample. Since the sample (six coated and six uncoated pipes) is small, methods of *statistical inference* will be important here. What you really need to do is to predict what the mean difference in yearly weight loss would be between a coated and uncoated pipeline, based on the experimental data from Apex (the sample) at a 95% degree of certainty.

1. Determine the mean, standard deviation and square of the standard deviation values for the pipe weight loss. Then, using the methods of statistical inference, determine the range of difference in weight loss between pipelines built of coated and uncoated pipe. There are two procedures to follow in making this prediction.

2. Perform an *F-test*. This is a pre-testing process that lets you know whether or not the second technique, the *confidence interval*, needs any adjustments.

3. After the F-test is "passed," use the *confidence interval* procedure to make your prediction. (Procedures to follow if the *F-test* is not passed are examined in the next example.)

Notice that the *F-test* and *confidence interval* procedures examined here involve mathematical manipulations that will put your advanced business calculator "through its paces".

For Uncoated Pipe

Action	Press	Display
1. Clear calculator and select four-decimal display.	CLR 2nd CM 2nd FIX 4	0.0000
2. Enter statistical data.	3.68 Σ+	1.0000
	1.28 Σ+	2.0000
	1.84 Σ+	3.0000
	3.68 Σ+	4.0000
	1.83 Σ+	5.0000
	6 Σ+	6.0000
3. Determine mean weight loss.	2nd MEAN	3.0517
4. Determine standard deviation.	2nd S.D.	1.7653
5. Determine square of standard deviation.	x^2	3.1163

For Coated Pipe

Action	Press	Display
1. Clear calculator.	CLR 2nd CM	0.0000
2. Enter statistical data.	2.68 Σ+	1.0000
	.45 Σ+	2.0000
	.92 Σ+	3.0000
	1.69 Σ+	4.0000
	.05 Σ+	5.0000
	.16 Σ+	6.0000
3. Calculate mean.	2nd MEAN	0.9917
4. Calculate sample standard deviation.	2nd S.D.	1.0213
5. Calculate sample square of standard deviation.	x^2	1.0430

Note: Based on the samples, the mean weight loss for the standard pipe is 3.0517 and the mean weight loss for the Neverust pipe is 0.9917. From these results (without using statistical inference) it appears that the Apex claim of about three times less weight loss for Neverust pipe is justified. But how much can you depend on this result?

Now, for purposes of the *F-test* you need to identify the data with the greatest standard deviation as the "high" data, and the data with the lowest value standard deviation as the "low" data. Use the subscripts "H" for high and "L" for low to tell these apart. So, because the uncoated pipe data has the greatest standard deviation, it will be called the "high" data. The F-test here is said to be a "one-tailed" test, because the test is to see if Sx_H^2 is greater than Sx_L^2. Now, tabulate what is known at this point, along with all the necessary labels.

Yearly Weight Loss Data (oz./ft./year)	*Uncoated Pipe*	*Coated Pipe*
Sample mean	$3.0517 = \bar{x}_H$	$0.9917 = \bar{x}_L$
Standard deviation	$1.7653 = Sx_H$	$1.0213 = Sx_L$
Square of standard deviation	$3.1163 = Sx_H^2$	$1.0430 = Sx_L^2$
Number of samples	$6 = n_H$	$6 = n_L$

Now, to conduct the *F-test,* calculate the value of $\dfrac{Sx_H^2}{Sx_L^2}$, and compare this to an *F-value* found in *Table E* in the *Appendix.* The F value you look for in the table should be for $n_H - 1$ degree of freedom (in this case $6 - 1$ or 5) for the numerator, and $n_L - 1$ degrees of freedom (in this case $6 - 1$ or 5) for the denominator; and a 95% degree of certainty. The F value from the table is F = 5.05. If this F value is greater than your calculated value for $\dfrac{Sx_H^2}{Sx_L^2}$, the F-test is "passed" and you can proceed to the prediction using *confidence interval* procedures. So, the value of $\dfrac{Sx_H^2}{Sx_L^2} = 3.1163 \div 1.0430 = 2.9878$. Since the F value of 5.05 is greater than your calculated value for $\dfrac{Sx_H^2}{Sx_L^2}$ of 2.9878, the F test is "passed".

Now use the *confidence interval* procedure to determine the range of difference in mean weight loss between the coated and uncoated pipe.

To find the range, look in *Table C* in the *Appendix* and find the t value for the degree of surety you want (here 95%), and for $n_H + n_L - 2$ degrees of freedom ($6 + 6 - 2 = 10$). The t value you will find is 2.228. Now you can calculate the range of predicted difference for the means, using the following complex-looking formula.

Range of difference between means =

$$(\bar{x}_H - \bar{x}_L) \pm t \left[\left(\frac{((n_H - 1) \, Sx_H^2 + (n_L - 1) \, Sx_L^2)}{(n_H + n_L - 2)} \right) \left(\frac{1}{n_H} + \frac{1}{n_L} \right) \right]^{\frac{1}{2}}$$

In our case:

$\bar{x}_H = 3.0517$	$n_H = 6$	$Sx_H^2 = 3.1163$	$t = 2.228$
$\bar{x}_L = 0.9917$	$n_L = 6$	$Sx_L^2 = 1.0430$	

Action	Press	Display
1. Clear calculator and select four-decimal display.	CLR 2nd CM 2nd FIX 4	0.0000
2. Calculate upper limit of difference.	3.0517 − .9917 =	2.0600
	STO 1 +	2.0600
	(((((	2.0600
	6 − 1) × 3.1163 +	15.5815
	(6 − 1) ×	5.0000
	1.043) ÷	20.7965
	(6 + 6 − 2)	10.0000
	) ×	2.0797
	(6 1/x + 6 1/x)	0.3333
	)	0.6932
	2nd √x	0.8326
	× 2.228) STO 2 =	3.9150
3. Calculate lower limit of difference.	RCL 1 − RCL 2 =	0.2050

Based on this analysis you can be 95% sure that the difference in the means between a coated and uncoated pipeline will be between 3.9150 and 0.2050 ounces per foot per year (assuming Apex's data are valid). What this means is that you are 95% certain that the coated pipe will perform better than the uncoated pipe by as much as 3.9150 ounces per foot per year or by as little as 0.2050 ounces per foot per year (or any value in between). This is all you can tell based on only six experiments. Apex's claim of "up to" three times better performance seems to be technically sound, but they left out the other side of the claim which could read: "or as little as a few percent better performance". At any rate all you really have to base your decision on is a predicted range for the difference between the means.

With this information, closely scrutinize what extra costs are involved in changing to the coated pipe, how long the pipeline needs to last, and the other factors surrounding the decision. Your analysis of this data should put you in a better bargaining position with Apex and also lets you clearly see just how much (or how little) information can be drawn from a small series of experiments.

Corrected *Confidence Interval* Method

Example: A young biology student is testing to see whether or not a certain drug has any effect on the intelligence level of hamsters, as measured by the time it takes the hamsters to complete a simple maze. Nine hamsters were fed the drug and given the test, while a control group of 13, which were not treated, were given the same test. The student has already tabulated the data for the two groups of hamsters:

	No Drug	Treated with Drug
Number of hamsters in sample	13	9
Mean time to complete maze	110.02	101.58
Standard deviation	9.9116	2.8566
Square of standard deviation	98.24	8.16

The student wants to determine if he can go to his instructor and state that he's 99% sure that the drug really did improve the hamsters' performance on the test.

The student needs to determine all he can about the performance of the drug based on a small series of tests. Statistical inference provides the capability to calculate, at a certainty level he selects, a confidence interval (range) of difference in intelligence of hamsters treated with the drug and those not treated with the drug. The method used to calculate this range is a two part process. First, an F-test is used on the data. Based on the results of this test, calculate either a "corrected" or an "uncorrected" confidence interval.

To perform the F-test, identify the data with the greatest standard deviation as the "high" data, and data with the lowest value standard deviation as the "low" data. The subscripts "H" and "L" distinguish between these two groups. Tabulate the data with all of the necessary labels below.

	No Drug	Treated with Drug
Number of hamsters	$13 = n_H$	$9 = n_L$
Mean time on maze test (sec)	$110.02 = \bar{x}_H$	$101.58 = \bar{x}_L$
Standard deviation	$9.9116 = Sx_H$	$2.8566 = Sx_L$
Square of standard deviation	$98.24 = Sx_H{}^2$	$8.16 = Sx_L{}^2$

The F-test compares $\dfrac{Sx_H{}^2}{Sx_L{}^2} = \dfrac{98.24}{8.16} = 12.03921569$ to the appropriate F value for 99% level of certainty found in *Table F* in the *Appendix*. The F value is at the intersection for $n_H - 1 = 12$ degrees of freedom for the numerator and $n_L - 1 = 8$ degrees of freedom for the denominator or F = 5.67. Since the calculated value is greater than the value from the table, the test is said to fail and a *corrected* confidence interval procedure must be used. This involves adjusting the number of degrees of freedom as follows before calculating the confidence interval.

$$\text{corrected degrees of freedom} = \cfrac{1}{\cfrac{K^2}{n_H - 1} + \cfrac{(1 - K)^2}{n_L - 1}}$$

$$\text{where: } K = \cfrac{\cfrac{Sx_H^2}{n_H}}{\cfrac{Sx_H^2}{n_H} + \cfrac{Sx_L^2}{n_L}}$$

If the calculated value had been less than the value from the table, the F-test is said to pass and the above correction need not be made.

Once this corrected number of degrees of freedom is calculated, then the appropriate t value is used to calculate the predicted range of difference in the population means by:

$$(\bar{x}_H - \bar{x}_L) \pm t \left[\left(\frac{(n_H - 1)\, Sx_H^2 + (n_L - 1)\, Sx_L^2}{(n_H + n_L - 2)} \right) \left(\frac{1}{n_N} + \frac{1}{n_L} \right) \right]^{\frac{1}{2}}$$

Action	Press	Display
1. Clear calculator and select three-decimal display.	CLR 2nd CM 2nd FIX 3	0.000
2. Calculate value for K.	98.24 ÷ 13 = STO 1 ÷	7.557
	(RCL 1 + 8.16	8.16
	÷ 9)	8.464
	= STO 2	0.893
3. Calculate corrected number of degrees of freedom.	1 ÷	1.000
	(RCL 2 x^2 ÷ (	0.797
	13 − 1) +	0.066
	(1 − RCL 2)	0.107
	x^2 ÷	0.011
	(9 − 1 =	14.734

Now to continue the analysis, the corrected number of degrees of freedom is used to find a t value from *Table D* in the *Appendix*. The exact t value for 14.734 degrees of freedom must be interpolated between 2.977 (the value for 14) and 2.947 (the value for 15).

Action	Press	Display
4. Interpolate t value.	2.977 ⊟ .734 ⊠	0.734
	⟮ 2.977 ⊟ 2.947 ⟯ ⊟	2.955
	STO 3	2.955
5. Calculate upper limit of range of	110.02 ⊟ 101.58 ⊟	8.440
difference in population means.	STO 1	8.440
	⟮ ⟮ ⟮ ⟮	8.440
	13 ⊟ 1 ⟯ ⊠	12.000
	98.24 ⊞	1178.880
	⟮ 9 ⊟ 1 ⟯ ⊠	8.000
	8.16 ⟯ ⊟	1244.160
	⟮ 13 ⊞ 9 ⊟ 2	2
	⟯ ⊠	62.208
	⟮ 13 1/x ⊞ 9	9
	1/x ⟯	0.188
	⟯ 2nd √x̄ ⊠	0.434
	RCL 3 ⊟	10.106
	STO 2 ⊞ RCL 1 ⊟	18.546
6. Calculate lower limit of range of		
difference in population means.	RCL 1 ⊟ RCL 2 ⊟	− 1.666

Based on the data he has, the student can state with 99% certainty that the difference between the means lies between 18.546 and − 1.666. Now if the drug had no effect on the hamster's performance, he would expect no difference (zero difference) between the means. Since the range of predicted values of the difference between means includes the value zero, he cannot be sure (at a 99% degree of certainty) that any real change has taken place when the hamsters are treated with the drug. There is no "statistically significant" difference between the two groups at the 99% confidence level. Possibly, more data need to be taken at this point.

Would this analysis predict a significant difference between the two groups at the 95% confidence level? The answer is "yes."

An *Economic Order Quantity* Inventory Model

9

The *Economic Order Quantity (EOQ)* is the quantity which should be ordered to minimize inventory costs during a specified time period, assuming no stock outs. Inventory costs consist of ordering costs plus carrying costs, and this model determines the EOQ and the minimum inventory costs for the time period. In addition, you can go on to find the number of times to order by dividing the number of units to be used during the time period by the EOQ.

$$EOQ = \sqrt{\frac{2KL}{M}} \text{ and}$$

$$\text{Minimum Costs for Time Period} = \sqrt{2KLM}$$

$$\text{Number of Times to Order during Period} = \frac{L}{EOQ}$$

where:
EOQ = economic order quantity
K = cost of placing each purchase order
L = total number of units used during time period
M = cost of carrying one unit in inventory for the time period

Since this is a procedure you may want to evaluate with several different cost estimates, you can use a program to avoid repetitive keystrokes.

Program Memory	Key Sequence	Program Memory	Key Sequence	Program Memory	Key Sequence
00 02	2	11 03	3	22 42	R/S
01 55	×	12 85	=	23 41	RST
02 61	RCL	13 19	2nd √x	24 00	
03 01	1	14 42	R/S	25 00	
04 55	×	15 61	RCL	26 00	
05 61	RCL	16 04	4	27 00	
06 02	2	17 55	×	28 00	
07 45	÷	18 61	RCL	29 00	
08 51	STO	19 03	3	30 00	
09 04	4	20 85	=	31 00	
10 61	RCL	21 19	2nd √x		

AN *ECONOMIC ORDER QUANTITY* INVENTORY MODEL

Example: A company has annual requirements for 30,000 units, with an $18 cost per purchase order placed. The cost of carrying one unit of inventory for a year is estimated to be $.15. What is the economic order quantity (EOQ), and what are the minimum annual inventory costs? If carrying costs rose to $.25 per unit, how would EOQ and inventory costs be affected?

Action	Press	Display
1. Clear calculator and enter program.	[2nd] CA [2nd] LRN	00 00
	Program [2nd] LRN [RST]	0.
2. Select two-decimal display.	[2nd] FIX 2	0.00
3. Enter cost per purchase order.	18 [STO] 1	18.00
4. Enter number of units required annually.	30000 [STO] 2	30000.00
5. Enter carrying cost per unit.	.15 [STO] 3	0.15
6. Calculate economic order quantity.	[R/S]	2683.28

Each purchase order should consist of approximately 2683 units.

7. Calculate annual minimum inventory costs.	[R/S]	402.49
8. Enter revised carrying cost per unit.	.25 [STO] 3	0.25
9. Calculate revised EOQ.	[R/S]	2078.46
10. Calculate revised annual cost.	[R/S]	519.62

Cost-Volume-Profit Analysis

Cost-Volume-Profit analysis is a common technique used to determine the breakeven point and sales level necessary to earn a given income after taxes. This model assumes that sales units equal units purchased or produced and takes into account constant sales prices, variable costs, and fixed costs. The relationships can be expressed either in terms of units or sales dollars, and the formulas are:

Formulas for units method

$$SP\,(X) = VC\,(X) + FC + \frac{I}{(1 - T_x)}$$

$$\text{Units to earn specified income (I)} = \frac{FC + \dfrac{I}{(1 - T_x)}}{(SP - VC)}$$

$$\text{Income (I) with specified unit sales} = \left[X\,(SP - VC) - FC\right](1 - T_x)$$

Formulas for sales dollars method

$$S = R \times S + FC + \frac{I}{(1 - T_x)}$$

$$\text{Sales dollars to earn specified income (I)} = \frac{FC + \dfrac{I}{(1 - T_x)}}{(1 - R)}$$

$$\text{Income (I) with specified sales dollars} = \left[S\,(1 - R) - FC\right](1 - T_x)$$

where:
SP	=	sales price per unit in dollars
VC	=	variable costs per unit in dollars
FC	=	fixed costs in dollars
T_x	=	tax rate as percent (in decimal form) of income before taxes
I	=	desired after-tax income
X	=	units
S	=	sales dollars
R	=	ratio of variable costs per unit to sales price per unit

Reference: Horngren, *Cost Accounting: A Managerial Emphasis,* pp. 62-63.

The same program can be used to evaluate both the unit method and the sales dollar method, depending on which data is stored in the memory registers before executing the program.

Program Memory	Key Sequence	Program Memory	Key Sequence	Program Memory	Key Sequence
00 61	RCL	11 00	0	22 85	=
01 01	1	12 85	=	23 55	X
02 75	+	13 42	R/S	24 61	RCL
03 61	RCL	14 61	RCL	25 02	2
04 03	3	15 00	0	26 85	=
05 45	÷	16 55	X	27 42	R/S
06 61	RCL	17 61	RCL	28 41	RST
07 02	2	18 04	4	29 00	
08 85	=	19 65	−	30 00	
09 45	÷	20 61	RCL	31 00	
10 61	RCL	21 01	1		

Note:

To solve for the breakeven point, enter a zero for income (I). Also, if you want before-tax results, enter a zero for the tax rate (T_x), i.e., $1 - 0 = 1$.

Example:

A canoe company sells its paddles for $20 each. The unit variable cost is $15, and fixed costs are $3,000. The company's tax rate is 40%. Assuming that all paddles produced are sold and all prices and costs remain the same, how many paddles must be sold to earn $2500 after tax? What is the after-tax income for sales of 1700 paddles? What is the breakeven point in number of paddles? What sales volume (in dollars) must be reached to earn $2500 after tax? What after-tax income will be produced by $34,000 in sales? What is the breakeven point in sales dollars?

First, approach the problem from a unit standpoint.

Action	Press	Display
1. Clear calculator and enter program.	2nd CA 2nd LRN	00 00
	Program 2nd LRN RST	0.
2. Select two-decimal display.	2nd FIX 2	0.00
3. Deduct variable unit cost from selling price (SP − VC) and store in memory 0.	20 − 15 = STO 0	5.00
4. Enter fixed costs in memory 1.	3000 STO 1	3000.00
5. Calculate 1 − 40% (tax rate) and store in memory 2.	1 − 40 % = STO 2	0.60
6. Store specified income in memory 3.	2500 STO 3	2500.00
7. Store specified unit sales in memory 4.	1700 STO 4	1700.00
8. Calculate unit sales necessary to earn specified income ($2500) after tax.	R/S	1433.33
9. Calculate after-tax income for sales of specified units (1700).	R/S	3300.00
10. Calculate breakeven point in units.	0 STO 3 R/S	600.00

Now, to answer the remaining questions, solve the program with the sales dollars method (using the program still in the calculator).

Action	Press	Display
1. Clear display and memories.	CLR 2nd CM	0.00
2. Subtract ratio of variable costs to selling price from 1, and enter in memory 0.	1 − (15 ÷ 20	20
	= STO 0	0.25
3. Enter fixed costs in memory 1.	3000 STO 1	3000.00
4. Calculate 1 − 40% (tax rate) and store in memory 2.	1 − 40 % =	0.60
	STO 2	0.60
5. Store specified income in memory 3.	2500 STO 3	2500.00
6. Store specified dollar sales volume in memory 4.	34000 STO 4	34000.00
7. Calculate sales in dollars needed to earn specified after-tax income ($2500 net).	RST R/S	28666.67
8. Calculate after-tax income for specified sales volume ($34,000).	R/S	3300.00
9. Calculate breakeven point in sales dollars.	0 STO 3 R/S	12000.00

Learning Curve Analysis

The learning curve ($y = ax^b$) has many applications in modern business. Scheduling production, projecting unit costs and labor hours, and setting cost and labor standards are only a few of the applications of the learning curve. Your calculator can help you determine the learning curve, if necessary, and project results based on your data.

The examples that follow deal with direct labor hours, which are a common application for learning curve analysis. However, this model could also be applied to machine hours. The model to determine the average number of labor hours needed to produce x cumulative units is:

$$y = ax^b$$

where: y = average number of labor hours required for production of x cumulative units

a = number of labor hours needed to produce the first unit

x = number of units produced

b = learning rate factor expressed as $\dfrac{\ln (\text{learning rate})}{\ln 2}$

The total number of hours required to produce x units is expressed as:

$$yx = ax^{b+1}$$

while the incremental hours required to produce the xth unit are:

$$\text{manhours} = a(b+1)x^b$$

You can use two programs, one to enter the data for calculating the number of hours required to produce the first unit and the learning rate, and a second program to compute the cumulative average number of hours to produce x units at a given learning rate, the total number of hours to produce x units, and the number of hours required to produce the xth unit.

Program for data entry

Program Memory	Key Sequence	Program Memory	Key Sequence	Program Memory	Key Sequence
00 13	$\ln x$	11 00		22 00	
01 34	$x{:}y$	12 00		23 00	
02 42	R/S	13 00		24 00	
03 13	$\ln x$	14 00		25 00	
04 35	$\Sigma+$	15 00		26 00	
05 42	R/S	16 00		27 00	
06 41	RST	17 00		28 00	
07 00		18 00		29 00	
08 00		19 00		30 00	
09 00		20 00		31 00	
10 00		21 00			

Program for computing the cumulative average number of hours needed to produce x units at a given learning rate, the total number of hours to produce x units, and the number of hours needed to produce the xth unit.

Program Memory		Key Sequence		Program Memory		Key Sequence		Program Memory		Key Sequence	
00	51	STO		11	61	RCL		22	01	1	
01	02	2		12	02	2		23	44	)	
02	37	2nd	y^x	13	85	=		24	55	×	
03	61	RCL		14	42	R/S		25	61	RCL	
04	01	1		15	61	RCL		26	02	2	
05	55	×		16	00	0		27	37	2nd	y^x
06	61	RCL		17	55	×		28	61	RCL	
07	00	0		18	43	(		29	01	1	
08	85	=		19	61	RCL		30	85	=	
09	42	R/S		20	01	1		31	42	R/S	
10	55	×		21	75	+					

Example: Determining learning rate and number of labor hours to produce the first unit

A company has started a new product line and has made the following observations:

Cumulative Units Produced (x)	Average Cumulative Labor Hours (y)
50	31
80	24
100	22
125	19.50
160	17.30

Is there a learning curve relationship? If so, what is the learning rate, and how many hours did it take to produce the first unit?

LEARNING CURVE ANALYSIS

Action	Press	Display
1. Clear calculator and enter data entry program.	[2nd] [CA] [2nd] [LRN]	00 00
	Program [2nd] [LRN] [RST]	0.
2. Select two-decimal display.	[2nd] [FIX] 2	0.00
3. Enter your observed x and y values.	50 [R/S] 31 [R/S]	1.00
	80 [R/S] 24 [R/S]	2.00
	100 [R/S] 22 [R/S]	3.00
	125 [R/S] 19.5 [R/S]	4.00
	160 [R/S] 17.3 [R/S]	5.00
4. Calculate the correlation between your x and y values.	[2nd] [CORR]	−1.00

This result indicates a good negative relationship — that is, as your x values increase, your y values decrease proportionately.

Action	Press	Display
5. Calculate the number of hours required to produce the first units.	[2nd] [INTCP] [2nd] [e^x]	216.17
6. Calculate learning rate factor (b).	[2nd] [SLOPE]	−0.50
7. Calculate learning rate.	[×] 2 [lnx] [=] [2nd] [e^x]	0.71
	[×] 100 [=]	70.81

The learning rate is 70.81% and the time needed to produce the first unit is 216.17 hours. With these values you can go on to calculate your learning curve values, using the second program listed above.

Example: Given the learning rate and number of hours to produce the first unit

Your company manufactures a labor intensive product. The time required to produce the first unit was 352.33 hours. Based on past experience, you have either a 75% or 80% learning curve effect on average hours to complete a unit.

With an 80% and a 75% learning rate, calculate the following.

 (a) average number of hours to produce 100 units.
 (b) total number of hours to produce 100 units.
 (c) number of hours to produce the 100th unit.
 (d) the same information as above for 150 units.

Action	Press	Display
1. Clear calculator and enter program for average number of hours, total number of hours, and hours to produce the xth unit.	2nd CA 2nd LRN Program	0
2. Select two-decimal display.	2nd FIX 2	0.00
3. Enter time required to build first unit.	352.33 STO 0	352.33
4. Calculate and enter learning curve factor.	80 % lnx ÷ 2 lnx = STO 1	−0.22 −0.32
5. Enter number of units you want to produce (100) and calculate average number of hours to produce those units.	100 R/S	80.00
6. Calculate the total number of hours needed to produce the units.	R/S	8000.06
7. Compute the hours required to build the 100th unit.	R/S	54.25
8. Reset and repeat *Steps 5* through 7 for 150 units.	150 RST R/S R/S R/S	70.21 10531.64 47.61
9. Calculate and enter the 75% learning curve factor.	75 % lnx ÷ 2 lnx = STO 1	−0.29 −0.42
10. Reset and repeat *Steps 5* through 7 for 100 units.	100 RST R/S R/S R/S	52.10 5210.44 30.48
11. Reset and repeat *Steps 5* through 7 for 150 units.	150 RST R/S R/S R/S	44.03 6605.13 25.76

With this procedure, you can easily perform a sensitivity analysis to determine the effects on your project from various estimations of your learning rate and the time required to build the first unit, as well as predicting the learning curve values.

Reference: "The Learning Curve as a Production Tool," *Harvard Business Review*, pp. 87–97.

TABLE A

Number of Samples	(df) degrees of Freedom	Level of Certainty 80%	90%	95%	99%	99.9%
3	1	0.951	.988	.997	1.000	1.000
4	2	0.800	.900	.950	.990	.999
5	3	0.687	.805	.878	.959	.991
6	4	0.608	.729	.811	.917	.974
7	5	0.551	.669	.755	.875	.951
8	6	0.507	.621	.707	.834	.925
9	7	0.472	.582	.666	.798	.898
10	8	0.443	.549	.632	.765	.872
11	9	0.419	.521	.602	.735	.847
12	10	0.398	.497	.576	.708	.823
13	11	0.380	.476	.553	.684	.801
14	12	0.365	.457	.532	.661	.780
15	13	0.351	.441	.514	.641	.760
16	14	0.338	.426	.497	.623	.742
17	15	0.327	.412	.482	.606	.725
18	16	0.317	.400	.468	.590	.708
19	17	0.308	.389	.456	.575	.693
20	18	0.299	.378	.444	.561	.679
21	19	0.291	.369	.433	.549	.665
22	20	0.284	.360	.423	.537	.652
23	21	0.277	.352	.413	.526	.640
24	22	0.271	.344	.404	.515	.629
25	23	0.265	.337	.396	.505	.618
26	24	0.260	.330	.388	.496	.607
27	25	0.255	.323	.381	.487	.597
28	26	0.250	.317	.374	.479	.588
29	27	0.245	.311	.367	.471	.579
30	28	0.241	.306	.361	.463	.570
31	29	0.237	.301	.355	.456	.562
32	30	0.233	.296	.349	.449	.554
42	40	0.202	.257	.304	.393	.490
62	60	0.165	.211	.250	.325	.408
122	120	0.117	.150	.178	.232	.294

TABLE B

z values

Degree of Sureness	Column I For Checking Only an Upper or Lower Level	Column II For Checking Both an Upper and Lower Level
60	0.26	0.84
65	0.39	0.94
70	0.53	1.04
75	0.68	1.15
80	0.84	1.28
85	1.04	1.44
90	1.28	1.65
95	1.65	1.96
99	2.33	2.58

TABLE C

t values

(For Checking Only an Upper or a Lower Limit)

Degree of Freedom	Level of Certainty			
	90%	95%	99%	99.5%
1	3.078	6.314	31.821	63.657
2	1.886	2.920	6.965	9.925
3	1.638	2.353	4.541	5.841
4	1.533	2.132	3.747	4.604
5	1.476	2.015	3.365	4.032
6	1.440	1.943	3.143	3.707
7	1.415	1.895	2.998	3.499
8	1.397	1.860	2.896	3.355
9	1.383	1.833	2.821	3.250
10	1.372	1.812	2.764	3.169
11	1.363	1.796	2.718	3.106
12	1.356	1.782	2.681	3.055
13	1.350	1.771	2.650	3.012
14	1.345	1.761	2.624	2.977
15	1.341	1.753	2.602	2.947
16	1.337	1.746	2.583	2.921
17	1.333	1.740	2.567	2.898
18	1.330	1.734	2.552	2.878
19	1.328	1.729	2.539	2.861
20	1.325	1.725	2.528	2.845
21	1.323	1.721	2.518	2.831
22	1.321	1.717	2.508	2.819
23	1.319	1.714	2.500	2.807
24	1.318	1.711	2.492	2.797
25	1.316	1.708	2.485	2.787
26	1.315	1.706	2.479	2.779
27	1.314	1.703	2.473	2.771
28	1.313	1.701	2.467	2.763
29	1.311	1.699	2.462	2.756
30	1.310	1.697	2.457	2.750
40	1.303	1.684	2.423	2.704
60	1.296	1.671	2.390	2.660
120	1.289	1.658	2.358	2.617
∞	1.282	1.645	2.326	2.576

(For Checking Both Upper and Lower Limits)

	← Level of Certainty →				
	80%	90%	95%	99%	99.9%
1	3.078	6.314	12.706	63.657	636.619
2	1.886	2.920	4.303	9.925	31.598
3	1.638	2.353	3.182	5.841	12.941
4	1.533	2.132	2.776	4.604	8.610
5	1.476	2.015	2.571	4.032	6.859
6	1.440	1.943	2.447	3.707	5.959
7	1.415	1.895	2.365	3.499	5.405
8	1.397	1.860	2.306	3.355	5.041
9	1.383	1.833	2.262	3.250	4.781
10	1.372	1.812	2.228	3.169	4.587
11	1.363	1.796	2.201	3.106	4.437
12	1.356	1.782	2.179	3.055	4.318
13	1.350	1.761	2.160	3.012	4.221
14	1.345	1.761	2.145	2.977	4.140
15	1.341	1.753	2.131	2.947	4.073
16	1.337	1.746	2.120	2.921	4.015
17	1.333	1.740	2.110	2.898	3.965
18	1.330	1.734	2.101	2.878	3.922
19	1.328	1.729	2.093	2.861	3.883
20	1.325	1.725	2.086	2.845	3.850
21	1.323	1.721	2.080	2.831	3.819
22	1.321	1.717	2.074	2.819	3.792
23	1.319	1.714	2.069	2.807	3.767
24	1.318	1.711	2.064	2.797	3.745
25	1.316	1.708	2.060	2.787	3.725
26	1.315	1.706	2.056	2.779	3.707
27	1.314	1.703	2.052	2.771	3.690
28	1.313	1.701	2.048	2.763	3.674
29	1.311	1.699	2.045	2.756	3.659
30	1.310	1.697	2.042	2.750	3.646
40	1.303	1.684	2.021	2.704	3.551
60	1.296	1.671	2.000	2.660	3.460
120	1.289	1.658	1.980	2.617	3.373
∞	1.282	1.645	1.960	2.576	3.291

Degree of Freedom

Values of F for 95% Level of Certainty

Degrees of Freedom of the Numerator →

Degrees of Freedom of the Denominator ↓

	1	2	3	4	5	6	7	8	9	10	12	15	20	30	60	120	∞
1	161.4	199.5	215.7	224.6	230.2	234.0	236.8	238.9	240.5	241.9	243.9	245.9	248.0	250.1	252.2	253.3	254.3
2	18.51	19.00	19.16	19.25	19.30	19.33	19.35	19.37	19.38	19.40	19.41	19.43	19.45	19.46	19.48	19.49	19.50
3	10.13	9.55	9.28	9.12	9.01	8.94	8.89	8.85	8.81	8.79	8.74	8.70	8.66	8.62	8.57	8.55	8.53
4	7.71	6.94	6.59	6.39	6.26	6.16	6.09	6.04	6.00	5.96	5.91	5.86	5.80	5.75	5.69	5.66	5.63
5	6.61	5.79	5.41	5.19	5.05	4.95	4.88	4.82	4.77	4.74	4.68	4.62	4.56	4.50	4.43	4.40	4.36
6	5.99	5.14	4.76	4.53	4.39	4.28	4.21	4.15	4.10	4.06	4.00	3.94	3.87	3.81	3.74	3.70	3.67
7	5.59	4.74	4.35	4.12	3.97	3.87	3.79	3.73	3.68	3.64	3.57	3.51	3.44	3.38	3.30	3.27	3.23
8	5.32	4.46	4.07	3.84	3.69	3.58	3.50	3.44	3.39	3.35	3.28	3.22	3.15	3.08	3.01	2.97	2.93
9	5.12	4.26	3.86	3.63	3.48	3.37	3.29	3.23	3.18	3.14	3.07	3.01	2.94	2.86	2.79	2.75	2.71
10	4.96	4.10	3.71	3.48	3.33	3.22	3.14	3.07	3.02	2.98	2.91	2.85	2.77	2.70	2.62	2.58	2.54
11	4.84	3.98	3.59	3.36	3.20	3.09	3.01	2.95	2.90	2.85	2.79	2.72	2.65	2.57	2.49	2.45	2.40
12	4.75	3.89	3.49	3.26	3.11	3.00	2.91	2.85	2.80	2.75	2.69	2.62	2.54	2.47	2.38	2.34	2.30
13	4.67	3.81	3.41	3.18	3.03	2.92	2.83	2.77	2.71	2.67	2.60	2.53	2.46	2.38	2.30	2.25	2.21
14	4.60	3.74	3.34	3.11	2.96	2.85	2.76	2.70	2.65	2.60	2.53	2.46	2.39	2.31	2.22	2.18	2.13
15	4.54	3.68	3.29	3.06	2.90	2.79	2.71	2.64	2.59	2.54	2.48	2.40	2.33	2.25	2.16	2.11	2.07
16	4.49	3.63	3.24	3.01	2.85	2.74	2.66	2.59	2.54	2.49	2.42	2.35	2.28	2.19	2.11	2.06	2.01
17	4.45	3.59	3.20	2.96	2.81	2.70	2.61	2.55	2.49	2.45	2.38	2.31	2.23	2.15	2.06	2.01	1.96
18	4.41	3.55	3.16	2.93	2.77	2.66	2.58	2.51	2.46	2.41	2.34	2.27	2.19	2.11	2.02	1.97	1.92
19	4.38	3.52	3.13	2.90	2.74	2.63	2.54	2.48	2.42	2.38	2.31	2.23	2.16	2.07	1.98	1.93	1.88
20	4.35	3.49	3.10	2.87	2.71	2.60	2.51	2.45	2.39	2.35	2.28	2.20	2.12	2.04	1.95	1.90	1.84
21	4.32	3.47	3.07	2.84	2.68	2.57	2.49	2.42	2.37	2.32	2.25	2.18	2.10	2.01	1.92	1.87	1.81
22	4.30	3.44	3.05	2.82	2.66	2.55	2.46	2.40	2.34	2.30	2.23	2.15	2.07	1.98	1.89	1.84	1.78
23	4.28	3.42	3.03	2.80	2.64	2.53	2.44	2.37	2.32	2.27	2.20	2.13	2.05	1.96	1.86	1.81	1.76
24	4.26	3.40	3.01	2.78	2.62	2.51	2.42	2.36	2.30	2.25	2.18	2.11	2.03	1.94	1.84	1.79	1.73
25	4.24	3.39	2.99	2.76	2.60	2.49	2.40	2.34	2.28	2.24	2.16	2.09	2.01	1.92	1.82	1.77	1.71
26	4.23	3.37	2.98	2.74	2.59	2.47	2.39	2.32	2.27	2.22	2.15	2.07	1.99	1.90	1.80	1.75	1.69
27	4.21	3.35	2.96	2.73	2.57	2.46	2.37	2.31	2.25	2.20	2.13	2.06	1.97	1.88	1.79	1.73	1.67
28	4.20	3.34	2.95	2.71	2.56	2.45	2.36	2.29	2.24	2.19	2.12	2.04	1.96	1.87	1.77	1.71	1.65
29	4.18	3.33	2.93	2.70	2.55	2.43	2.35	2.28	2.22	2.18	2.10	2.03	1.94	1.85	1.75	1.70	1.64
30	4.17	3.32	2.92	2.69	2.53	2.42	2.33	2.27	2.21	2.16	2.09	2.01	1.93	1.84	1.74	1.68	1.62
40	4.08	3.23	2.84	2.61	2.45	2.34	2.25	2.18	2.12	2.08	2.00	1.92	1.84	1.74	1.64	1.58	1.51
60	4.00	3.15	2.76	2.53	2.37	2.25	2.17	2.10	2.04	1.99	1.92	1.84	1.75	1.65	1.53	1.47	1.39
120	3.92	3.07	2.68	2.45	2.29	2.17	2.09	2.02	1.96	1.91	1.83	1.75	1.66	1.55	1.43	1.35	1.25
∞	3.84	3.00	2.60	2.37	2.21	2.10	2.01	1.94	1.88	1.83	1.75	1.67	1.57	1.46	1.32	1.22	1.00

TABLE E

Values of F for 99% Level of Certainty

Degrees of Freedom of the Numerator

df (denom)	1	2	3	4	5	6	7	8	9	10	12	15	20	30	60	120	∞
1	4052	4999.5	5403	5625	5764	5859	5928	5982	6022	6056	6106	6157	6209	6261	6313	6339	6366
2	98.50	99.00	99.17	99.25	99.30	99.33	99.36	99.37	99.39	99.40	99.42	99.43	99.45	99.47	99.48	99.49	99.50
3	34.12	30.82	29.46	28.71	28.24	27.91	27.67	27.49	27.35	27.23	27.05	26.87	26.69	26.50	26.32	26.22	26.13
4	21.20	18.00	16.69	15.98	15.52	15.21	14.98	14.80	14.66	14.55	14.37	14.20	14.02	13.84	13.65	13.56	13.46
5	16.26	13.27	12.06	11.39	10.97	10.67	10.46	10.29	10.16	10.05	9.89	9.72	9.55	9.38	9.20	9.11	9.02
6	13.75	10.92	9.78	9.15	8.75	8.47	8.26	8.10	7.98	7.87	7.72	7.56	7.40	7.23	7.06	6.97	6.88
7	12.25	9.55	8.45	7.85	7.46	7.19	6.99	6.84	6.72	6.62	6.47	6.31	6.16	5.99	5.82	5.74	5.65
8	11.26	8.65	7.59	7.01	6.63	6.37	6.18	6.03	5.91	5.81	5.67	5.52	5.36	5.20	5.03	4.95	4.86
9	10.56	8.02	6.99	6.42	6.06	5.80	5.61	5.47	5.35	5.26	5.11	4.96	4.81	4.65	4.48	4.40	4.31
10	10.04	7.56	6.55	5.99	5.64	5.39	5.20	5.06	4.94	4.85	4.71	4.56	4.41	4.25	4.08	4.00	3.91
11	9.65	7.21	6.22	5.67	5.32	5.07	4.89	4.74	4.63	4.54	4.40	4.25	4.10	3.94	3.78	3.69	3.60
12	9.33	6.93	5.95	5.41	5.06	4.82	4.64	4.50	4.39	4.30	4.16	4.01	3.86	3.70	3.54	3.45	3.36
13	9.07	6.70	5.74	5.21	4.86	4.62	4.44	4.30	4.19	4.10	3.96	3.82	3.66	3.51	3.34	3.25	3.17
14	8.86	6.51	5.56	5.04	4.69	4.46	4.28	4.14	4.03	3.94	3.80	3.66	3.51	3.35	3.18	3.09	3.00
15	8.68	6.36	5.42	4.89	4.56	4.32	4.14	4.00	3.89	3.80	3.67	3.52	3.37	3.21	3.05	2.96	2.87
16	8.53	6.23	5.29	4.77	4.44	4.20	4.03	3.89	3.78	3.69	3.55	3.41	3.26	3.10	2.93	2.84	2.75
17	8.40	6.11	5.18	4.67	4.34	4.10	3.93	3.79	3.68	3.59	3.46	3.31	3.16	3.00	2.83	2.75	2.65
18	8.29	6.01	5.09	4.58	4.25	4.01	3.84	3.71	3.60	3.51	3.37	3.23	3.08	2.92	2.75	2.66	2.57
19	8.18	5.93	5.01	4.50	4.17	3.94	3.77	3.63	3.52	3.43	3.30	3.15	3.00	2.84	2.67	2.58	2.49
20	8.10	5.85	4.94	4.43	4.10	3.87	3.70	3.56	3.46	3.37	3.23	3.09	2.94	2.78	2.61	2.52	2.42
21	8.02	5.78	4.87	4.37	4.04	3.81	3.64	3.51	3.40	3.31	3.17	3.03	2.88	2.72	2.55	2.46	2.36
22	7.95	5.72	4.82	4.31	3.99	3.76	3.59	3.45	3.35	3.26	3.12	2.98	2.83	2.67	2.50	2.40	2.31
23	7.88	5.66	4.76	4.26	3.94	3.71	3.54	3.41	3.30	3.21	3.07	2.93	2.78	2.62	2.45	2.35	2.26
24	7.82	5.61	4.72	4.22	3.90	3.67	3.50	3.36	3.26	3.17	3.03	2.89	2.74	2.58	2.40	2.31	2.21
25	7.77	5.57	4.68	4.18	3.85	3.63	3.46	3.32	3.22	3.13	2.99	2.85	2.70	2.54	2.36	2.27	2.17
26	7.72	5.53	4.64	4.14	3.82	3.59	3.42	3.29	3.18	3.09	2.96	2.81	2.66	2.50	2.33	2.23	2.13
27	7.68	5.49	4.60	4.11	3.78	3.56	3.39	3.26	3.15	3.06	2.93	2.78	2.63	2.47	2.29	2.20	2.10
28	7.64	5.45	4.57	4.07	3.75	3.53	3.36	3.23	3.12	3.03	2.90	2.75	2.60	2.44	2.26	2.17	2.06
29	7.60	5.42	4.54	4.04	3.73	3.50	3.33	3.20	3.09	3.00	2.87	2.73	2.57	2.41	2.23	2.14	2.03
30	7.56	5.39	4.51	4.02	3.70	3.47	3.30	3.17	3.07	2.98	2.84	2.70	2.55	2.39	2.21	2.11	2.01
40	7.31	5.18	4.31	3.83	3.51	3.29	3.12	2.99	2.89	2.80	2.66	2.52	2.37	2.20	2.02	1.92	1.80
60	7.08	4.98	4.13	3.65	3.34	3.12	2.95	2.82	2.72	2.63	2.50	2.35	2.20	2.03	1.84	1.73	1.60
120	6.85	4.79	3.95	3.48	3.17	2.96	2.79	2.66	2.56	2.47	2.34	2.19	2.03	1.86	1.66	1.53	1.38
∞	6.63	4.61	3.78	3.32	3.02	2.80	2.64	2.51	2.41	2.32	2.18	2.04	1.88	1.70	1.47	1.32	1.00

Degrees of Freedom of the Denominator

TABLE F

Selected Bibliography

Chisolm, Roger K., and Whitaker, Gilbert R., Jr.
    Forecasting Methods. Homewood, IL: Richard D. Irwin, Inc., 1971.

Croxton, Frederick E.; Cowden, Dudley J.; and Bolch, Ben W.
    Practical Business Statistics, 4th ed. Englewood Cliggs, NJ: Prentice-Hall, Inc.
    1969.

Grawoig, Dennis E.; Fielitz, Bruce; Robinson, James; and Tabor, Dwight.
    Mathematics: A Foundation for Decisions. Reading, MA: Addison-Wesley
    Publishing Company, 1976.

Horngren, Charles T. *Cost Accounting: A Managerial Emphasis,* 4th ed.
    Englewood Cliffs, NJ: Prentice-Hall, Inc., 1977.

Hummel, Paul M., and Seebeck, Charles L., Jr.
    Mathematics of Finance, 3rd ed. New York: McGraw-Hill Book Company, 1971.

Kieso, Donald E., and Weygandt, Jerry A. *Intermediate Accounting,* 2nd ed.
    Santa Barbara, CA: John Wiley and Sons, 1977.

Kinnard, William N., Jr. *Income Property Valuation.* Lexington, MA: Heath
    Lexington Books, 1976.

Meigs, Walter B., et al. *Intermediate Accounting,* 3rd ed. New York: McGraw-Hill
    Book Company, 1974.

Miller, Merton H., and Orr, Daniel. "A Model of the Demand for Money by
    Firms." *Quarterly Journal of Economics* 80 (August 1966): 413-435.

Parsons, Robert. *Statistical Analysis: A Decision-Making Approach.* New York:
    Harper & Row, 1974.

Paton, W. A., ed. *Accountant's Handbook,* 2nd ed. New York: The Ronald Press
    Company, 1936.

Spence, Bruce M.; Graudenz, Jacob Y.; and Lynch, John J.
    Standard Securities Calculation Methods. New York: Securities Industry
    Association, Inc., 1973.

"The Learning Curve as a Production Tool." *Harvard Business Review,* January-
    February 1954, pp. 87-97

Welsch, Glenn A., Zlatkovich, Charles T., and White, John Arch.
    Intermediate Accounting, 4th ed. Homewood, IL: Richard D. Irwin
    Incorporated, 1976.

Weston, J. Fred, and Brigham, Eugene F. *Managerial Finance,* 5th ed. Hinsdale, IL:
    The Dryden Press, 1975.

Index